ROOTS AND FENCES

A GENERATIONAL STORY OF FRIENDS, FAMILY AND DISABILITY

SHARON GREGORY DUNCAN ED.D

outskirtspress
DENVER, COLORADO

Roots and Fences
A Generational Story of Friends, Family and Disability
All Rights Reserved.
Copyright © 2013 Sharon Gregory Duncan Ed.D
v3.0 r1.1

Cover Photo © 2013 Cynthia Kristufek. All rights reserved - used with permission.

Outskirts Press, Inc.
http://www.outskirtspress.com

Paperback ISBN: 978-1-4787-0710-3
Hardback ISBN: 978-1-4787-0709-7

Library of Congress Control Number: 2013907822

Outskirts Press and the "OP" logo are trademarks belonging to Outskirts Press, Inc.

PRINTED IN THE UNITED STATES OF AMERICA

Dedicated to the memory
of
Ed, Dorothy, and Jacqueline Sheehan
and
My Dad, Art Gregory
with love.

ACKNOWLEDGEMENTS

I have been writing forever, but writing this story took me to a place in my soul that I had never been before. I am grateful to my professors from my doctoral program at National Louis University, who challenged me to employ phenomenology. I was encouraged by my students at Purdue- Cal. They provided feedback, encouragement, and came to love Jackie, Chuck, Jon and Jamee almost as much as I do. I am so proud to have taught so many passionate special educators.

There would not be a book if it were not for my forever friend, Laura. She originally convinced me that our story had merit for dissertation research. Besides putting up with all my drama for over 50 years, she saw to it that I finished this book. Thank you does not seem enough.

I am fortunate to have siblings: Tom, Ed, Colleen,and Kathy who enhance my life. You were there in the beginning and are always there for me. My mom opened her heart to me and talked about her personal feelings in regard to her sister Jackie and her parents. I know this was emotional and difficult. I love and appreciate her. While my Dad was not "here" to interview, I know he was beside me each step of the way.

To all of those who let me into their homes, hearts, and lives through the interviews: My Aunt Lovie, Mr and Mrs E. Debbie, Colleen, Jenna, Amy, and Laura. Thank you!

Thanks to my Mount Assisi sister, Cindy Kristufek for her beautiful photography. She is so talented !

I only knew Dave Duncan a few days when I fell in love with him. Thirty six years later, I love him even more. He is my constant.

This is a true story. People who know us and our community will recognize people and places. The names used in the story are with the permission of those interviewed. Agencies and school names have been changed for privacy purposes.

Proceeds from this book will be donated to Abide in Me, a not for profit organization which supports individuals with disabilities live active and engaged lives. Visit abideinme.org.

Chuck, Jonathon, and Jamee, you all have such a special place in my heart. Without you, there is no story. I am forever proud of the three of you! Thanks!

Once upon a time there were three little girls; Laura, Debbie and Sharon who grew up to tell a story.

With love and gratitude,
Shar

Table of Contents

Our Rhizomic Connection

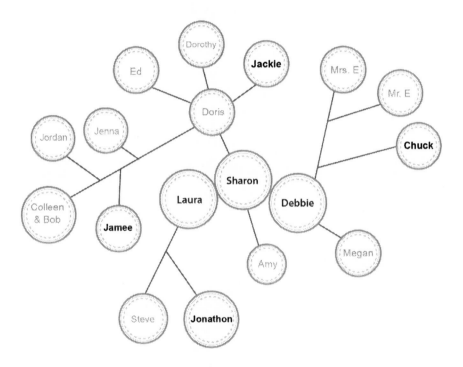

CHAPTER ONE

Revelations and Fractured Fairy Tales

Once upon a time...

I have a thing for Barbies. For me, Barbie dolls conjure up warm memories. I can close my eyes and see my little girl self playing Barbies on a blanket in the backyard with my friends, living in our little fantasy world. Barbie and Ken living the good life, oblivious to reality. With our childhood innocence, we were pretty oblivious as well. I may have been even more naive than the other girls, not having older siblings and well protected by all the adults that lived in my home. My maternal grandparents and Aunt Jackie lived with us, so my two younger brothers and I were outnumbered by the grownups.

My Barbie collection afforded me an elevated social status among the girls in the neighborhood. As a chubby, seven year old, bright redheaded, drama queen I definitely needed some assistance in this area. I had all the dolls: Barbie, Ken, Midge, Allen, Skipper, Tootie ... you name them, I had them. My grandmother (Mere)was always buying me the latest doll to add to my collection. My Aunt Jackie and I would play Barbies in her bedroom for hours on end. In the neighborhood of my childhood, the picnic table in the backyard of the twins house was the gathering place for the best Barbie action on the block. Massive pretend Barbie towns were created out of old cardboard boxes. Since I had the "real" Barbie house, cases, and dolls and I was eager to share, I was typically included as part of the picnic table group.

"Go home Sharon....goodbye, go home...., we already started", Bernadette and Nancy made faces as they told me to leave.

"But, but I have all my Barbie stuff."

"Take your Barbies and just go!"

My lip starts to quiver and tears come to my eyes.

"You're a big crybaby! You act retarded, just like your mongoloid Aunt Jackie, AND we don't want to play with you!"

The twins, Mary Jo and Mary Ann sneered those words at me in a mean sing -songy voice. I did not hear the words as much as I felt the rejection. I was hurting in side and my stomach felt tight.I really wanted to play Barbies that day. As I stood there with tears coming to my eyes and my lip quivering, I was going to ask them again if I could PLEASE play and even offer them one of my dolls or cases.It suddenly hit me, I actually heard the words they said. They called my Aunt Jackie RETARDED. They called her Mongoloid.

"No, Jackie's not retarded, my friend Debbie's brother Chuck is retarded, and I heard him called Mongoloid, too." Those words described Chuckie, not my Aunt Jackie. Jackie could talk. Jackie took care of me. Jackie liked to play Barbies with me and my friends. I loved Jackie. Nothing made sense and I started to tremble. A big gulp sound came from somewhere and I started to sob as I ran back towards my house.

Running towards home it seemed like the gate to my yard was miles away. Tears blinding my eyes and dragging my Barbie cases, and finally, I reached my yard. I dramatically threw the cases on the ground. I heard the girls laughing at me in the background.I ran faster through the yard and into the house. By now, I was crying loudly.

Throwing open the back screen door, I yelled into the house, "M-o-o-o-om, the Twins said Jackie is retarded." My grandmother was sitting at the end of the kitchen table in her usual spot and gave me a scary dirty look. My voice was bellowing through the house. At this point, I was crying hard and loud, bent over and sobbing with tears pouring down my face. My mom ushered me out of the kitchen and kept saying"Shhh,Sharon, calm down."

"I, I, I can't."

"I am trying Moooom."

"They are so mean."

"Why,(deep breath) did they say that?"

I continued to cry and blubber and kept trying to explain what I heard them say. I was loud and hysterical. My mom pushed me into Aunt Jackie's bedroom. Looking back, I'm now thinking Jackie might have been right there in the kitchen or in hearing distance as the first floor of our house was not large.

My mom closed the door and said, "Oh, Sharon I should have told you, but I couldn't." I calmed down enough to listen, but the tears kept coming to my eyes. I swiped one from my cheek and looked into my mom's concerned eyes. She told me Jackie was slow and that is why she lived with us and never got married. She did not say retarded, she did not say Mongoloid. She really did not give me an explanation I could understand. She told me that I shouldn't listen to mean people. I was told to stop crying and to NOT say anything to Jackie or in front of my grandmother (Jackie's mother).

I stamped up the stairs to my bedroom and plopped on the bed, continuing to cry and talk to myself. I had only wanted to play pretend that day. I did not want to hear bad things about my Aunt Jackie. I loved my Aunt Jackie. I pictured the event in my head and thought about who was sitting at the table. My friends Laura and Debbie were not there. Maybe I will go and play with them. I will never let the twins play with my Barbies again. So there! I felt confused, sad and angry all at once. As a seven year old whose world was turned upside down, I guess I was entitled to be a bit dramatic.

On the inside, my fairytale world would never be the same. My innocence was taken away that day on so many levels. What is wrong with my Aunt Jackie? I kept those questions to myself, not asking them out loud to anyone. I tucked them in a place deep in my soul, but the questions were always nagging. I would continue to have many inner conversations trying to figure it out. I needed the wisdom and advice of my Aunt Jackie, but I could not ask. I was specifically told not to say anything to Jackie and the secrets were about her.

Does Jackie know she is retarded?

Since I could not figure "it" out. I wiped my face and ran down the stairs to the living room. Out of the house I went. I purposely went out the front door to avoid the twins and went off to see if Laura or Debbie wanted to play.

Roots Planted: Fairy Tales Stories

Once upon a not so distant time, and in a not so distant land, lived three little girls. Their lives revolved around playing Barbies, games of "ghost beware" at dusk, sewing lessons, riding the bus to Ford City Shopping Center, buying penny candy at the pet shop and square-scooped sherbet cones at Prince Castle. At times their lives seemed to them idealistic and somewhat fairytale; as they were growing up in a middle class suburban neighborhood in the 1960s, with stay-at-home moms, and dads who arrived home at five for family dinner. The girls were connected by proximity, living in houses separated only by cyclone fences and a grassy alley. They lived so close you could call out "Yo Laura", or "Yo Sharon" or "Yo Debbie"…and someone would answer the door. They shared the same Catholic faith, attended the same parish school and were all about the same age. They shared dreams and made up fairytale stories while lying on blankets under Sharon's big backyard tree, sipping cherry Kool-Aid from shiny metal tumblers, while munching on sugar wafer cookies.

"So what do you want to be when you grow up?"

"'Where do you think we will live?"

"Think we'll still be friends when we're old and married?"

Laura declared her husband was going to look like President Kennedy. She stared at her gum ball ring that switched from JFK's picture to the American flag when she moved her hand. Debbie said maybe he'd be from Chicago, because that's where she used to live, you know, and Granny Opal still lives there. Sharon knew her husband would definitely not have a thick mane of auburn hair, as she hated her own red hair, and he wouldn't be obnoxious like her brother Tommy, who kept hitting Debbie with his boot bag on the way home from school. The stories were the tales of seven year old girls with nary a care on a warm summer's day.

In the distance, Sharon's mom was ironing clothes on the back porch, drinking a Pepsi. Laura's mom was busy in the kitchen preparing dinner for her family of nine with the help of her oldest daughter. Debbie's mom was sitting in a chair on her driveway watching Debbie's brother Chuckie, swinging on his homemade swing in the garage, while her nephew is inside taking a nap.

Laura, Debbie and I shared many childhood adventures. One of our favorite past times revolved around going to the store. For kids today walking to the store with a quarter to purchase penny candy sounds pretty lame, but for us in 1969, it was the best.

The nine-year-old me runs through the kitchen, pulls open the pantry door and grabs an eight pack of empty Pepsi bottles from the pantry floor. I have a shiny quarter in my pocket just waiting to be spent. With the sixteen cents I would get from the bottles, I would be able to get a lot of penny candy.

"Mom, I'm going," I yelled.

"Where are you going young lady?" my grandmother, Mere inquires.

"Just up town with Laura and Debbie."

"Be careful."

"Don't worry Mere." I run by my Aunt Jackie washing dishes at the sink. I grab her apron string pretending to untie it and she slaps my hand.

"Oh, Sharon, what a kidder."

"See ya!" I run out the screen door and it slams behind me. I hear Mere yelling in the distance, but I'm off... across the porch ...down the steps... criss-crossing my fenced backyard, running through the back gate, which is hanging slightly open. I give it an extra shove to open it all the way and I head across the alley to Laura's yard.

"Yo Laura." She comes to the door with a brown bag in her hand holding two empty quart bottles from beer. (She will get five cents each for those).

"Ready? Let's go get Debbie."

"I asked her this morning if she could go uptown for candy with us".

We travel down the driveway toward Central Avenue to go next door to Debbie's.

We approach the fenced- in yard. A locked double gate extending across the driveway stops us in our tracks. Laura takes her free hand and opens the latch while I take my free hand and pull up the pole. In we go. We are sure to lock the gate again or face the wrath of Mrs. E., Debbie's mom. The gate must remain locked at all times.

"Yo Debbie," we call out on her back stoop.

"Hi guys! I can go, but I have groceries to buy for my mom at Freshline." She goes back in the house and comes back out with her mom's old brown wallet and a list in one hand, and her little brother Chuckie's small chubby hand tightly clenched in the other.

"I gotta bring Chuck; my mom gave me money so we can get sherbet cones from Prince Castle on the way back."

We walk down the drive. Laura and I open the gate and Deb pulls Chuck through. We lock it behind us. Looking both ways, we cross Central Avenue. Mere's "be careful" rings in my brain. Laura and I take the lead.

"Come on Chuck, walk faster," Deb says... As we make our way from our neighborhood and the safety of the locked gates and cyclone fences into the vast world... we called: UP TOWN.

Our Story

Fast forward 40 plus years. I am having lunch with Laura, pouring my heart out about not having a topic for my dissertation. I am in a doctoral program for disability studies and I want to do something impressive, cutting edge or new to the field. Every time I sit down to start writing I can't seem to get started. As I tell Laura, I keep thinking about Jackie. Laura reminds me that Jackie's story is unique. Then she says "What about our story? We have a pretty impressive story. You need to find a way to tell it."

Story Making

As I embarked on my quest to reveal our story, I returned to the past; to the relationships, the values, the truths, that connected our experiences. I felt compelled to provide a visual to represent the people and the relationships, which represent the roots of our story. A family tree immediately came to mind. A tree has a central trunk, and a main root system; however, it is very divisionary, both visually and philosophically as the branches reach out to the sky. The tree proved to be too rigid and hierarchal, providing a linear structure. I was determined to seek a fluid representation for the connected history. Visually, I was drawn to a root structure and all the little threads that come from and connect to the root. The root could well represent the connectiveness of our circumstances. There was also this protective aura that surrounded our lives and I searched for a means to portray this feeling. The cyclone fences which surrounded my backyard and Debbie's whole yard came to mind. I visualized the fences and the gates, keeping us in, locking us out, but still allowing us to see out to the other side. The fence provided safety, but was imprisoning at the same time. We could lift the lock, pull up the pole and get out from time to time, but we were compelled to go back in... to the safety that existed within those fenced boundaries. Within the safety of the fence was the yard, my tree, the swing set, the back porch, the house; my home, the place of safety.

In my childhood home I was known by name. I was Sharon, the firstborn, Doris and Art's daughter, Ed and Dorothy's grandchild, Jackie's niece, Tom, Ed, Colleen and Kathy's older sister. I was not redheaded, or big-eared or chubby or a crybaby, but Sharon Marie or Rose-red, as Daddy would say. My family may have called me stubborn or sassy or dramatic or moody, but that was all right most of the time, because no matter what, I felt loved. The love and concern showered on me by my parents, Grandparents, and Aunt Jackie served as a protective fence. I could go home and emotionally remove myself from mean kids like the twins. Safe in my home, I could forget that they made fun of me and called my Aunt Jackie *retarded*.

Metaphorically Speaking

Picturing the cyclone fence and searching for a visual and philosophical representation to provide cohesion for our story, I looked again at the root, the rhizome. In botany, the rhizome is a horizontal, subterranean plant stem that is thickened by deposits of reserve food material. It produces shoots above and roots below (Merriam-Webster, 2008). In the philosophy of Gilles Deleuze (1983), the rhizome serves as a symbol for multiple becomings, referring to the dimensions of growth of human beings. He utilizes this unique root to serve a metaphor for multidimensional growth. The dimensions demonstrate moral, intellectual growth and individual and collective consciousness (Deleuze, 1983). Rhizome theory provides an open structure and a process for becoming. One can see the correlations with the structure of a chain link fence in the view point of Kurokawa (2001) in an essay covering Deleuzio-Guallaria Architectural Theory: "A rhizome is an interlocking web. It is a conjunction of dynamic relations producing bulbs here and there, interweaving with great complexity, reaching outward in its continuing growth. It represents the principle of dynamic varied pluralism that absorbs the hierarchal structure of the tree" (p. 1031).

This story is a personal revelation, an uncovering, a phenomenological search, linking the past to the present, with implications for the future. Deleuze, together with his research partner Guattari, (1987, 1994) a psychoanalyst, referred to their philosophical method based on the rhizome concept as geophilosophy; privileging geography and history and emphasizing the value of present- becoming. Phenomenology is about revealing, uncovering, exposing and connecting. So the present-becoming perspective of the rhizome metaphor is well suited for portraying this particular story. Deleuze gives meaning to spatial temporal dynamics that embody the idea of difference versus identity. The process is dynamic, an uncovering. The rhizome symbolizes the linkages.

The folds of experience (Deleuze, 1983) are formed at critical connections, where different rhizome lines cross and interact.

The rhizome, the root, starts here and now. There are roots in place, grounded in friendship, family, proximity, history, and disability.

The rhizome is fluid and has the ability to grow and change, tiny threads will emerge from the root, linking to other threads, which will grow and flourish over time. Rhizomes are about possibilities. Our story is full of possibility, but simultaneously there were the fences serving as protective physical and emotional boundaries. There is an eb and flow of possibility and innocence along with boundaries and stigma.

While we had fences and families who loved us none of us were totally protected from facing reality. The "Barbie" day changed my life. I had this inner struggle with the whole "retarded" thing. It did not feel right and it did not feel good. Yet being with my Aunt Jackie felt right, hanging out with Chuck seemed normal. Could I or should I let the twins mean words change how I felt about Aunt Jackie or Chuck? Over time, I came to realize both Jackie and Chuck were born with Down Syndrome. I am not sure who or when anyone explained it to me, I just must have figured it out. By the time I did, it was no longer an issue. In the sixties we had so many issues that were left unspoken. Without the benefit of social media, hundreds of cable channels and reality TV, people were very private in general. So Chuck and Aunt Jackie actually were the same, as far as a disability category, anyway. My eight year old self never imagined that Jackie and Chuck would have a profound impact on my occupation, my values, my future, my life. THEY were my ROOTS.

I now realize I was situated in a particular circumstance of disability. I lived in a home where disability and "retard- ness", as it was referred to in the 60s, was somewhere else, not in our house. Although my Aunt Jackie had an intellectual disability, my grandmother refused to call or label her disabled. The norm when my aunt was born in the late 1930s was for children who were declared retarded or mongoloid to be put away. Children like *those* were sent to institutions. The professionals there would know how to care for *them*, and babies like Jackie would not live long anyway. My maternal grandparents, but most especially my grandmother (Mere) defied the norm and made Jackie "fit". She taught Jackie to walk, talk, count, read, close her mouth (drooling was not an option) and was determined that she reached those milestones in typical developmental stages.

Although, as a young child, I never thought of Jackie as different, I always knew Chuckie, my friend Debbie's brother, was "different". He could not read; he needed help with everyday tasks and went to a "special" school. I thought the experience of disability was beyond my fenced yard. It was over there; in Debbie's fenced- in house on the next block. However, as I grew older, the words of the twins especially the way in which they said Retarded and Mongoloid became more relevant to me. Disability was part of our lives and fences could not protect us from a world who looked at Jackie and Chuck with disdain or pity. People would stare at us when we had to get Chuckie off the ground, because he refused to walk. Grownups would actually "tsk" when we would wipe the drool off his chin as he slurped on his Prince Castle ice cream cone. Or they would look away, as if he was scary to look at. When we would go to the movies with Aunt Jackie, people moved to other rows with their kids. The teenager selling the tickets would talk to me, instead of adult Aunt Jackie, when she tried to purchase the tickets. My world was not so perfect any more.

Life and human reality gets in the way of fairytale stories and dreams. We never dreamed that Debbie would have five children and have a son die from a brain tumor. We never dreamed that Laura would confront disability by giving birth to a baby boy Jonathon, missing an eye and part of his brain. We never dreamed that my little sister Colleen would have a child (Jamee) with cerebral palsy and labeled profoundly retarded, and Laura would then give her advice about doctors, therapy, and legal issues. Our fairytale stories never had my dad getting sick and dying so young, or Jackie having Alzheimer's and my mom always having to be her guardian. We never dreamed Laura's daughter would then have a brain tumor. I never thought I would spend my life working in special education and my daughter and Debbie's daughter (my God daughter) would become special educators, too.

As Laura reminded me, there is a profound story here; a story that crosses generations and stereotypes. This is a multifaceted story of lives, labels, and perceptions. It is the story of Jackie not being allowed to have a label. It is the story of Chuck receiving a label shortly after birth. It is also the story of Laura, demanding inclusion for her son despite having a label. It is the story of Jamee needing a label.

This is a revelation process for those of us whose lives were changed, simply because we were present; living with everything life put before us. This story is "our social construction of what happened" (Ferguson et al., 1992, p. 5).

Connecting Phenomenologically

As an emerging disability scholar with a story burning in my heart, phenomenology provided me with the means to reveal the story. A broad theme of phenomenology is intentionality. Intentionality, according to Pollio, Henley and Thompson (1997), "is a basic structure of human existence that captures the fact that human beings are fundamentally related to the contexts in which they live" (p. 7). There are three central intentionalities that phenomenological interpretists typically draw from: life-world, place, and home (Van Manen, 1990).

Lifeworld

Life-world refers to the content in the context of everyday life. It is all the little day-to-day goings-on that are not typically thought about. It is all that life encompasses, from exciting events to typical routine happenings. A way to reflect on this is through the events that "just happen." It is the constant flow of inner and outer life. Dilthey (1985) describes this phenomenon as in its most basic form:

> A lived experience does not confront me as something perceived or represented; it is not given to me, but the reality of lived experience is there- for- me because I have a reflexive awareness of

it, because I possess it immediately as belonging to me in some sense. Only in thought does it become objective. (p. 223)

The life-world shared by Sharon, Laura, and Debbie is reflected in the moments the girls spent daydreaming under the tree, or venturing uptown with Chuck, or teasing with Aunt Jackie. Their life-world was the day to day moments that occurred in their everyday lives.

Place

A critical dimension of life- world is the human experience of place. Casey (1997) ascertains that place is a central ontological structure of the human experience: "Place serves as a condition of all existing things... to be, is to be in the place" (pp. 15-16). Merleau-Ponty (1962) emphasizes that place is central to phenomenology, because of our existence as embodying beings. It is a critical structure of being- in -the world. In order for anything to occur, we, as human beings, must be in a particular place. We have to be *here* in order to have the lived experience. The girls in the story were in a place. They had to be in that particular place for their particular story. As humans we are bound to a particular place. The disabled have a particular place in the world, because of their particular situations and physical or cognitive challenges. Throughout history individuals with disabilities have been designated to a *place*. Our story sheds light on the place of disability.

Home

The life- world is often expressed through a return to home. Home and in-home experiences have been covered by many phenomenologists. It is the place where the lived experiences occur. Day (1996), a human science researcher, studied the area of "at- homeness", and concluded that home involves a timeless quality; home involves a positive attunement to the present moment; home relates to a lived interplay between safety and familiarity; home offers an attunement into oneself in relationship to others; home relates to healing and personal well-being. There is an unconscious but very real bond between lived experience and home.

Home for the girls was more than houses on Central or Parkside Avenue. Home was an emotional place where they felt protected and loved. Home is the sense of "no matter what occurs around me, I have a place where I am safe; emotionally, physically and psychologically". Home is where a person can truly be free, just to be. Through phenomenology, the personal connection to the place called home can be revealed. Being immersed in the story, I connected intimately to the others, hearing their stories, relating to their lives, feeling their feelings. The "other" is no longer, but one of us. Jackie and Chuck were one of us.

CHAPTER TWO

Soil, Roots, Rhizomes, and Fences

A rhizome has not beginning or end; it is always in the middle, between things, interbeing, and intermezzo. Between things does not designate a localizable relation going from one thing to the other again, but perpendicular direction, a transversal moment that seeps one and the other a way, a stream without beginning or end that undermines its banks and picks up speed in the middle. (Deleuze & Guattari, 1987, p. 25)

The rhizome represents all the possibilities, whereas the cyclone fence and locked gates exemplify a connectiveness that closes off the outside world, and provides a physical and symbolic protective circle for those who abide within, while at the same time locking them out. Just as the rhizome needs rich soil to grow and flourish, story gathering is rooted in theory and thought. Growing a rhizome is about questioning, reflecting and writing. The cyclone fence must be supported by posts which are pounded deep into the soil for support. This story is "grounded" in the soil of reflexive epistemology and the lived experiences of those who share this connective experience with disability. The fence and the rhizome are juxtaposed in a beautiful, complicated life dance.

Fences

As I went back to the beginning... to my childhood; my roots, images came to my mind and pressed on my heart. I kept seeing the fence, the fence around Debbie's and Chuck's yard. The fence that kept me separated from the alley; my path to Laura's and Debbie's yard.

The fence was ever present, both physically and metaphorically, in the lives of the families dealing with disability. The neighborhood of my child self had only two fenced yards; the yards of Jackie and Chuck, both individuals with Down Syndrome. Fences structurally are an enclosure, a barrier or boundary. Fences keep people in and lock people out. Fences have supports such as posts or stakes, which hold sections together. Fences can also give a sense of false security; all may not be well inside the fence. Just because people are inside the structure it does not mean they are safe emotionally or physically. Fences are barriers to opportunities, blocking out the world. Some fences are not as thick as others. A cyclone or chain link fence is an opaque structure. It serves as a border, but one can see in, or look out from within. There is safety, yet the inside and the outside is not hidden from view. Fences have an opening, typically a gate. The gate locks or latches. At times the gate may be opened to let the world in or at other times locked tight to block the world out. The fence serves as a metaphor both for me and is representative for the lived experience of disability. The disabled are a marginalized group, typically blocked from participation in society as a whole. The gate is often closed, in terms of opportunities, education, and validation. The fence also represents the safety within the structure; the family who protects their family member with a disability, closing them off from the cruelty or stereotypes of the world beyond the fence; keeping them safe from harm. The fence serves as a symbol of boundaries, safety and restrictions ever present in the lives of people with disabilities.

As a child, when I was troubled or worried; I wanted the fence. If my grandparents were arguing in the house or someone made fun of me outside in the neighborhood, I just wanted to be by myself in my fenced yard. I would sit on my swing and sing silly songs that I would make up. I would sing those songs out loud to block out whatever problems that lurked on the other side of the fence. Physically and emotionally I could close the gate, swing and sing and go into my own safe world.

Rhizomes

When people go back to their origins, it can be said they return to their roots. Seeking clarification, one can analyze the "root" of the problem or situation. The rhizome is a root structure, but it is distinguished from the true root, because it possesses buds and nodes and shoots. It has extensions above and below the true root. The rhizome is able to make connections with diverse ways of coding. Resultantly, a rhizome structure does away with vertical hierarchies. A rhizome is never static. It is alive and welcomes other elements as it breaks down and makes new linkages. The concept of becoming is rhizomic.

The connections of three little girls, now grown women are well portrayed by a rhizome. The linkages that crossed time, place and circumstances are beautiful, revealing, and intricate. Roots reached out to touch others;whether it was Laura giving Colleen advice about doctors, or Mrs E. hugging my mom at my Aunt Jackie's funeral, the roots always connected us. Life for families dealing with disability issues can be represented by both of these symbols. The fence and the rhizome are juxtaposed metaphorically. Life situations and internal forces are full of fences and rhizomes, dancing beautifully choreographed steps. As in Resistance Theory, there is a pushing (rhizomic possibility) and holding back (fences) happening simultaneously. Fences are pounded into the soil to stay strong; rhizomes need the soil to grow.

Reflections on Perceptions

The eight year old me had no thoughtful concept of disability. Rarely were people with disabilities in the public eye in the early 1960s. I never thought of my Aunt Jackie as disabled. The word people used to describe people with intellectual disabilities at the time was "retarded," but even that term was rarely said out loud in my personal experience. Sometimes I noticed Jackie did and said silly or inappropriate things. One of my favorite childhood "Jackie" stories revolved around Jackie's reaction to passing gas. (Young children always get a kick out of bathroom humor, for some strange reason.) If Jackie would pass gas around me or my girlfriends, she would slap herself on her back end and say, "Oops stop that." That would send us into fits of embarrassed laughter. Yet, for some reason Jackie did not do those "not so adult-like things" around my Grandparents or other adults. She seemed to have two distinct personas, the one who acted like an adult and the other who was my own personal silly friend.

Jackie had a very matter of fact way of dealing with things and often took things literally. When she would toss a salad for instance, she would put the Tupperware lid tightly on the bowl and toss the bowl in the air. When I tried that once when my mother was around, I got in trouble for throwing the salad. I defended myself and told my mom Jackie had tossed salad that way. My mom responded by telling me to not listen to Aunt Jackie about everything.

I had this internal nagging tension about when to listen to Jackie or not, or why Jackie did things at times that most adults did not do in public. There was also an unspoken rule in my household not to ask about Jackie, especially around my Grandmother. Chuckie, Debbie's brother with Down Syndrome, was not discussed either. Chuck was the only person I knew as a young child with a disability. Jackie, (who often said out loud what she was thinking), did talk about Chuck and very sympathetically called him "poor 'tarded Chuck." I did hear my Grandmother say back to Jackie one time, "Do not say that about Chuck," but she did not provide any clarification to her comment.

Children should be seen and not heard was engrained in my personal make-up. I knew to never question my Grandmother, because she especially, amongst the five adults in my household, was the one to stay quiet around. Keeping my mouth shut was very difficult for me, and I was always saying, "but, but" in an attempt to ask another question and maybe get an answer; and then promptly shushed by an adult. I felt uncomfortable, but realized I had to keep my questions to myself.

I share these vignettes about life as I knew it then, because as an adult, I have come to realize that my childhood experiences with Jackie served as a catalyst in forming my own theory about disability. The nagging questions of the little girl, who was to be seen and not heard, are ever present in this adult, as I engage in thoughtful introspection. I have come to the realization that I look at the disability experience from a particular point of view. A viewpoint which is rooted in my past life experiences as a little girl hanging out with Jackie and Chuck. My past cannot be disregarded or set aside, but serves as a connective root strand now watered by a disability studies perspective.

A Disability Studies perspective encouraged me to look at the entire picture of disability as it related to families and time. Anthropology, sociology, and aesthetics were drawn upon to reveal the personal stories of the experience of disability. While much of the views and definitions of disability is socially constructed, I could not rely only on a strict social model of disability (Oliver, 1990) for this story. Oliver suggests the social model places disability squarely in society. He believes:

> It is not individual limitations, of whatever kind, which are the cause of the problem but society's failure to provide appropriate services and adequately ensure the needs of disabled people are fully taken into account in its social organization. (p. 32)

Indeed individuals with disabilities are oppressed and marginalized in society, but the experience of disability is more complex. By looking at disability only from a social perspective, the body and cognitive abilities are disregarded. The disability experience crosses politics, culture, identity and physicality. A strong social model tends to have a fairy tale type belief that when social constructs are broken down, individuals with disabilities will be able to independently access their world. Individuals with significant intellectual and physical disabilities, such as my niece Jamee, are still excluded.

I cannot ignore the social aspects of disability, especially as they have occurred in particular historical times. I am compelled to embrace a theory of disability which embraces the richness of the full disability experience. The experience of disability has to do with voices and silences, oppression and power, medical supports, labels, and societal expectations. Resistance Theory exposes and embraces the story of the disability in its entirety.

Resistance Theory affords me the opportunity to draw on the social model's focus on the "politics of disablement" (Gabel, 2005, p. 8) and yet embrace the possibilities. There is Resistance Theory embodied in our story. It is a story of families linked through friendship, each experiencing a unique relationship with disability. It is a story of limits and yet it is a story of possibility. Resistance Theory goes beyond strict social theory and is all about possibility. According to Gabel (2005), "A resistance theory of disability maintains the social model's focus on the politics of disablement and adds to it recognition of the complexities of resistance" (p. 8). Resistance Theory looks at the whole picture, the entire experience; not one side or the other but the entire experience of disability. Looking at the totality of the experience is imperative when uncovering the meaning of disability. In Resistance Theory, the body and medical support cannot be totally disregarded. Elements of disabled identity are the voice that cannot be heard in a typical manner, the brain that works in a particular way, or ambulation with a wheelchair. Individuals with disabilities have been given assistance because of medicine, and science. Medical science is embraced as a support but does not define a person's entity of humanness.

Jamee utilizes an augmentative communication device to answer questions and ambulates via a wheelchair that requires specific measurements to fit her body in a precise manner. The wheelchair is medical and scientific, yet it is not limiting, it enables her to get where she needs to go, so she can physically join society. The Dynovox gives her a voice, a voice that needs to be heard, so she can tell *her* story. Through this form of technology, Jamee can voice her choices and opinions. She is able to resist the societal stereotype often assigned to a person with significant intellectual disabilities. Gabel and Peters (2004) discuss the complexities of Resistance Theory, and ascertain it connotes a push and pull situation occurring simultaneously. People with disabilities such as Jamee can push against the status quo and at the same time pull society in to their way of seeing the world. Gabel (2005) stresses that Resistance Theory "connotes an open ended negotiation of meaning" (p. 8). The experience of disability has to do with voices and silences, oppression and power, medical supports, labels, and societal expectations. Resistance Theory exposes and embraces the story of disability in its entirety.

The rhizome and the fence metaphorically represent the resistance scenario, as they are juxtaposed in "a push me- pull me" connectiveness; the fence with the shutting out, but providing protection, and the rhizome, open to all the possibilities that occur in the lived experience of disability. A theory of resistance embraces disability in its complexity and entirety. My perspective of disability is grounded in Disability Studies and rooted in Resistance Theory.

Looking Back, Going Forward-Phenomenologically

This story is a return to my roots, it serves as an opportunity to dig into the soil and let it run through my fingers. I delved into the memories, the thoughts, and the lived experiences. Posing a question relating to lived experiences compelled me to call on a particular method of qualitative research. Phenomenology is the "till" for my uncovering. Founded by Edmund Husserl, phenomenology is considered to be one of the most important philosophical movements of the twentieth century (Morse & Richards, 2007). By definition, phenomenology is the study of human experience (Moustakas, 1994; Van Manen, 1990; Seamon, 2000). This definition, however, does not capture the full range or value of phenomenological inquiry. The aim of phenomenology is to examine and clarify human situations, happenings, meanings and experiences "as they occur in the course of every day life" (von Eckartsberg, 1998, p. 3). Phenomenology serves as a means to give "a rigorous description of human life as it is lived, and reflected upon, in all of its first person concreteness, urgency, and ambiguity" (Pollio, Henley, & Thompson, 1997, p. 5).

The rhizome symbolizes endless possibilities; through phenomenological inquiry the possibilities can be uncovered. Phenomenology studies the lived experiences. In effect, Pollio et al. (1997) believe the phenomenological "root strands" of an event are more clearly understood when we bring ourselves:

> Wholly to the transparency of the imaginary, think about it without the support of any ground, in short withdraw to the bottom of nothingness. Only then could we know what moments positively make up the being of experience. (p. 111)

My story is so much a part of me; the roots and fences were firmly planted. I was drawn to place myself inside the fence and outside the fence, to a philosophical, subjective zone so I could engage in deep reflection on the historical and contemporary lived experiences. Phenomenology offers the opportunity to uncover and explore the generational lived experience of disability. (Richards, 2007, p. 49). As a hermeneutic phenomenologist, I evoked culture, language, and experiences to understand and interpret the lived experiences.

In utilizing hermeneutics to understand the story, Gadamer (1989) describes the circular connectiveness of understanding: "We must understand the whole in terms of the detail and the detail in terms of the whole" (p. 258). Van Manen (1990) refers to this as the life world: "phenomenology attempts to explicate the meanings as we live them in our everyday existence, our life world" (p. 11). Hermeneutics was a tool for digging into MY earth. Hermeneutic phenomenology links the written word to recording the story of *the* experience. Words are written to share with contemporaries, and saved to share with future generations. We cannot go forward until we know and embrace where we have been.

Labels as Rhizomic Threads

Terminology describing individuals with disabilities is troublesome and those without disabilities have used terms like "differing abilities", "challenged" or "handi-capable". Members of the disability community themselves find these words condescending, and believe they are used to "sugar coat" so called "normal people's" uncomfortable-ness. Labels are just words until they serve as a means to objectify a person. This objectifying aspect prevents society (and sometimes the person with a disability herself) from experiencing the person for "who she is." At times family members in this story would hear the word "retarded" and just let it go. However, when someone actually called or described Chuck or Jackie as "retarded" it was very hurtful and never went unnoticed. When a person becomes objectified she is no longer a physical, spiritual, and emotional being, but the blind girl or the "retarded" girl or the "crippled" girl. Labels are consistently used to separate or categorize people. The process of labeling people results in an expectation of looks, performance, mental abilities and other human attributes. Since disability is a social role, labeling someone as disabled creates a self-fulfilling prophecy. Mercer (1973) clarifies: "People with disabilities are rewarded for behavior that conforms to social expectations associated with the disability role and punished for behavior that departs from these expectations" (p. 73). For those with disabilities, labels further increase feelings of oppression (Wilde, 2004).

Labeling confers identity and with it comes social responses. For individuals with disabilities the label can be the all defining characteristic of who they are and who they can become. The label and the implications derived from the label determine where children attend school, the classrooms or programs they are in, or the sports teams they join. The social construct of disability has the label as its root. Bogdan and Taylor (1982) note that the labeling of a person developmentally disabled also creates a self-fulfilling prophecy.

What does a label of developmentally disabled or retarded or cognitively impaired mean? For individuals with labels, their family, friends, caregivers, and teachers this is a critical question. Is the label the person? Is the person a label? Why have labels? Who needs a label? An individual who was labeled "mentally retarded" explains: "We don't want the label anymore. Certainly, you people have control… You're experts, but I'm an expert in my own field" (Monroe, 1994, quoted in Smith, 1999, p. 130).

Thoughts on Labels

As communicators, humans feel the need to identify people, objects, and things. I have a name, Sharon, but I carry many other labels or names: mother, wife, teacher, friend, daughter, sister. These labels are relatively neutral and do not carry negative or positive implications. I have been labeled with names not so-neutral like obese, loud, persistent, or moody, which have negative connotations. I have also been called helpful, friendly, dedicated, and creative which are of a more positive note.

Perhaps it is the type and connotation of the label that is important. A label can denote power, authority, and identity. Labels have scientific, social, and political usage. Teams have names; people have names. A name is in reality a label. Medicine labeled appropriately can save a life or labeled inappropriately can cause more problems. Labels are important in medicine. We all have alliances to our home team, school, or town, and when hearing their name or label it invokes a personal, emotional response. The label on the medicine bottle or the name of the school mascot, are seen as positive or helpful. It is a natural human activity to give names or labels to things and people. People have a sense of pride about their family name, and parents choose particular names for their children.

Many well meaning individuals have worked to label people with intellectual disabilities in ways that will not be harmful to them. We, as human beings, cannot stop labels, but those of us who experience disability on a personal level can actively reject the objectivity and presumptions constructed through the labeling process, and should be compelled to do so.

Jackie either never heard the words used to describe her intellectual abilities, or chose to ignore them. My mother asked Jackie if she had ever heard of the word Down Syndrome, or wondered why she had difficulty with money or lived with my mom all her life. Jackie just looked back at my mom with a puzzled expression. My mom felt the need to address it more bluntly.

"So Jackie, do you think anything is wrong with you?"

Jackie thought for a moment, then clearly replied, "I'm short."

I personally have gained a clearer understanding of the affect of labels on Jackie, and Chuck, and Jonathon and Jamee as well. The families all had experiences with labels. Chuck was labeled "special" shortly after birth. It was apparent he was an individual with Down Syndrome at birth. He went to "special" school, rode a "special" bus, and played on "special" teams. Jonathon was labeled the day after he was born as having severe brain damage. This label had profound implications as initially he was sent home to die. When it became apparent that he was going to live, it was the medical label that served as the gate to access much needed medical and therapeutic attention, and early intervention services. The label also served as a fence which the educational system in his community used to try to corral him into a special preschool, and a separate education. The fence was broken down because his mother refused to give into the social and educational presumptions. Jonathon was then included throughout his education. Yet, medically the label was needed to assure his physical well-being. The field of medicine relies on labels, and these labels can actually have life saving implications. For Jonathon, medicine improved his quality of life and aided his independence. He was able to receive occupational, physical, and vision therapy, since he had a labeled medical condition.

Jamee looked "fine" at birth, not displaying any apparent physical impairment, but shortly after birth her mom noticed her frail looking hands, and her body trembled. Upon consulting the best medical experts available in the area, her parents were assured that she was "fine," and the experts reminded them that all children develop differently. A year and a half later it appeared Jamee was not–so fine. She was unable to roll over, crawl, and could not sit independently. After assessing her on a develop-mental scale, the medical experts labeled her "malnourished" and "failure to thrive." Those labels entitled her to some medical attention, but for all intents and purposes did not qualify her for therapy. Finally at age 2 ½, upon receiving a new label, "cerebral palsy," magically (or so it seemed) the gate was opened. She could now receive speech therapy, physical therapy, and occupational therapy, and insurance would cover the expense. It also served as a means to enter early childhood special education services. Since Jamee could now receive the assistance she needed for accessing her world, the label was embraced. The label was a relief as it stood for opportunity, possibility, and hope. Cerebral palsy served as the key to open the gate for services, validation and monetary support.

Jackie never had a label in her inner family circle, although she was obviously a person with Down Syndrome. The term "mongoloid idiot" (Kliewer, 1998; Trent, 1994) was common when she was born. By acknowledging the label, she could have been sent to an institution but instead remained with her family and attended the neighborhood Catholic school, without an official label.

The danger may not lurk in the label, but in its use, a label can be a tool, a means to help and assist. A person is, however, more than the label; just as I am more than a mother, teacher, or obese, or creative. Jamee, Jonathon, Chuck and Jackie's "being", their lived experience, is more complex and intricate than a single label. Parents and individuals with disabilities often times have resisted the labels of disabilities. Jackie and Jonathon's families rejected the label.

The Paradox of Labels

When a parent or individual with disabilities totally resist a label, then services to provide equal access can be denied. Individuals who philosophically dispel labels need the label in order to receive educational, therapeutic, and medical assistance. This situation poses a conundrum for both people with disabilities and those who love them. Colleen, the mother of Jamee explains:

> We needed a name for whatever was "wrong" with Jamee. It would almost be easier if she had Down Syndrome. They (medical, insurance, and educational professionals) would know what Down Syndrome is. we would know what to do then, too. Colleen stated this after another session when a specialist was unable to determine the reason why Jamee was exhibiting "failure to thrive." I don't care about the label as much as I care that she gets whatever she needs. We call her Jamee; whatever they put on the paper is fine, as long as she gets the therapy.

If the definitions and labels assigned to individuals with disabilities are not oppressive enough, there are also disability stereotypes that permeate dominant culture.

What is Normal?

The categorizing of individuals with disabilities is entrenched in the deficit model of disability stemming from a curative approach (Snyder & Mitchell, 2001). This model is based on the premise that the individual's deficits must be corrected or fixed. Normal is a relative term. Special Education, government services and supports, and insurance are all based on the medical model premise. Laws for disability rights were designed to empower individuals with disabilities, but the methods utilized to gain access to programs and supports to "balance the field" further separate individuals with disability. People must "qualify" in order to receive assistance. In order to qualify, the disability must have a specific name based on what a person "lacks." Individuals with disabilities, their parents and families get to the point that they almost desire the label so they can have access to the world (Phillips, 1993).

When families and individuals with disabilities choose to use the label, it does not necessarily mean they philosophically embrace it. Individuals with disabilities have the right to determine their personal construction of normal without others being judgmental of their choices. Many individuals with disabilities embrace their disabled image, or "crippled" bodies (Charlton, 1998; Siebers, 2006). It is their choice in how they view themselves, and they can create their own individual definition of success (Phillips, 1993).

Throughout history the ontological reality of disability was impairment. Disability activists in the 1970s helped create a paradigm shift which resulted in separating impairment from disability. Biological domain and social experience became two distinct entities. The ontology of disability shifted from a physical or mental deficiency to the essence of exclusion and discrimination. To be a disabled individual was to be an oppressed individual. This distinction between disability and impairment was the theoretical framework for the social model of disability (Barton, 1998; Oliver, 1990). According to Oliver (1990) "Disability can be defined as a form of oppression and marginalization" (p. 65).

It is troublesome to only look at disability from one side or the other. The biology of the body is an essential piece of the lived experience of disability. The body and the physicality of disability can be instead embraced, dispelling old notions of disability, vulnerability, and negativity.

To truly uncover the full lived experience a different tactic may be needed; one that not only acknowledges the body, but embraces it, in all of its beauty; whatever that may look like, and at the same time embraces the possibilities. Over time changes may occur.

History According to Jackie, Chuck, Jonathon & Jamee
1937-2012

Men make their own history, but they do not make it just as they please; they do not make it under any circumstance chosen by them-selves, but under circumstances directly encountered, given and transmitted from the past.

Karl Marx, 18ᵗʰ Brumaire of Louis Bonaparte (1851)

Jackie, Chuck, Jonathon and Jamee made and are making their own histories. As stated so eloquently in Marx's quote they were not able to do it on their own. Society, cultural factors, family situations, and their particular place in time, had much to do with the formation of their personal histories.

Jackie's Place in Time

Jackie was born in the era of eugenics and fear of disability. History has not been kind to individuals with disabilities. Those considered different or abnormal have been ostracized, persecuted, sterilized and killed for centuries. Individuals were deemed subnormal and were considered sub-human. Jackie was born in 1937, the time between the two world wars. During World War One the IQ test was administered to men in the army. Half the men tested below normal. Instead of acknowledging a flawed test, the proponents of this testing saw it as an indicator that the country was being overwhelmed by feeble-minded people (D'Antonio, 2004). This finding only fueled the eugenic movement which was in full bloom in the United States as well as around the world. Opinions about people with disabilities were influenced by Darwin's theories of natural selection and interest in Mendel's work with genes. Many people believed that human traits, including intelligence, character, and morality were ideologically rooted. From this perception, it was thought that individuals with disabilities could never be adequately trained to live by their own means. If people with disabilities were allowed to reproduce, they would continue to breed more mentally deficient offspring, thus putting a burden on society (Ferguson, 1994; Noll & Trent, 2004; Rosen, Clark, & Kibitz, 1976).

The American eugenics movement campaigned to build institutions in order to house all the mentally and physically defected people. Institutions such as the Fernald School in Massachusetts and the Willowbrook School in New York were built along with hundreds more throughout the country to house individuals deemed "sub-normal" (Wolfensberger, 1975). Hundreds of thousands of children were part of a national effort to eradicate the subnormal for over 50 years. Physicians, bureaucrats and other socially minded professionals applied the principles of animal husbandry to weed out the bad stock and segregate individuals with disabilities (Kevles, 1995).

The institutions held children and adults that were unsuitable for procreation, yet perfect for experimentation and forced labor. Once locked away, those considered subnormal were isolated from society, endured overcrowding, malnutrition, and physical abuse. Medical procedures, such as the lobotomy, electroshock and sterilization were carried out with the residents serving as medical guinea pigs. World War II brought with it Nazism and genetic engineering. Some of these barbaric practices and institutions continued until the 1970s. As late as 1974, individuals without cognitive disabilities were discovered living in state training centers, "for the retarded" in Florida. Some of the individuals residing there had been placed there inappropriately for over 20 years (Rothman & Rothman, 2004).

During the 1930s and1940s, the definition of mental retardation basically focused on one of three areas of development: the inability to perform daily common tasks, deficits or delays in social development, or low IQ (Yepsen, 1941). Edgar Doll (1936) applied the social competence definition when he proposed that mental retardation, "referred to social incontinence due to mental sub normality, which has been developmentally arrested, which obtains at maturity, is of constitutional origin, which is essentially incurable" (p. 38). As a person born and raised in this era, Jackie, according to Doll's definition, bore the label ;*mentally retarded.*

Myths

Many myths were propagated about disabled people in the postwar era. People of the time worried that disability was something they could "catch". Society looked to find something or someone to blame for producing sub-normal individuals. If retardation is biologically propagated, what is the best way to stop this? Parents and siblings often wondered what they did to deserve this fate, or if it was catchy, or if they did something wrong or sinful for this to occur in their family. Intellectual disability, according to Brockley (2004) "acted as a magnifying lens, revealing the cultural constructions of American family life, including hidden tensions and fears" (p. 133).

Fears

The parents of disabled children in the 1940s faced a society that thought their children were difficult, unteachable, helpless, belligerent, subhuman or criminal (Castles, 2004). Doctors often assumed that parents would reject a child born with Down Syndrome: "The parent is repelled by the unfortunate child's mental inadequacies, by his grotesque physical appearance, by awareness of the social stigma which he is brought on the family" (Bakwin, 1956, p. 487). Parents were encouraged to give their child up. Doctors assumed the stigma would be so difficult for their family that the best way to deal with this, to avoid attachment, and undue stress by the mother, was to take the baby immediately away at birth. The baby would be brought to an institution right from the hospital. Families who chose to keep their child at home were often worried they would be shunned for their choice. Some worried that (because it was physically obvious that their child was disabled) the child could be snatched and then sent off to an institution. A parent describes this fear:

When Janie first came home to stay, I developed an irrational, but nevertheless horrifying fear of arrest each time I took Janie beyond the boundaries of our property. Coupled with this was the fear that she would be snatched away from me, and hustled off to an institution. (Castles, 2004, p. 363)

Parents were often taught by doctors and other professionals to fear their children with Down Syndrome (Meyer, 1956). Parents worried that although they accepted the child in their home and family, society did not accept their child. They pondered just how to accomplish this task of social acceptance for their children. Schwartzenberg (2005), in her book of life stories of families and disabilities, *Becoming Citizens* explains:

The World War II generation is often called the pioneering parent advocates. Invisible to most of us, they rode a wave of both social and human rights activism during the postwar decades, activism that transformed life in America. A quiet undercurrent of the civil rights movement, their first act was to challenge their doctors and pediatricians by saying, "No, I will not institutionalize my child." Nor would they abandon their children to the jurisdiction of the medical/professional establishment. (p. ix)

Tiny seeds of new ideas were being planted. Parents were quietly doing what they felt was right for them and their children. Without drawing much attention, they were keeping their children home with the family. Unbeknownst to them, the seeds planted after the war would grow into fruition a generation later as parents and people with disabilities themselves would loudly demand social acceptance.

Educational Issues

Teachers and researchers who felt that students with Down Syndrome (like Jackie) could learn to read or write were often dismissed or their research was considered invalid. Educational theory of the time ascertained that feebleminded children and children with Down Syndrome would never be able to read or learn academic skills. When teachers or educational researchers proved otherwise, it was difficult to get their work published or recognized (Kleiwer, Bicklen, & Kasa- Hendrickson, 2006). In the late 1940s and early 1950s, educational programs began to emerge to support students with disabilities. Still, in 1956 (Winzer, 1993) only 18% of students with any type of disability were in educational programs. Jackie, although she could read and write, would not have been in those programs, because in 1956 she was already 20 years old.

Chuck's Place in Time

Chuck was born in the early 1960s. This time period, in the history of disability, is typically thought of as the age of parent involvement and societal awakening. The previous decade of the 1950s was a critical decade for legislative advocacy of parents of mentally retarded children. Parents came together to fight for their children's rights and to share ideas and information. The National Association for Retarded Children (ARC) was formed in 1950 (ARC, 2008). A group of parents in Pennsylvania rallied together to fight for their children's right to an education. During this time "little was known about the condition of mental retardation or its causes, and there were virtually no programs or activities in their communities to assist in the development and care of children and adults with mental retardation and to help families" (ARC, 2008). This parent group lobbied for educational rights and community services for their children. They set out to educate government officials about the needs and rights of their children, and to demonstrate that adequate provisions must be made for them. Though the faction started as a small group of parents, the group gained national public recognition and divisions of ARC were developed nationwide (ARC, 2008).

The human factor associated with the 1960s created a new climate. People began to question the old stereotypes as they pertained to the disabled. Winzer (1993) explains:

The 1960s ushered in a series of exposés about society's treatment of disabled persons, of studies of the efficiency of

31

segregated classes, and a massive infusion of funding into the growth of professional and community interest in the problems of social disadvantages. (p. 376)

Still many children with intellectual disabilities were being sent off to institutions because parents thought it was the best place for them. Carleen Ashley (Shapiro, 1994) recalls the day her twin sister went to live far away: "It felt like someone had died" (p. 10). She explained how on a sunny day in the spring of 1965 her mother carried her "severely disabled" sister in a red and white party dress out to the family station wagon. Her mom cradled her sister in her arms while her Dad drove on in silence, more than 100 miles to the New Hampshire Hospital for Children with Mental Retardation.

In 1966, Burton Blatt, a professor of special education from Boston College, ventured into institutions which housed the "mentally retarded" over his Christmas break. He took along a friend as a photographer and the atrocities of institutional living were exposed in all its glory. Their documentation later took the form of a book filled with compelling black and white photos of the stark reality and brutality which was found within the walls of the fenced properties. Blatt and Kaplan (1966) in the introduction of the book shares:

> Our *Christmas in Purgatory* brought us to the depths of despair. We now have a deep sorrow, one that will not abate until the American people are aware of and do something about the treatment of severely mentally retarded in our state institutions. We have again been caused to realize that "Man's inhumanity to man makes countless thousands mourn." (p.vi)

The citizenry of the United States were becoming aware of what lurked within the fenced-in edifices. Blatt commented in his book that all the institutions had one element in common. All of them were behind fences made of iron or barbed wire. There were also locks on the gates, and bars on the windows. Exposing the lived experiences that occurred behind the fences brought about some changes for people with disabilities. The fences were beginning to come down both physically and symbolically.

The Kennedy presidency marked an era of interest in special education, vocational rehabilitation, and supportive services. This was due in part to the fact that the president's sister had cognitive disabilities, and later during Lyndon Johnson's reign, the Vice President Hubert Humphrey had a granddaughter with Down Syndrome. Kennedy formed a panel, The President's Panel on Mental Retardation, to study programs for people with mental retardation which made decisions about guardianship and social security benefits. In his address to the panel he stated:

Although we have made considerable progress in the treatment of physical handicaps, although we have attacked on a broad front the problems of mental illness, although we have made great strides in the battle against disease, we as a nation have too long postponed an intensive search for solutions to the problems of the mentally retarded. That failure should be corrected. (Murdick, Garten, & Crabtree, 2002, p. 3)

Kennedy's challenge served as a catalyst for change for the people known at the time as mentally retarded. In 1963, Public Law 88-164 (Minnesota Mental Retardation Planning Council, 1966) was signed, which broadened educational opportunities for children who required special education.

Institutions and special schools were the norm in the 1960s. Many of the schools were private schools which were formed by parents and governed by parent boards. Standards were developed to protect the individuals living in institutional environments.

Chuck's world was a safer world for the disabled. His parents were not directly told to put him away. By 1962 there was a scientific explanation for his "condition of Down Syndrome". While the social understanding of disability had improved, Chuck was not welcome at his sister's parochial school, and when he entered school at age 6, the local public school did not have a program for him. He instead had a special school to attend. Chuck was considered trainable mentally handicapped or TMH (Kliewer, 1998), so he could be grouped accordingly at his special school.

People began to see children with disabilities in the community with their families. White, middle-class, parent advocacy groups were able to help society make the shift from disability being thought of as undesirable, sinful, or lower class (Trent, 1994). Since these families were "normal" their disabled members were thought of as individuals who needed medical or charitable support. Disabled children were emerging from the shadows as visible members of their families and communities (Metzel, 2004).

Jonathon's and Jamee's Place in Time

Jonathon and Jamee were born in the era of integration. Jonathon, born in 1986, and Jamee, born in 1990, is reflective of another generation of disability. Many changes had occurred since the late 1960s and 1970s. The 1970s continued to bring to the forefront the dehumanizing conditions of the institutions which housed and educated people with disabilities via the media. In February 1972, TV commentator Geraldo Rivera gained entry to The Willowbrook School for the Developmentally Disabled (Rivera, 2008). With cameras rolling, Rivera exposed the appalling conditions in this institution which was reflective of many institutions throughout the nation. The institution was overcrowded, lacked hygiene facilities and little or no educational practices were evident (D'Antonio, 2004; Fisher & Fisher, 2002). Children and adults were filmed naked and living in their own excrement.

The atrocities portrayed in photos in *Christmas in Purgatory* a decade before now came via television right into the homes of America. While improvements had occurred in that people with disabilities were more visible in the community, the majority of individuals with disabilities, especially with significant intellectual disabilities, were still housed in institutions. This televised exposé occurred at the "right" time. The public outcry, in combination with the support of the legislators, assisted in bringing to the forefront the de- institutionalization phase for individuals with disabilities. In 1975, a consent decree compelled the State of New York to establish group homes for the Willowbrook residents (Rothman & Rothman, 2004). The tides were turning; a shift from institutionalization to community-based services. Jonathon and Jamee live in the time of community-based programs.

"Community" became the goal for social policies as they related to people with disabilities. The local issues relating to community was emphasized in the Developmental Disabilities Assistance and Bill of Rights Act of 1984; Public Law 98 – 527 (Minnesota Governor's Council on Disability,2008) which stated that persons with mental retardation have the same opportunities for community resources available to all persons, and be able to partake in the same community activities as non-handicapped individuals, and residences for people with mental retardation should be in homes or home-like settings, which are in proximity to the community resources. This law opened doors for the visibility of people with disabilities in the community. Being true community members, however, was still a subject of consternation. Relationships are also elements of community involvement as identified by Bogdan and Taylor (1982):

> Being IN the community is not the same as being OF the community... being in the community points only to physical presence; being part of the community means having the opportunity to interact and form relationships with the other community members. (p. 210)

Laws were being put in place for inclusion for people with disabilities. Laws did not, however, guarantee that people with disabilities were socially embraced as true contributing members of the community.

Of the Community?

Passage of federal special education law was revolutionary and had many positive effects and outcomes. Children with disabilities who had been left out of the public system were guaranteed an education. However, passage of the law did not fully address all the layers of educating students with disabilities, and it did not curtail the debates about the appropriate programs to support students with disabilities. Despite strong legislative backing and the empirical evidence of the benefits of inclusive education, schools and school districts still had a difficult time providing a learning experience which included all children, especially those with significant disabilities (Dowling, 2008). The interpretation of the law could vary from school to school, district to district, or state to state. Parents continued to invoke law and obtain lawyers to ensure that their children's educational and social and emotional needs were being met appropriately (Friend, 2008).

The passage of ADA opened doors for individuals with disabilities both figuratively and literally. ADA legislation directly addressed communication, requiring close captioning and also insured that buildings have ramps and elevators and that public transportation must accommodate wheelchairs. It also had an impact on employment accessibility. Employers may not refuse to hire an individual because that person has a disability, and as in the educational setting, reasonable accommodations must be made in the work setting (Fleischer & James, 2001).

Progress had been made for including and accepting individuals with disabilities in school and the community. Inclusion in the community and in school was declared the right of all individuals with disabilities, yet negative terminology and labeling were still in vogue. The federal term for individuals with cognitive disabilities was still mental retardation (Friend, 2008). Individuals with intellectual disabilities voices became louder in attempting to change the terms to describe them. A man with intellectual disabilities explains, "…we don't want that label anymore. Certainly you people (the professionals) have control… you're the experts in your field, but I am an expert too, in my own field" (Monroe, 1994, quoted in Smith, 1999, p. 130).

Many children with disabilities were physically included in the neighborhood schools but they were not "of the school." Friend (2008) found that kindergarten children tended to conceptualize disability in terms of physical abilities, and that they generally were positive toward people with disabilities; however, less than half of the children in the study could identify a classmate with a disability as a friend. As children enter middle school and high school, they are less likely to have a friend with a disability. In a study researching friendship between middle school age children and middle school children with disabilities, only 10% of the students said they had a friend with a disability (Siperstein, Parker, Norins-Bardon, &Widamon, 2007). They were even more reluctant to engage in any outside social activities with the students with disabilities. Much of the literature in the field supports the evidence of the lack of friendships and social inclusion for children with disabilities (Siperstein, Leffert, & Wenz-Gross, 1997; Zetlin & Murtaugh, 1988).

Inclusion and what is considered inclusionary practices varies widely, depending on local policies, teacher attitudes, administrator's commitment, parent and community support (Friend, 2008). Many school administrators are apprehensive about inclusionary practices. For example, Praisner (2003) surveyed elementary principals about their attitudes toward inclusion. She found only one in five principles were positive about inclusionary practices and the others were uncertain. According to The United States Department of Education, as of 2004, 52.61% of students with intellectual disabilities were educated outside of the general education classroom more than 60% of the day (United States Dept. of Education, 2004). In some schools inclusionary practices were thought of as exemplary and in others the term inclusion was employed, but corresponding practices were not in place (Friend, 2008). I personally witnessed an example of this situation:

> I was observing in the school which called their inclusion program "push in". Students with physical and intellectual disabilities were included via being "pushed in" with their general education grade level peers. As I was walked down the hall, I witnessed a general educator push the classroom door open, while loudly exclaiming "I'm not putting up with this anymore," and she aggressively "pushed out" a second grader in a wheelchair

with physical and cognitive disabilities. She reprimanded him loudly in the hall, telling him he was not going to make "moaning sounds" in her classroom because she had children who were trying to learn.

Just as parents and individuals fought for true community involvement, parents and disability advocates continued to fight for true educational involvement; to be "of the school," not just "in" the school. Jonathon's and Jamee's temporality affected their lived experiences. Their social and educational experiences were shaped and constructed by the times in which they lived. Their lived experience will continue to be affected by the viewpoints and social constructs in the years to come.. Social constructs, temporality and spatiality will continue to shape their destiny.

Throughout history, parents and families have played key roles to bring about change in the lives of their children with disabilities. Situations and viewpoints have changed over the decades. Yet parents and families have remained key threads in the rhizome of the disability experience.

The Stories

Somewhere in the deepest part of my being I knew I needed to tell this story, our story. Throughout my life I would share little vignettes in conversation with people about my life growing up with my Aunt Jackie. I was always told "you should write that down" or "that would be a great book", but because it was my life, it did not seem important enough to share. Perhaps the determined spirit of my grandmother whispered in my ear to capture the words before there was no one left to tell them. Or it was Laura reminding me that there is something unique about our friendship and the ties to disability? Whatever the reason, I am compelled now to share the connected lived experience of Jackie, Chuck, Jonathon, and Jamee.

CHAPTER THREE

Jacqueline is a Nice Name

Jackie, 1937

Jacqueline is a nice name, but it by no means describes the woman I knew as Aunt Jackie. In fact the only time I heard Jackie called "Jacqueline" was when my grandmother would give her a look, and say "Jacqueline Marie", when Jackie would be doing something inappropriate in my grandmother's eyes, such as having her mouth hanging open. The name; Jacqueline was mentioned over and over again by Jackie herself when I was pregnant with my children. The conversation would be as follows:

J. (Jackie):	Mmmm, so when are you having that baby? (As she patted my protruding belly.
S. (Sharon/me):	Oh, in a couple of months.
J.:	So have you thought of names yet?
S.:	We are thinking of some; Matthew for a boy and maybe Shannon for a girl.
J.:	(With a contemplative look) You know, Jacqueline is a nice name. (Looks up with a hopeful expression).
S.:	Oh, that is a nice name; I wonder whose name that is anyway?
J.:	You kidder you, that is my name!
S.:	Oh really, no I never knew that. (Jackie laughs)

S.: So anyway, we want the baby to have his or her own name. We are not naming the baby after anyone.

J.: Oh shucks, Jacqueline is a nice name anyway.

This same dialogue or something similar went on with my next two pregnancies, as it did when my sisters and sister-in-law were pregnant. Jackie kept saying "Jacqueline is a nice name" whenever she got the opportunity. As life went on and the years went by, Jackie experienced dementia, and she rarely knew us by name. She would call our children cute puppies. One day we were visiting Jackie at her Community Integrated Living Arrangement (CILA) home, where Jackie lived with caretakers and five other women with intellectual disabilities. As we visited, Jackie was busy petting my niece and calling her cute. Jackie began to focus her eyes on my very pregnant sister-in-law's stomach; which was housing twins. I heard her mumble as she gazed at Pattie's stomach: "Jacqueline is a nice name." My emotions came to the surface and tears came to my eyes, as I realized for that fleeting moment my Aunt Jackie had returned to us. I thought to myself, yes Jackie, Jacqueline is a nice name.

Beginnings

Life for Jacqueline was not always nice or neat or easily explained. Jackie's lived experience was complicated, multilayered, influenced by her place in time, her physicality in her environment, and her relationality with those who shared her life. Jackie's story begins on a blustery November day in the year of 1937.

Jackie was the second daughter of Ed and Dorothy, a couple in their twenties residing in a rented home on the south side of Chicago. Her two year old sister Doris was excited to have a new sister born the day after her birthday. Black and white photos, framed with scalloped white borders now yellowed with age, show Doris dressed in her Sunday's best for her sister's homecoming day. My grandmother's dark hair is blowing in the wind and she is bent over trying to get low enough so little two year old Doris can see her sister. The picture depicts Doris peering lovingly into the face of her sister as her mom pulls the blanket away for her to get a peak.

Looking carefully at the photo I notice, even at seven days old, Jackie has the facial characteristics of a baby with Down Syndrome. I know, just by looking at the photo, that Jackie manifests a certain set of identifiable traits that places her in a particular category. By virtue of my life experiences, I gaze at the picture with an educated lens. As she gazed at her child, my grandmother saw Jackie, not Down Syndrome. With a big smile on her face, the adoring big sister saw her sibling, not Down Syndrome, and my Pa was just enjoying the moment, taking in the beauty of his three girls. Lived time or temporality has to do with the past changing itself because we are already looking toward the future (Van Manen, 1990). The family was forever changed by the arrival of their new baby Jackie. A feeling of anticipation and joy filled this moment.

Children who we currently label as Down Syndrome, were called "mongoloid idiots" in 1937, the year of Jackie's birth. The majority of children with disabilities were institutionalized and cared for by ill trained and uninformed attendants (Trent, 1994). Most institutions or training schools in the late 1930s merely housed the children called imbeciles, idiots, or morons. When World War II started, the institutions were extremely understaffed as many staff members went to join the military or left to seek government employment. This was the corporality of children with visible disabilities when Jackie was born. I asked my mother, Doris, what she may have heard about Jackie's birth.

"My mother told someone the story, she never told me about Jackie's birth, but she told someone, because I heard the story somewhere. You know, she never explained anything to me really about Jackie, and I never really asked." My mom is looking off in the distance somewhere and is looking confused.

"You never asked about Jackie, even as an adult ?" (I am thinking this is bizarre)

"No, I didn't, I guess I just knew it was something Momma would not want to talk about. Anyway, right after Jackie was born in the hospital, the nurse brought her in and Jackie had scratches on her. My mom asked why she had scratches and the nurse told her Jackie had scratched herself. Years later, when my mother was trying to figure out what happened to Jackie, she told someone, not sure who she told, maybe someone dropped Jackie in the hospital. She remembered that Jackie was scratched. She was trying to figure it out, I guess."

"Mere didn't know it was a chromosome thing?"

"No, no one knew that, or they never explained that. My mother insisted for awhile they dropped Jackie and that was why she was the way she was. But my mother never talked about it, she never referred to her by anything(disability label) ever, ever, ever, you know. She just was Jackie. That was all there was to it."

My mom strongly said "That was all there was to it." It was if my mother was reminding herself never to question her Momma about her sister. My mom was still answering to her mom internally, and Mere was dead for 40 years.

This is the first evidence of the internal struggle and outward resistance portrayed by my grandmother. Often times mothers who give birth to a child with disability, long before a true diagnosis, have an intuition that something just does not feel right to them (Spiegel & van den Pol,1993;Ferguson,2002).My grandmother possibly was feeling anxious, but did not understand her own anxiety.

Aunt Laverne (Lovie) is my grandmother's youngest sister and the only living sibling (of five) in my grandmother's family. Aunt Lovie believes she was around nine when Jackie was born. Throughout our conversations, she stressed how young her sister was when my mom and Jackie were born. I posed a similar question about Jackie's birth to her.

My aunt paused, gathered her thoughts, tskd a bit, then proceeded to tell me all in one breath:

"Well, we all went to this Doctor Mc Cory when she (Jackie) was born and no one knew anything was wrong...and Dorothy was so young and you know your mom was still a baby, too. She (Dorothy) should have been told, someone should have known, if they (medical people) knew, someone should have told her, but no one did, no one said. I do not know if they really did know...people did not know it was a chromosome thing then, I guess, right?... because it is a chromosome thing, but no they did not tell her anything. She went home thinking nothing was wrong, that she (Jackie) was fine."

Looking retrospectively at this situation, my grandmother spent a great deal of her life trying to convince herself and the rest of the world that Jackie really was Jackie. Her child was not "mongoloid" or "idiot" (Noll & Trent, 2004) or any of the other words utilized to label people with intellectual disabilities in the 1930s. Ferguson (2002) explains the way in which a family interprets disability, or their reaction to giving birth to a child with a disability, cannot be separated from the socio-historical context of when this occurred. My grandmother was looking to the professional to provide her with information, but the reality was that the professionals of the time had very little information themselves (Featherstone, 1980). The socio-historical constructs of the times were also fences to getting accurate information.

In my short conversation with my great aunt I received so much information. I kept asking questions and just wanted to take it all in.

"Do you have any specific memories about Jackie as a baby?

"I remember when I was a little girl; I thought Jackie as a baby was so adorable. I would sit and watch her because she was so cute. She would just lie in her crib and the light from the bedroom window was shining on her, and she would just look at the light and she would hold her one hand out and look at it for so long, she was so adorable and happy. Then someone gave her this little gold bracelet, and they put it on the one hand. She would look at it and she was so happy looking at the bracelet. She was cute and had shiny brown hair; she would look at each and every finger, and then do it all over again. I just found that so adorable, my little niece, and after all this time, I can still see her doing that, it is such a clear memory. She was so beautiful, my little niece."

My Aunt Lovie went back to her child-self in this recollection. Young children have an innocent interpretation of life. They have yet to be tarnished by societal expectations or categorizations. Ferguson and Asch

(1989) said "the most important thing that happens when a child with disabilities is born; is that a child is born" (p. 108). Lovie was sharing this celebratory experience. She was excited to have a new baby niece to love, and she was immersed in the excitement of a new birth. This was one of the clearest descriptions in my conversation with my aunt, her tone denoted happy reminiscing from a place back in time.

Reality

Life went on for the family and Jackie was now around six months old. Dorothy set out with her daughters to go to the grocery store. She put the girls in the buggy and walked to the local grocery store. Aunt Lovie reflects on the day her sister, Dorothy began to look at her daughter, Jackie, differently.

"Do you remember when my grandmother came to realize that there was something *wrong* with Jackie? (My Aunt had referred to "something being wrong" with Jackie when describing when Jackie was born)

My aunt describes my grandmother's very public confrontation with her new reality.

"I remember that clearly, I do not know if I was told about the whole story then as a little girl, or I learned all of this later, but yes, I know the story...Dorothy had Jackie in her buggy, I do not know if your mom was there too, she could have been because she would have been little too. She (Dorothy) was pushing the buggy through the store and a woman came up and looked in the buggy and said to her (while she was looking at Jackie who was probably around 6 months old at the time). "Oh you have a child like that, my sister has one like that too". Your grandmother left the store crying and called my mother up hysterical, begging her to tell her if something was wrong with Jackie. I think she was herself starting to think something might be wrong. I remember her coming over then and she was hysterical and crying, she kept pleading: "Tell me, tell me". My mother said that she thought she might be like *those* children. I do not recall what she called what was wrong with Jackie, just that she, my mother, was starting to think something may be wrong. They both kept saying they wondered why nobody said anything. It was awful. I remember because my sister was crying so hard. Oh Dorothy, poor Dorothy."

As human beings we tend to have a dualistic point of view, thinking in terms of good-bad, bright-dull, normal-abnormal, and right-wrong. The words "wrong" or "something was wrong" are said over and over by the story tellers in this uncovering. The word "wrong" could be replaced by "different", but no matter the term used, Jackie was being defined as a person lacking "something". In early disability research individuals who looked like Jackie and were categorized as mongoloids were considered sub human (Wright, 2004). I would never propose that a person with an intellectual disability such as Down Syndrome is sub human, yet immersed in the moment of conversation with my great aunt, I, myself, used the word, "wrong" to describe my Aunt Jackie. Words used as descriptors for people are powerful, and represent more than a word. There is nothing "wrong" with Jackie. She was the person she was destined to be.

The words now used to describe Jackie were "a child like that" or "those children". My Aunt's retelling of the story is using words reflective of the times. Children like "those" were sent away, they were not thought of as worthy to be included in society (Trent, 1964; Wolfensberger, 1975). This could account for the reaction of my grandmother. She may have had an opinion of what life would be like for Jackie as one of "those" children. This event was a moment when any worries anyone may have had were exposed. It is also the only time anyone talks directly about my grandmother breaking down externally. A myriad of feelings must have been running through her very being. If she was similar to other parents dealing with the revelation of having a child with a disability, she may have felt confused, scared, guilty, and inadequate or uniformed (Bailey & Simeonsson, 1988; Ferguson, 2002).

Secrets

My mom verified Aunt Lovie's story and reminded me that these stories were told to her by her aunts after her mother had passed away. My grandmother kept her thoughts about giving birth and confronting disability to herself, yet she was confronting it every day of her life.

She put up internal and external fences, which kept her from having people to confide in and inflicted deep internal struggles. My mother, as an adult, still never questioned her mother. As a child, my mother could never voice her opinions; this fence was ever present through my mother's adult life as well. My mother and grandmother never discussed the reality of disability. I asked my mother more than once if my grandmother ever said anything to her about her concerns, or if she ever called Jackie mongoloid or a person with Down Syndrome. My mother's reply was "No, never." My mom does think she overheard at times her parents talking about their concerns for Jackie but they always used vague terms like "how she is." The fence of protection was not always blatant, but sometimes very subtle as reflected in the words, "how she is"; keeping the descriptors used for disability away from describing Jackie.

My aunt went on to describe the next stages, reflected in the life of her sister's family when Jackie was still an infant. Based on the stories shared with me, my grandmother needed to have a reason why this happened to her baby. Evidence of this is the story about the nurses dropping her, or the fact that my Grandfather's (Pa) mother was not married to Pa's natural father. Since the medical professionals had not given my grandmother an explanation she could accept, she was still searching for an answer that was logical to her. During this time in history, illegitimacy was thought of as a social liability that bred idiots or people who would not contribute to society. Adoption records were closed in 1930 so that families of adoptive children would not be subjected to the "stigma of illegitimacy" (Roberts, 2001, p.1). This fact served a perfect excuse for my grandmother, who felt inadequate next to an over powering mother-in-law.

My aunt told me that my grandmother and grandfather met in high school (which I was aware of). She said when my grandfather entered high school he had a different last name and initially that was the last name they knew him by. She said at some point during high school he started using a different last name (the family name we continue to use).

My mother did not know that the man she knew as her Grandpa was not her natural grandfather, nor was she aware that her Irish last name was not reflective of her true nationality. My aunt said she personally found out through the grapevine that my grandfather's natural father was a drinker and in her words, "died on skid row or something". He and my great grandmother were never married.

There were emotional issues that lurked under the surface; family secrets that were not discussed. My grandmother never discussed Jackie with my mom, nor did she ever tell my mom about the situation with my grandfather's birth. All these stories came out after my grandmother and great grandmother passed away and my grandmother's sisters came over to help my mom clean out my grandmother's belongings.

I remember the day my great aunts came over to help pack up Mere's things. I recall that Jackie and I kept being sent out of the room. They were guarding the secrets that 10 year old me and Jackie did not need to know. So many "things" no one ever talked about.

Seeking a clearer understanding and trying to decide if the triangular relationship with my grandmother, grandfather, and his mother had a bearing on my grandmother's insecurity or self assurance, I asked my mom about what she remembered about the situation with her parents and grandmother.

"Mom, can you describe the relationship with Grandma Sheehan and Mere and Pa?"

"Well, I know Grandma Sheehan treated Daddy like a little boy and that made my mom mad. It was always…My Ed this or my Ed that. I suppose since he was her only child she thought he did no wrong. She would also just show up where my parents were, when they would go out, and take over. If my dad would get drunk she would always have excuses for him. She would try to tell my mom what to do. I do not think my mom confronted her about anything or the way she felt. In fact Momma would go out of her way so that Grandma did not know anything was wrong. I know she (Grandma Sheehan) never knew that I stayed home from school to take care of my mom, and my mom made sure Grandma did not know if she was mad at Daddy about something. She tried to keep things to her self. My mother did not approve of the life Grandma Sheehan led."

"How do you know that she did not approve of her life?"

"Well, like me singing, my mom wanted me only to sing at family things. She told me over her dead body would I ever be a bar room singer like my grandmother, look what that got her."

There was obviously underlying tension, which may never be revealed. The situation between my grandmother and her mother-in law may have caused feelings of insecurity, resistance, and determination in my grandmother, as she dealt with her marital situation and her role as mother to Doris and Jackie.

After the confrontation with the woman in the grocery store and exhausting all the other reasons real or imaginary for Jackie's slow development, my aunt told me that my grandmother started going to different doctors for clarification on whatever was "wrong" (my aunt's word) with Jackie. My grandmother was told by the doctors to put Jackie away, to put her in an institution and forget about her. The physicians said she would not live long anyway, and she would never learn how to walk or talk. These same words were spoken to Mrs. E almost thirty years later about her son Chuck. One doctor told my grandmother she was young and the best thing she could do was forget Jackie and have more children. Another dwelled on the harm that it would cause the family to keep this child in the home. Children with Down Syndrome were also prone to heart defects and breathing difficulties. Those conditions were left untreated in institutions allowing the children to die a natural death. The advice of the doctors was typical of this time period (the late 1930s early 1940s). Doctors and professionals continued to give this same advice to parents for decades.(Ferguson, 1994; Noll & Trent, 2004; Trent, 1994)

My grandmother took their words as a personal challenge. While not receiving an answer, she now knew what she would not do with her daughter. She was not going to let those people tell her what her child, Jackie, could or could not do. My grandmother may have not realized it at the time, but she was embarking on a personal journey, one that would lead her to finding ways to change the dominant cultural perceptions about disability on a very personal level as it related to her Jackie. She was intent on breaking down the societal fences of disability and, unknowingly, was instead looking at the rhizomic possibilities. In other words, she would find a way for Jackie to be part of the world.

According to my Aunt, my Mom, and stories shared with me by my grandfather when I was a teenager, my grandmother took her daughter home and began to figure out ways to help Jackie be more independent. I cannot be sure of her reasoning or deep personal thoughts, but I think my grandmother felt she needed to prove herself on some level. She felt compelled to prove to the doctors, her mother-in law and to herself, that Jackie would be the child to defy the odds. Perhaps she was trying to convince everyone (even herself) that her daughter was not really "one of those people." Despite having only one or two years of high school, my grandmother employed many techniques and methods to teach her daughter. Aunt Lovie talks about my grandmother's teaching methods and determination that Jackie would indeed walk.

"But she never ever would put Jackie away and made sure she would walk. In fact, she kept practicing with her. I was a little girl and remember her putting Jackie out in front of her with a belt and tying men's ties and teaching her to walk. And Jackie did walk and not much later than anyone else would and she could talk as clear as anyone else."

School for Jackie

My Pa was driving me to college one day in the late 1970s and was feeling particularly reflective as we were discussing my career choice of becoming a teacher. I enjoyed these quiet times with Pa because when it was just the two of us he would share stories of Mere (my grandmother) with me. By this time Mere had been deceased for over eight years and Pa had remarried and moved out of our shared home. Although Pa had remarried it was evident, even to my teenage self, that he missed his high school sweetheart/wife desperately, and had to bring her back for a moment for both of us. He told me teaching was in my blood. Pa explained that my grandmother had an old chalkboard in their kitchen and before she sent Jackie to school she made sure Jackie knew her ABC's, and how to print her name. Night after night they would sit at the kitchen table and play school. Jackie was drilled using flashcards made with scraps of paper and counting was taught using match sticks. With tears in his eyes and a sense of pride in his voice, he went on to say my grandmother figured out what Jackie needed and just did it. My grandmother quietly was preparing her daughter for entering the local Catholic school. She was determined that Jackie would attend the same school as her big sister Doris.

Children with any type of disability were typically sent away during the 1940s and did not attend the public or private schools of the day. I questioned my mom about how Jackie came to attend the parish Catholic school.

"When she got old enough to go to school, not to kindergarten, because she never went to kindergarten; but then they went over to church and they (her parents) wanted to put her in school but they didn't have kids like her at school. They didn't do that. But because Father Fennessy knew my mother and father, he said of course she can come to school. She did not go to school at six though; I think my mom sent her once she was able to do some schoolwork."

After my mom told me the story of Jackie going to school, I went rummaging through the family pictures. I knew Jackie's treasured class pictures were somewhere. According to the date on the first class picture, I realized Jackie did not go to first grade until she was nine years old. My poor Grandma, for three years she worked night after night to get her sweet child ready to go to first grade.

I asked my mom for further clarification of how Jackie was able to go to school considering the times and the fact that Catholic schools were selective. My mom revealed that Father Fennessy had been a friend of my grandmother's family. He had actually married my maternal great grandparents and assisted with my great grandfather's conversion to Catholicism. My great grandfather had also donated work to the construction of St. Nick's. It just so happened that Father Fennessy was named pastor of St. Nick's when my grandparents lived there. If it was not for this coincidence, Jackie may never have gone to school.

My mom goes on to tell how Jackie almost could not continue at school.

"But when she was in 2ⁿᵈ grade, I think it was. But, um, when she was in 2ⁿᵈ grade, a nun, Sister Loretta, that I had for second grade decided Jackie did not belong there. I overheard this at home and I couldn't figure out that nun because she was somebody I had in 2ⁿᵈ grade and I loved her to death. She decided that Jackie was (my mom pauses and looks away)…she didn't need to be there. She…I don't know what she thought Jackie should do. And Sister went to the principal, Sister Somebody or other, then the principal called Mom and Dad up there to school and told them that Sister Loretta felt Jackie did not belong there. My mother got furious. So, she and Daddy went over to the rectory and talked to Father Fennessy and he said, "Jackie will be in the school as long as I'm here." So, that's why she got to stay there as long as she did."

My grandparents would not let Father Fennessy forget his promise. I can just picture them ringing the door at the rectory, demanding to see the pastor, reminding him of his promise, and telling him in no uncertain terms that their daughter would remain in school. It took true courage to defy the institution of the church. Practicing Catholics, especially in the 1940s when Jackie attended school, would never argue with the "good sisters" or the priests. By the time Jackie was 10 years of age, my grandmother had stood up to two dominant social institutions; the medical doctors and now the church. Again, my grandparents were breaking down the fences, this time by knocking at the rectory door. This was an act of resistance. Resistance can blur the boundaries and open the possibilities for people with disabilities. My grandparents were coming to know the experience of disability through an aesthetic lens of resistance. Through an aesthetic view, meaning is "constructed through lived experiences" (Gabel, 2005, p. 35). The emotional meaning making event of going to the rectory and demanding a Catholic education for Jackie was an aesthetic experience. My grandparents were confronting the oppressive construct of educational exclusion and through their actions, Jackie gained an opportunity to go to school.

My mother gives her interpretation of Jackie's school experience:

"And they gave her…, they would just give her busy work I think; they would give her whatever she could do. You know, she sang as flat as a pancake but they'd say to her (at choir in church) just mouth the words sometimes. And she would get very upset about that, because to her there was no difference between her and anybody else. Even if she was very slow in the things she did, which of course she was, uh…it didn't seem to make any difference. She could kind of keep up in spelling; she was in the lowest reading group; she was very poor at math, she couldn't do math very well at all, especially money. But the only way…she had a good memory and because she had a good memory that was how she would remember things. That's how she'd remember spelling words and how to print certain things. She never was very proficient at printing, she could print, but was…and she did everything phonetically. …if the word was "call" she would write "col" the way it sounded. So, she sounded everything out … but they kept her there all those years."

My mom goes on to describe more of Jackie's school experiences and her responsibilities as the big sister:

"My mother was very protective of her, terribly protective. In fact, she used to walk us to school and she would walk home, 'cause we lived a long way from school. She'd walk us to school, she'd walk home, she'd walk back at lunch time pick us up, walk us home again and then walk back again. So, my mother would walk back and forth like six to eight times a day until she finally, I think when Jackie was in maybe 2nd grade, she would let Jackie stay for lunch. But then I would have to have Jackie sit with me. They wanted me to have her sit with me, which was alright by me because she'd eat what I didn't eat. So, I'd feed her what I didn't want to eat 'cause the nuns used to watch to see if you ate your food. But, she was really always a part of me you know. I'd wait for her after school and then when I got to be in like 7th grade I rode my bike. She'd ride on the back of the bike and that's how we got to school when it was nice out, to ride bikes. My dad made a special seat for Jackie and my mother made a beautiful (laughing) tufted rug and there she would sit on the back of my bike."

This recollection from my mother is revealing on many levels. She first describes my grandmother's protectiveness of Jackie. As they walked back and forth, did my grandmother look out for people who looked at Jackie in a particular manner? Did she scope out the safest route, both physically and psychologically? The literature portrays parents in the 1940s who worried because their child had a disability that could be seen, such as Down Syndrome (Castles, 2004; Meyer, 1956). Since people could see their child's disability, they were afraid that their child would be snatched up and put in an institution. I wonder if my grandmother was dealing with those same insecurities and worries. I believe the "walking back and forth" and my mother's childhood intuition that her mother was protective of her little sister, is indeed indicative of such feelings. My grandmother was putting up a safety fence.

There is another story imbedded in my mother's quote. My mother may be painting a more positive picture of the situation, now that her little sister is deceased and she is reflecting from the stance of a woman in her seventies. I personally would not have liked to have my sibling attached to me in seventh grade, or to have to sit with my younger brother in the lunch room, so I questioned my mother further about this situation. She was insistent that riding Jackie to school on her bike was not a problem, and it did not carry any social stigma with her peers. My mother said this may have had to do with the times and the "whole Catholic school obedience thing." I asked her to explain her statements. She told me that this was right after the war ended and most families, no matter how many children they had, only owned one or two bikes, and so riding a sibling to school was common. To own a bike of your own was a "big deal" in itself. She also said that kids did not "see" people with disabilities in the community in those days. Jackie, with her hair fixed, wearing her glasses and catholic school uniform, looked like all her other classmates. My mom said she personally had never seen another person with Down Syndrome until she was older, so this factor may have contributed to her naiveté. She knew that Jackie struggled in school, and that she should watch out for her, but as a seventh grader she did not think she was disabled in any way.

My mother also shared with me that the most embarrassing part of having to ride Jackie to school had to do with the seat cover my grandmother had fashioned from a handmade tufted rug. My grandfather tried a number of homemade seats trying to find one that would not collapse with Jackie's weight. Finally, he concocted a stainless steel seat. My grandmother wanted to have it comfortable for Jackie so she made a custom seat cushion. The trouble was that the seat cushion had this tufted rug covering which was bright orange and royal blue with a large red "S" (for the family name Sheehan) embroidered in the center. My mom said when Jackie was physically on the seat, at least the *lovely* tufted rug was covered up, but whenever my mom rode her bike without Jackie, it was a source of embarrassment for her.

I pressed on questioning my mom further about having to sit with Jackie in the lunchroom.

"Well, if the nuns told you to do something you would do it. We would not dare question the nuns. If they told you to do something you did it. I would get in trouble at home, too, if I did not listen. Somehow our parents always found out. Like I said, Jackie would eat whatever I did not want to eat, so it was ok, really."

Sing Out, Sing Strong

Jackie rushed home from school on a warm autumn day. She was all excited and kept running ahead of Doris..

"Slow down Jackie."

"Wait." Doris was trying to keep Jackie near, because she knew she would be in big trouble if something happened on the way home.

"I have to tell Momma something." Jackie's pig tales were going up and down as she ran and skipped down the sidewalk. As soon as they reached the house Jackie ran up the front stairs. She couldn't wait to get in and tell Momma.

"Momma, you will not believe it, (trying to catch her breath), ahh mmm guess what? I have to go to children's Mass on Sunday, umm at what time, Doris? Not that she gave Doris a chance to answer... and I get to sing with my classmates. All the kids have to go." Moomm I have to go, ok?"

Jackie loved to sing, so she was thrilled to be part of the children's singing group for mass.

'All the kids'..... Jackie was part of the class. She had to fulfill all the requirements and take part in anything that was mandatory for the students of St. Nick's. If she ever felt excluded she never said anything. There were many rules and laws in the Catholic Church and school. As a child Jackie followed each and every rule with grave seriousness. Anything the nuns or priests said she internalized it as *the* profound truth. Singing at church may have been just another obligation to the other fourth graders, but to Jackie this was a very serious undertaking, after all Sister said she had to go.

Singing was part of who Jackie was. Jackie's Grandma Sheehan was a professional singer and her big sister Doris had solos in choir and sang all the time. Grandma Sheehan had even brought the girls to a recording studio and Doris and Jackie made a record. Grandma Sheehan had a friend from the "business" who had a studio, and he let my great grandmother come in with a piano player to "cut" a record with her family. When I was a little girl I often listened to the songs they recorded. There was a special ritual when we listened to the old 78's. Jackie carefully opened the lid of the black record player and moved the arm so we could put the record on the turn table. We reverently removed the record from its white paper sleeve. It was really heavy and made of a material more like glass. So taking it out of the package was almost a religious experience. I was full of wonder and awe. We put the record on the silver bar, and with a click it slowly went down and the bar was placed on the record just so. With a "shhh" sound the needle engaged and the record went round and round, and crackly sounds gave way to the voices of little girls.

Jackie closed her eyes and smiled as she listened to herself singing. I thought it was really cool that she was able to sing on a record. My great grandmother was singing on the record and sounded really good. My mom's little girl voice was strong and sweet. Listening to the songs brought joyful memories to Jackie's heart and, as usual, I went along with the flow. I was Jackie's shadow much of my young childhood.

Jackie sang songs to me all the time. I usually just sang along. Sometimes we made up even silly songs as we did chores together. We had dusting and vacuuming songs. Usually we lifted the tune from Broadway musicals and changed the words to match what we were doing.

"I am going to wipe the dust right off the table" was sung to the tune of "I am Going to Wash That Man Right Out of my Hair" from *South Pacific*.

"This is the way we vacuum the house, vacuum the house, vacuum the house, here on Parkside Avenue." Jackie took her hankie out of her pocket (or sometimes it was tucked inside her bra) and waved it in the air in between verses.

I really never gave it a thought if Jackie sang well. We were just being goofy and having fun. My mom, however, sang really well. People even asked her to sing when we were at family parties or if we were at the local Elks Club. When we went to parties at the club, people said, "Give us your "Bill Baily", Doris, or how 'bout, "I Left my Heart in San Francisco?" My mom's friend Ruthie went over to the organ and played and Mom sang. It seemed like she was a star or something. My Dad, grandparents, and we kids were so proud of her. We clapped loud when she finished. Some old man at the bar bought me a kiddie cocktail, since my mom was such a good singer. To this day I have to have a cherry in my drink. I think it is because of the "sweetness" of those childhood memories. I loved going to the Elks Club. Jackie and I put money in the Juke box and sang along to the latest hits in the corner, whenever my mom was not singing. There I was in my little princess dress, patent leather shoes and ruffly anklet socks, swaying to the music. I liked to move in a certain way so my slip made a swishing sound and my skirt swirled in the air. Jackie had this butt wiggle move that she did to most songs.

My stardom at the Elks Club and singing with Aunt Jackie did not go over so well at the very strict Bible school I attended for kindergarten. Neither our local public school or our Catholic school offered kindergarten, so my mom enrolled me at a Bible church program. At kindergarten graduation, I clearly disgraced my teacher by saying I wanted to be a model or singer when I grew up (I have proof via the look on her face in old family movies). All the other 5 year old girls wanted to be mommies or missionaries or nurses. I was the heathen, Catholic girl that spent Sundays (after Mass) singing next to the bar at the Elks, applauding my mom, and twisting and singing with Aunt Jackie.

One morning all of us kids had to be really quiet, because a radio station called and said my mom was a finalist in a singing contest and she had to sing over the phone. (Kinda like old school"American Idol") My mom was barely awake, yet there she was singing "Bill Baily" in the bedroom. Holding the old black, square dial phone base in one hand and using the handle mouthpiece as a microphone, she belted the song out as well as she could. She even did this growl thing as she sang. "Won't you come home Bill Baily, won't you come home....

She took second place. My dad was excited because he heard her singing on the car radio on his way to work, so that was better than the marble paper weight with her name engraved in it, anyhow. Previous to "You Tube" anything on the radio was really impressive. Jackie was very proud of her sister's talent. She told me all about my moms' singing in plays and showed me programs from my mom's shows and choir recitals. Jackie was so animated as she talked of my mom's talent, but her demeanor changed when she told me the real story about her choir participation at St. Nicks.

Jackie went to church to sing in the choir at Mass. She went every Sunday and took her spot in the pew at 8:30 am children's Mass. She was right in the first row, because for some reason the nuns always lined everyone up by height and Jackie was shorter than most of her peers. Jackie memorized all the songs, since sometimes the words were hard for her to read. She practiced all the songs and the sung parts of the Mass in the mirror in her bedroom. She was really proud to remember all of the words.

After a few weeks of Sunday children's choir, the "Singing" Sister asked Jackie to stay after Mass because she needed to talk to her. Jackie was worried about what Sister was going to say. She had a hard time concentrating on Mass that day. She was sooo worried what Sister would say when Mass was over. She wondered if she did something wrong. Sister told Jackie she did not want to dismiss her from the choir because she knew that Jackie liked to come to Mass with her classmates. She informed Jackie that in order for her to stay in the choir, she could no longer sing the songs, she was told just to "mouth the words". Sister offered no explanation as to why Jackie could no longer sing out loud. Jackie knew she should not talk back or ask why. Good Catholic school girls never questioned nuns. Jackie strived to be a good girl.

When Jackie told me the story as a child, I told Jackie I thought the nun was mean and it was not right that Jackie could not sing. I told her I would not have gone if I could not sing. Jackie just shrugged her shoulders in response to my tirade about the unfairness of it all. As I got older and realized that Jackie could not sing any song in tune, and she sang out really loud and flat, I realized why the Sister had asked her not to sing. In fact, Jackie's lack of talent was even a subject of family jokes with her as time went on. Jackie just brushed off the ribbing from me and my siblings with a chuckle and a shrug. She never failed to remind us how we were all sung to sleep by her, so she just knew we *always* enjoyed her singing. My brother Tommy would tease her back and tell her we fell asleep quickly so we did not have to listen to her anymore.

"Jackie, we made ourselves go to sleep because your voice was painful to our ears."

Tom had a smirk on his face.

Jackie took it in stride and replied, "Oh Tom, you are such a kidder."

Jackie stayed in the children's singing group for Mass on Sundays until she transferred from St. Nicks. She was there every Sunday mouthing the words with drama and enthusiasm. Once and awhile she would slip up and actually sing out and Sister would give her a look to remind her not to sing. She did not tell her parents or my mom that she was told not to sing until years later when she was telling me about her choir days at St. Nick's. She kept her thoughts to herself for all those years. My guess is that she was afraid her mom would have said something. No kid wants her parents talking to the teacher.

Whenever things got dramatic in life, Jackie knew to slip into the background. I think she was accepted in her school and as a silent choir member because she did not draw attention to herself. While Jackie never verbalized that she had an intellectual disability, I wonder now how she internally rationalized her life situation. While being asked to mouth the words in the choir may seem like something simple, it was really very telling about how Jackie was able to function in her world. Jackie could quietly "blend in", putting herself in the background to avoid any confrontations.

Elementary school was a good experience for Jackie. She spoke of school with fond memories. She poured over her class photos, looking carefully at each face in the class and she recalled something very specific about each classmate. In those days Catholic schools had 40 plus students in each class, so it was pretty amazing that she had a special memory about each individual.

Jackie loved to tell me and anyone who would listen - usually my friend Laura, then as the years went by, my younger sisters and then my daughter Amy - about her school days at St. Nicks and St. Mary's. I did not come to truly realize the social relevance of her being included in school in the 1940's and 1950's until I was in my 40s and in a doctoral program for disability studies. Jackie's story was interesting to me, but now when I think deeply about what she accomplished long before advocates had even imagined integrating kids with disabilities, it is really inspiring. Until I looked at her situation with an enlightened mind, I had never realized the amount of courage it took on my grandparents part to get Jackie out into the world. They not only put her out there, they had expectations once she was there. Jackie **would** go to the local Catholic school with her sister, she **would** be in choir, she **would** play with the kids in the neighborhood. These everyday childhood experiences are commonplace for so called typical kids, but for Jackie living in her time and place, her situation was amazing.

During the 1940's most children with disabilities were hidden at home or were living in institutions. While Jackie was not really singing with her classmates she was still **there** in the first row, in the choir loft, lip syncing her heart out for the glory of God. I can guess that there may have been hushed whispers from some of the other parents or parishioners as to why there was a mongoloid girl in the choir. I am sure some of the Sisters did not think she should be there either.

In a strange way the choir Sister provided (in special ed terms) an accommodation for Jackie to still be included in the choir.So for as much as it sounds cruel that she could not sing out loud, she was still there. It was really more about being with her classmates than anything, but I do think Jackie harbored a quiet grudge against the choir sister for not letting her sing, her entire life.

Jackie, by virtue of having to keep quiet, developed her lip syncing skills right there in the choir loft at St. Nicks. Strange coincidence, my first teaching position was at St. Nicks. My husband and I moved into the city when we married and lived in St. Nicks parish. As a new teacher and also a young 21 year old mom, I took a teaching position there to be close to home when the position was offered to me right out of college. So I actually taught in the same building where my mom and Jackie had gone to school. I brought my 6th graders to sing at mass in the big church choir loft for special occasions. I actually stood in that same choir loft with my students, where Jackie and her classmates had been 35 years before.

Jackie was so impressed that I was teaching at St. Nicks. When I visited her at my parents it would lead to more and more stories, and she told me the choir story over and over again. I told her I had heard it all before, from the time I was a kid. I told her I could tell the story in my sleep. I treasure the Jackie stories since she is not here to tell them any longer.

Another revelation about the choir story occurred when I was sitting at my moms with my infant son Tim. I was feeding Tim in his high chair and Jackie was at the sink finishing supper dishes, my parents were sitting in the family room right off the kitchen. When Jackie started talking about St. Nick's yet *again*, my mom called out from the family room, "And do you know that my grandfather helped build the big church at St. Nicks?"

"Of course I know that Papa Walter built it, and Mama told me that years ago," Jackie said, "And some of the nuns use to tell me that, too."

Driving with my mom in the car just the other day, I started asking again about Jackie's school years. My mom explained that she now believes the only reason Jackie was allowed to go to St. Nicks was because of Jackie's grandfather's (Mere's Father) contribution. We know my great grandfather was friendly with the pastor and his construction company built the church at St. Nicks. He must have given them a great deal or something. I have often wondered if Father had a member of his family that had a disability, and his reasons for keeping Jackie in his school were more personal than we may ever know. Father Fennessy had said Jackie was always going to attend St. Nicks as long as he was Pastor. When Father was transferred to the neighboring parish, St. Mary's, Jackie transferred right along with him. The family then attended Mass there and Jackie finished her last couple of years of schooling at St. Mary's.

My Great-grandfather and Father Fennessy had much to do with Jackie ever attending school. Since the Catholic pastor in the 40's pretty much served as the king of the kingdom, I am sure he controlled much of Jackie's participation in school activities.

For what ever reason she was in the choir, Jackie was able to use it as a training for finessing her lip syncing. It was a source of great pleasure and entertainment to me, my friends and my siblings. Her skills did not go unnoticed when she joined "club". When Jackie finally was able to be in a social group, she was over fifty years old. My mom had a co-worker who had an adult son with a disability and she had started a social group called "Place in the Sun". The name of the club came from a song by that title which talks about a place where people are free to be themselves. Jackie was her best self when she hung out with her club. Jackie knew some of the club members had something "wrong" with them (in her words). After all there were some club people who could not walk or talk, but because many of the people attending could walk, talk and did not look "tarded" to Jackie, she thought it was just a group of adults getting together and having fun. She told me her club was like when my parents and grandparents had been involved with the Elks Club. Jackie had a way to explain anything that occurred in her life. Her life circumstances made sense to her. Her membership in a club for adults with disabilities was much the same. Since Jackie did not see herself as disabled, she did not see many of the club members as disabled either.

Every Tuesday evening a family member drove Jackie to club. At club they played sports, danced, watched movies, went on outings and oh yes, they sang. No one told Jackie she could not sing this time. Sometimes she sang out with joy, and sometimes times she would still lip sync, much to the enjoyment of her friends.

Each year in the spring, Place in the Sun presented a musical show. The adult volunteers and the club members all participated in the extravaganza. Jackie loved the musicals. She finally had her opportunity to be a star. She was involved in club for a few years and was typically part of the chorus for the shows. My mom went to pick Jackie up from club one evening from musical practice. Jackie was moving a bit more spryly than her usual slow shuffle as she approached the car.

"So Jack, anything new at Club? You seem a little excited about something."

There the two sisters were again, some 40 plus years later with Jackie having some news about singing with her friends. This time the results were a bit different. Jackie had been given a solo part in the musical.

"So Doris, guess what? I have a hint....Momma's name." Jackie had a mischievous grin on her face.

"Jackie, I have no clue what you are talking about and what Momma's name has to do with club."

"You know... the Tin man, and the lion and ... Dorothy. See Momma's name! I am going to be Dorothy in the Wizard of Oz number and I sing 'Somewhere Over the Rainbow.'

"Are you sure they heard you sing?"

"Don't be such a kidder. I even have a costume list, so you will have to get me the costume."

The night of the big show came and the whole family took up a couple of rows. We were more nervous for Jackie than she was. Would she remember the words? Would she be scared? My mom kept fidgeting and saying "Almost time, she comes up in a minute." It was actually pretty cute how excited my mom was for her little sister. All these years Jackie had been dragged along to my mom's singing events, and here was my mom, so nervous for Jackie's big moment.

The yellow brick road appeared and out strolled our Dorothy, red ruby slippers and all. Jackie had a wig with her hair in pig tales and was clutching her stuffed dog, renamed Toto for this evening. The musical introduction concluded. Softly and a little shaky at first, but then loud and clear, 'Somewhere Over the Rainbow' rang out throughout the theater. Jackie had this beautiful, peaceful look on her face and she sang almost in tune and with such feeling. When she finished we all jumped from our seats clapping loudly for our favorite star. I can still close my eyes and picture Jackie on stage that day, so full of joy. It is one of my treasured Jackie memories. Jackie had waited a long time to be able to sing out and sing strong. She really had her "Place in the Sun" that day.

Internal Struggles

While my grandmother appeared to know what to do for Jackie educationally, internally she had her own personal difficulties. Reflecting on my Grandmother's circumstance, my Aunt explains my grandmother's difficulty with marriage at eighteen, giving birth to my mom at 19, and Jackie's birth when she was 21 years old:

"It was so hard on her, she was never the same after realizing Jackie would need help, and she was so young, so very young when you think about it. Trying to figure this all out herself. She was at our house a lot with your mom and Jackie."

When my grandmother was confronting doctors, the church, society, and anyone else that fenced off Jackie she was in her late twenties. She was chronologically young, but determined and resistant to the prevailing norms of the time.

I had a frank conversation with Aunt Lovie about Mere's struggles.

"I know she had breakdowns and my mom would have to stay with her when she was in high school."

"Oh, I think it might have been sooner than that...I remember someone would drive her (my grandmother) over, either your grandfather or one of the guys from the dog food factory where he worked, and they would drop her off and we would watch her, she couldn't be left alone, nowadays they would give her Prozac or something, but then...You just lived with it. Someone would come back and get her then. She was always worried."

(My Aunt was talking slowly and sounded sad)

"And she was young then, I think everything with Jackie destroyed life as she knew it, but she loved her so much, she was always trying to figure it out, yet denying there was anything wrong at the same time."

This quote represents the internal struggle of a mother trying to come to terms with her child having a disability, yet simultaneously trying to determine how to help her be independent. In order to better understand this change in my grandmother, or to determine if she thought Jackie "destroyed life as she knew it." I asked Aunt Lovie to describe her sister's personality when they were growing up. Aunt Lovie described my grandmother as stubborn, and liked to get her own way. She also said my grandmother as a young girl was fun-loving and had a large group of friends. My grandmother was close to her older sister Isabelle who was only a couple of years older than her and when her brothers teased her she could stand up for herself. She dated my grandfather since she was 15 years old. When they married they belonged to a social club and she would watch my grandpa play semi-pro football and baseball. As young children, my mom and Jackie would take the trolley car with their "momma" to watch their "daddy" play.

The quality of stubbornness was an asset for my grandmother, and was represented in her determination to make sure Jackie was like every other child. I would assume that giving birth to a child with a disability at the age of 21 did change her life as she knew it, but I do not think my grandmother would have used the word "destroyed". The stories shared shows a woman with too much determination to totally let it destroy her, but her issues with depression did give evidence to her internal struggles. Often times mothers who have children with disabilities try to take everything on themselves (Rapley, 2004; Schwartzenberg, 2005). Today there are medical supports for depression. Twenty years later she would have the benefit of organizations like the ARC; an organization that supports and promotes people with disabilities and their parents. My grandmother could have shared her concerns with other parents who understood her situation (ARC, 2008). Later in the 1960s, The E's were members of the ARC through Chuck's school; they had the support of parents with shared experiences. As this was the 1940s, and there were not support systems for parents, my grandmother must have felt very alone.

Snapshots of Time

To get a better understanding of life for my mom and Jackie, I dug through all the old family photos my mom has stored in a big plastic bin. I found many pictures of my mom, grandparents and Jackie through the years. The corners of many of the pictures are torn and yellowed, glue remnants from photo corners line the backside of the pictures. There are pictures of all the typical milestones of life: First Communions, my mom's graduations, birthdays, summer vacations, and gatherings with extended family. I notice whenever my mom and Jackie are photographed with a group; they are always more dressed up than anyone else. My mom and Jackie were dressed meticulously with their hair perfectly combed and they always had hats or bows to match their outfits. I wonder if this was a way for my grandmother to show off her "perfect" girls to the world. Making sure that her girls always looked the best was a subtle form of resistance. My grandmother in her own way was rejecting the prevailing societal norms with this very outward expression. Again, she is resisting the dominating social construct (Gabel, 2005) which classified individuals with disabilities as not fully human or deviant. Not only did her daughters "fit in," they looked better. Dressing them up was another way she could protect her girls, another fence to separate them safely from the rest.

Another photo which struck me was Jackie's class picture from the school year 1949. Jackie is pictured sitting in her desk with her hands carefully folded, with a wide smile on her face. The students are pictured wearing their school uniforms, with the Sister standing in the back of the classroom in her full nun garb looking over the students. I initially had a hard time finding Jackie. She is in the fourth row, toward the back of the room, but not in the very back. She was very much in the middle of things, looking like her 7th grade peers. Considering that most other children with Down Syndrome in this era never attended school at all, this photo represents the ultimate in resistance and rhizomic possibility. Jackie was truly included in school.

Personally, Jackie's class photo could serve as a trophy in honor of my grandmother's determination. To Jackie, this photo was a treasured keepsake. Jackie showed me this same photo when I was a child. Jackie had a battered suitcase which served as her treasure box. She and I would often open it and Jackie would tell me about the items she had inside. She would show me the photo and one by one would name all the students, telling me something about each one. She would say something like, "He was mean." or "Joe was funny." and "There is Mary, she had a pretty coat." or "This girl is Judy, she lived on my block." Her school days were treasured memories for her, a time in her life when on many levels, she was accepted as *Jackie*.

Family

Through conversations shared and stories told by my mom, aunt and cousin, it is evident to me that my grandparents never kept Jackie home or felt the need to hide her. She went everywhere with the immediate family. Jackie enjoyed the company of all her aunts, uncles and cousins; all 26 of them on her mother's side of the family. On the paternal side of the family Doris and Jackie were the only grandchildren so they received the undivided attention from their paternal grandparents. They would take the girls to Riverview Amusement Park, or bring them to hang out at the tavern they owned. Jackie was in her element at the tavern. She would sit on a stool at the bar with the patrons sipping kiddie cocktails and holding court. My mom told me how Jackie would flirt with the patrons and carry on lengthy conversations, as well as entertaining everyone with jokes she memorized. When I was a child, Jackie told me that her Papa had a tavern on Archer Avenue in Chicago and she loved to go there.

I asked my mom about Jackie's relationship with her relatives, and she shared this about her maternal grandparents.

"Jackie was just always there. I think...when she was in about 3rd grade, I remember she had pneumonia, she was in the hospital, and I stayed at Grandma and Grandpa's and I heard something about Jackie having problems. Uh...I think they wanted her to die, because she, you know... she would go to heaven, and it would be all right because she'd be an angel, with her problems and all. I remember thinking she'll get better; I couldn't understand, why would she go to heaven because of her problems? What problems? She got better."

My mom said she wondered why they were talking quietly and why her grandparents referred to Jackie as having "problems". My mom thought they meant that Jackie was sick. Their conversation made her think and she tried to figure out in her child mind, what they (her maternal grandparents) meant about Jackie's "problems". This is another example of the difference between how things looked on the outside compared to what was going on within the family dynamic. My great grandparents were most likely thinking of their daughter's well being. They were the ones that held their daughter up when she cried for their help when she first realized Jackie was disabled. Their home was the place their Dorothy would go when she would be in the depths of depression. Individuals with disabilities were starting to be looked upon by charity minded individuals as helpless sinless angels (Noll & Trent, 2004). As practicing Catholics, my great grandparents may have truly felt it would be better for Jackie to be an angel in heaven and that would then cure their daughter Dorothy's demons on earth.

Later in the conversation my mom was contemplative and said she had just come to the realization that her maternal grandparents never invited Jackie to stay all night. My mom would stay, but Jackie never did.

Her maternal grandparents were nice to Jackie, but my mom went places with them, and Jackie did not go. This is representative of still more disconnections. If Jackie was treated the same as her sister, she would have stayed overnight, too. Being kind or nice to someone is not the same as embracing a person fully for who she is. Jackie was not treated the same as her sister, and my mother never realized this until she spoke with me for her interview. My mother was making connections now, as a 70 year old adult about the disconnections in her and Jackie's childhood experiences. As a big sister who loved her little sister very much, my mother was emotionally upset in the interview over this revelation.

After hearing my mom draw these conclusions about her maternal grandparents, I asked my Aunt if she had ever noticed that Jackie was treated differently by her parents as compared to my mom or other grandchildren. I asked if she ever heard my great grandmother advise her daughter to have Jackie go somewhere (an institution) out of concern for her daughter, especially since my grandmother had anxiety and emotional difficulties. My Aunt vehemently stated: "No. Never. My mother would never have told her that. She knew that Dorothy never would do that. Jackie was her daughter, that is how it was."

There were tensions all around, but no one, even years later, admits to them.

Jackie spent a great deal of time with her cousins, aunts, and uncles. She loved babies and was an eager and competent baby sitter. She acted as a care giver for her younger cousins and years later watched me and my siblings, as well as my own children. She was especially close to her cousin Barbara. Together they explored the open fields near Barbara's house out in the country. Jackie told me that Barbara tried to teach her to climb trees, but she was not too good at it. She also told me a story once about how Barbara could hang by her legs from the tree branches. Jackie seemed impressed by this. Barbara remained a treasured relative and friend throughout Jackie's life. As a young adult she would visit and she and Jackie would gossip at our kitchen table. When Barbara became engaged she told her parents, and then made her fiancé drive her to our house so she could tell Jackie. I was sitting on the front porch when they drove up. Barbara ran into our house yelling for Jackie. The fiancé stood on the porch looking at me, so I just looked up and said, "Hi". I brought him into the house with me and we could see Jackie and Barbara laughing, hugging and looking at the ring.

Now, I wonder how Jackie felt that day, Barbara was her only remaining childhood friend. Jackie must have had mixed emotions at that moment; envious, sad, and happy all at the same time. As a young child she would tell me the story about a guy she liked name Bill who she spent time with as a pre teen at the resort where the family vacationed each summer. She would say, "I wonder what happened to him?" She also wondered out loud to me why she never got married. If Jackie had been born in contemporary times, she may have had the opportunity to marry. People with disabilities would never have married in the1940s or1950s; in fact many people like Jackie with disabilities were sterilized so not to breed another generation of "feeble minded" during this era (Trent, 1994, p.222).

Jackie had a great time at Barbara's wedding. She told me all about it when she got home. Barbara had given Jackie a corsage to wear. She had her own pictures taken with the bride, and danced with the groom. Jackie brought me a piece of cake home from the wedding. She told me to put the cake under my pillow and dream of who I was going to marry. Jackie and I each put a piece of cake under our pillows that night. It saddens me that Jackie's dreams as far as marriage never came true. The pictures from Barbara's wedding went into Jackie's treasure suitcase. Barbara continued to visit with Jackie as a young married person, and held Jackie's hand at her mother's funeral. Jackie experienced another loss when Barbara's husband was transferred to California. Barbara wrote to Jackie through her adult life and sent Jackie pictures of her children. Jackie always looked forward to hearing from Barbara. My mother received a letter from Barbara after Jackie passed away. Barbara expressed her personal sense of loss and said how Jackie had always been her true friend. I think she was Jackie's only lifelong friend, and this friendship was genuine. Barbara was not being "nice" to Jackie, they connected.

Pictures depict Jackie playing board games with her cousins, and showing off her collection of story book dolls. Her cousin Nancy shared with me that as a child the only different thing about Jackie was that she had a great doll collection and that she (Nancy) was so jealous of those dolls and wanted them for herself. "Jackie was just, Jackie" are words said over and over throughout the interviews. Jackie was Jackie, but as I till the soil of this story there are layers of words on the surface, but there are so many more layers of tension just beneath. My grandmother never said Jackie was disabled, yet she protected her. My great grandparents loved Jackie, but Jackie did not stay overnight. My grandmother felt the need to dress her daughters perfectly for every occasion. Jackie saw herself as Jackie. Her cousins may have loved her for herself, and my mom saw her as her little sister, but the unsaid perhaps reveals more of the story than was verbalized. My grandmother sought possibilities for her daughter while simultaneously protecting her. There are fences and rhizomes, a pushing and pulling, a trying to come to terms with life. The existential of corporality is unconsciously both revealing and concealing.

Doris and Jackie, Together

My mom repeated throughout her telling of the story that it was always her and Jackie. She and Jackie were always together, that was just how it was. This togetherness actually led to my mom's realization that her sister was "different."

"Jackie was just always with me. Because I took her with me everywhere, I remember the one Sunday we went to the show. And, I went with my friend Lol and her sister and these twins that were in my room, in school, and their names were Jean and Joan. I'll remember them forever. I didn't much like them. Anyway, I thought they were snotty. But, they called Jackie a Mongoloid … Mongolian idiot. I just got furious and I said, "She is not, there is nothing wrong with her!" They said back, "Yes, she is an idiot." Jackie must have heard those words, too. When I got home I told my mother, and my mother said, "Don't pay any attention to them they don't know what they are talking about." My mother would never say she was retarded. My mother never said she was retarded."

"Do you recall anyone else who gave you or Jackie a hard time?"

"No, not really, Jackie had a best friend Trudy. Trudy was always good to Jackie. She went on vacation with us too. There were kids Jackie did not like and she would tell you who she liked. Maybe the kids she did not like had said something, but Jackie never said. We just did not talk about those things."

This quote is an example of tensions that existed below the surface. My mother over and over again said that "things" just were not talked about. Again, this is reflective of a particular era, of the "silent generation" (Strauss & Howe, 1992). Historically this was the time shortly after the Second World War.

People had lived through great tragedy and did not want to talk about the reality of their experiences. Raw, human emotion was buried deep inside. This was a crisis era. The young adults of this time were said to be lost and reactive and the children were suffocated, silent, and adaptive (Strause & Howe, 1992, p.79). I think of my mother as a child just doing what she was told. By not saying the words aloud, then possibly they would not have to face reality.

Discussing again the idea of naming Jackie's disability:

"So your mom never explained anything to you about Jackie?"

"She never ever told me what was wrong with her. She never said she was, well you know, retarded or anything."

"Never even when you were an adult…"

"No, NEVER even when she was dying, she called me into the room at the hospital… I'll never forget it. And she said take care of your sister. Then you know, she called your dad in by himself. He told me she told him to take care of her daughters, that Jackie needed to stay with us. Even then, she didn't say anything. Your dad was good to her (starting to cry, looking up)."

"I know Ma."

The words, "wrong with Jackie" are predominant in my aunt's and mother's interviews. They had difficulty naming Jackie's disability. There are positive and negative aspects of the conundrum posed by the naming of her disability. Jackie was a person with Down Syndrome, but the

Down Syndrome did not disable her as much as the time in which she lived, the societal implications and her family's expectations. My grandparents thought by not talking about "it" they could get society to look the other way. I keep thinking of the phrase "out of sight, out of mind," but it was always on their minds. The reality was always hovering over them and also hidden in the depths of their souls. Jackie was deeply loved by her parents, sister, and relatives. Limited by societal fences, a lack of true knowledge about the etiology of disabilities, and their own internal guilt and struggles they were never able to come to terms and see Jackie as a person and not a disability. The word, *retarded*, was not spoken directly, but is ever present, in their stories and life.

"High" (School) Fences

Jackie's mother, my grandmother, had emotional difficulties and she was also physically ill. She had emphysema, which was so acute she had a tank of oxygen in her bedroom. Although she was in her early forties, she tired easily. Her illness was the perfect excuse for Jackie not to attend high school. Jackie thought she would be going to high school. She started telling my mom about dances she would go to when she went to high school. Rather than telling her she could not go, she left eighth grade in the middle of the year. My grandparents did not have any connections for her to attend the local Catholic girl's high school, where most of Jackie's classmates would be attending. In fact, some of the nuns who taught there were so ill informed they made comments to my mother about Jackie when my mother attended school there. It was 1952, and children with disabilities did not have any educational rights (Winzer, 1993). When my grandmother had a bad bout with her breathing, and also needed surgery for stomach ulcers. Jackie was told by her parents that she would stay home from school and take care of her mother. Jackie may not have found this strange because my mother had to stay home sometimes and take care of their mother, when she was in high school.

By then my mom was out of high school and working, so Jackie felt it was her turn to help. Weeks went by and Jackie was told she was needed at home and she was not going to go back to school. She never went back to finish eighth grade. My grandparents were trying to do their best to protect Jackie. They knew she thought she was going to high school. They constructed a false situation, a "we need you to take care of momma" scenario to avoid talking about the lack of a high school program for Jackie. Rather than face reality, they worked hard to avoid it at all costs. The family put up another fence protecting Jackie from society, but they also fenced out her emotions. Jackie must have been upset; she liked school, and she had hopes and dreams for her life as a high school student. I do not feel sorry for Jackie being a person with Down Syndrome, but I am deeply sorry for the opportunities she did not have by virtue of the times in which she lived. Chuck, Jonathon, and Jamee by virtue of being born in a later time all had the opportunity to go to high school. They were able to go to the dances and join the clubs that for Jackie were only dreams.

Reflecting on the historicality of the era in regards to educating students with disabilities, Jackie received much more education than other children of the times. Jackie's speech was clear. She had an extensive vocabulary that upon testing as an adult was determined to be at an 11th grade level. Jackie could read and comprehend at approximately a fourth grade level and write simple sentences. She was included in school through 8th grade. Many children with Down Syndrome even today are not as fully included as Jackie was in the 1940s.

The next year the family purchased their first home in the Chicago suburb of Oak Lawn and moved there with Jackie staying home to care for her mom. A few years later my parents married and a year later I came along. It was now 1958, and Mere's (my grandmother) health was deteriorating. My parents, with baby Sharon, moved into my grandparent's two bedroom ranch home. As an infant I adored my Aunt Jackie. My mom said I would laugh whenever she came into the room. The house we lived in was way too crowded for all of us, and my mom was expecting another child. My grandmother needed more support than Jackie could provide. My grandmother also did not drive, and now living in the suburbs, she was dependent on my mother driving her to the doctor. My great grandfather was a builder and he had built a home on Parkside Avenue in Oak Lawn. My parents and grandparents purchased the house together and we all moved in.

Dancing and Ringing in the New Year

The stories that are in my heart and push on my brain, all begin and end with my Aunt Jackie.

"Dance faster Jackie, dance faster."

My parents were trying to take pictures of their baby girl in her Christmas pjs and the only way she even cracked a smile is when Jackie did a mean twist in front of her. The faster Jackie wiggled her butt to and fro the more the baby giggled and bounced in her bouncy chair. It is Christmas 1958. I have been told this story so many times by my Aunt Jackie and my parents it is as if I can actually remember being there at 5 months old.

The pictures turned out great. My parents' Brownie camera captured the moments well and they live on in fading Kodak color. Jackie must have danced fast enough. There I am in this one piece red polka dot sleeper with a goofy elf hat on my head, smiling ear to ear.

Jackie had so many roles... Auntie, sister, friend, playmate, confidant, maid. Roles that changed and fluctuated. It was a dance ; sometimes fast moving, sometimes dramatic and sometimes it was confusing as to who was leading who. At times Jackie was in charge, acting adult like, correcting me, helping me do important things kids should do like wash my hands or saying please and thank you. Other times I naturally took the lead and held her hand crossing the street looking all ways pretending she was taking care of me, but I was taking care of her. We did not discuss the role reversals they just happened naturally. Jackie and I always dancing. Jackie continued to dance for me and with me, both literally and figuratively her whole life. So many memories revolve around physically dancing,moving to the music and getting into the beat of a Four Lads, Chubby Checker or an Alvin and the Chipmunks song. Just as Jackie danced faster for the red-headed elf child, she danced and sang with me and Laura. We found her to be a great source of joyful entertainment.

It is New Years Eve and my friend Laura and I are seven years old. Laura's big sister, Nancy came over to help Jackie babysit us and my two brothers. No matter how hard I try I can barely remember my brothers being around on New Years, I know they were there, but the memories all revolve around the fun we had with Jackie. Since Tom was six years old and Ed was four, they must have gone to bed. Since I was the oldest child and grandchild I am thinking I did much more with the adults than my brothers. Laura's sister did homework, talked on the phone, helped get the chip and dip out, and left us to hang out with Jackie. I always wondered why she did not talk with Jackie more. She was polite and helpful, but she left us to play with Jackie, which was a little weird to us because one would think the grownups would want to talk. Nancy was probably a freshman in high school, but to us she was very old, and we really had little in common with her. We saw Jackie as a grown up but we never related to Jackie in terms of age or thought too deeply if she was an adult or a child. We connected with her; her spirit, her jokes, her sense of joy at basic things. She was very engaging to our seven year old selves.

New Year's Eve was a wonderful event in our childhood. It was a night full of anticipation for me, Laura, and even grown up Aunt Jackie. I was personally very excited about having chip and dip and Laura was glad to get out of her house, stay up late, and get away from her other five siblings. Jackie could not wait to listen to the famous band leader Guy Lombardo and his band of Royal Canadians on the New Year's celebration TV special televised live from the Waldorf Hotel in New York City. What seven year olds watch and enjoy a 1940s style big-band? Somehow Jackie made us enjoy it and look forward to ringing in the New Year with Guy.

There we were, the three of us dancing away in the living room to "Boogie-woogie Bugle Boy." Jackie imitated the singers and mouthed the words. We were truly enthralled with her talent. Her ability to mimic the singers and lip sync just amazed us. Dancing, singing at the tops of our voices, spinning around, giggling, falling on the couch in fits of laughter; the evening was full of joy.

There was such a sense of anticipation in our hearts. What would the new year bring? Soon we would venture out onto the snowy front porch and yell, "Happy new year!"

Time goes by and we watched the ball drop in New York and then switch to Channel 9, the Chicago station, for another hour of entertainment. But the local shows cannot compete with our favorite band, so we put Mitch Miller on the record player and sing-along. The TV stayed on in the background counting down to midnight. Laura's sister Nancy, emerged from the kitchen, shook her head and smiled at our antics. Then she provided us with some New Year's libations a.k.a. Seven- up floats. We continued to dance and sing out 1965.

"Dance faster Jackie!"

"Dance more Jackie!" Laura and I encouraged Jackie's silliness and efforts to entertain us with fits of girlish giggles.

"Show us how you sing like Leslie Uggams."

Jackie stood up, threw open her arms and imitated Leslie with gusto. Leslie was the best young singer in the Mitch Miller group. It didn't matter to us that Leslie was black (we said "Colored" then), skinny, and had an awesome singing voice. We thought my very petite, round, white Auntie was the perfect Leslie impersonator.

The pureness of our seven-year-old spirits saw Jackie as her authentic self; a fun-loving, vibrant, giving adult who was not afraid to share joy with a couple of silly little girls. The clock ticked on, the countdown on the TV showed it is getting closer to new year 1966. Twenty, nineteen, eighteen ... we ran to the kitchen and grabbed pots, pans, and spoons. Five, four, three...we threw open the front door and began yelling. In unison Laura, Jackie and I screamed out "Happy New Year!" as we banged on our pots and pans. Cars were honking on 95th Street. Some other neighbors were out yelling on their front porches and blinking their porch lights on and off. We waved to the folks next door and hurried in and out of the cold. Sharing a 7-up toast and clinking our jelly jar glasses, we toasted New Year 1966.

Nineteen sixty six will be an exciting year for Laura and I. We will be making our First Holy Communion, which is a major event in a Catholic schoolgirl's life. Jackie tells us about her First Communion and sharing the day with her best friend Trudy at St. Nicks. Laura and I will be just like Jackie and Trudy, celebrating in our fancy white dresses and receiving Jesus for the first time.

Jackie went to her bedroom and pulled out her black weathered cardboard suitcase from under her bed. We followed her into the room and plopped on the bed eager to look at Jackie's special treasures. She very carefully, almost with reverence, snapped open the gold latches. The case popped open and she dug through the contents until she came across her childhood photos. Jackie showed us black and white pictures with worn scalloped edges.

"Oh here is one of my favorites." Jackie handed me a photo. I gazed at the picture of Jackie and her friend Trudy. There they were looking very holy, standing next to each other, with their hands folded, gazing into the heavens with their rosaries wrapped around their fingers. Laura and I were in our "we want to be a nun" phase so we were extremely impressed by their holy state. Jackie had gotten our attention so she pulled out even more pictures. So many memories of her childhood were strewn all over the bed. Photos of Trudy and Jackie, some still in their fancy dresses but leaning against a backyard tree. Another with their arms wrapped around each other in the middle of the sidewalk as they mugged for the camera. Two friends sharing a very special day.

After a short time of reminiscing, Nancy reminded us that it was late. Laura and I admitted we were tired and marched upstairs to bed. Another new year of celebrating our friendship and hopes for the future. Our child selves really had no clue as to Jackie's true feelings on those nights. We were immersed in the excitement of the moment and were thrilled that we were able to stay up late, especially because we could stay up later than my younger brothers. Bedtimes are very important to seven-year-olds.

I wonder, now as I bring the memories to print if Jackie continued to look at those photos long after we went to sleep. Did she wonder why she and Trudy did not stay in touch once Trudy went to high school and Jackie moved to the suburbs? Did her heart ache for her best friend?

I have never heard when or why Jackie lost touch with her friend. Did Trudy at some point out grow Jackie emotionally and intellectually? As Trudy went to high school and Jackie was told she had to stay home and take care of her mother, did they just drift apart? At what point did Trudy realize Jackie was "slow?" Did her mom ever talk to her about that? There are photos of Jackie and Trudy together into their early teen years, but after that there are no more. Once Jackie moved to the suburbs, my grandparents would have had to help keep the friendship together. Jackie would have to use the telephone or get a ride into the city from her dad or sister. So many unanswered questions... Did my grandmother purposely not help Jackie see her friend, so that Jackie would not be disappointed if Trudy no longer wanted to hang out with her?

My grandmother created her own internal protective fences for Jackie. Was she trying to save Jackie from a broken heart, by trying to control the situation? Since Jackie had no idea she had an intellectual disability, did she wonder when Trudy did better in school or had new friends or interests? I'm sure she wondered why she no longer saw Trudy. Jackie, knew not to question her mother. So I can be relatively sure she never asked much about the situation. Now as an adult, who treasures my childhood friends, my heart hurts that Jackie did not have the love and companionship of her friend.

What could have occurred if Jackie and Trudy remained friends? At times maybe Trudy would not have wanted Jackie around. Maybe she would even have been embarrassed by having a friend with Down Syndrome. We'll never know. I think over time their friendship might have changed, but would still be a friendship. Jackie would have enjoyed helping her friend set up her home, or go to the movies, compare soap opera stories or babysit or play with her children. I could see her being doting Aunt Jackie to Trudy's children. I do not know anything about Trudy now, nor have we ever met. The families lost touch after the move to the suburbs.

Part of me thought she would someday arrive at Jackie's wake and see the pictures of them together. In fact, I really thought about that when Jackie passed away. I kept looking at the door waiting for Trudy to come pay her respects to her childhood friend. I had this feeling that she should be there.

My mom has said that Trudy was a good friend to Jackie. She explained that Trudy was always kind, but not too careful with her. They argued then made up, and played together as children do. My mom said she does not recall why they did not keep in touch. She guesses, it was all because the family moved. My mom also compartmentalizes issues that pertain to Jackie. She tucks them in some far away emotional place and doesn't like to speak about anything negative pertaining to her sister. It makes her sad and uncomfortable. Honestly, for me it isn't worth pushing my now 76 year old mom to face her feelings. The interviews and the reflections were emotional for her when I began to write our story. She often wishes Jackie had more opportunities. She deeply questions how she could have been a better sister or guardian to Jackie. She may be purposely blocking out why and when Jackie lost touch with someone that meant so much to her.

I personally wonder if Jackie's friendship impacted Trudy's vision about disability. I asked my mom for Trudy's last name and if she knew her married name. My mother gave me some information, but it did not lead anywhere. After internet researching I came up with nothing.

I would love to talk with Trudy. I think her story as Jackie's friend would be so interesting. Does she see someone with Down Syndrome and have memories of her childhood friend? Does she know that Jackie truly loved her and treasured their friendship throughout her life? I wonder if Jackie and Trudy banged pans together on New Year's Eve's long-ago? When the clock strikes 12 and a new year begins does the 70+year old Trudy recall moments with her childhood friend Jackie? I hope once in a while memories of her friend Jackie touch her heart and mind, and it is my wish that she does a little celebratory Jackie dance and smiles.

Fun with Aunt Jackie

Aunt Jackie was always present in my life. I knew she was different from other people's aunts because she played with me and my friends. She was the best babysitter because we had fun together. My childhood "Aunt Jackie" memories revolve around doing the twist to Chubby Checker songs, painting our nails with her special nail kit, playing Sorry and Barbies. I thought she was cool. As a young child, I did not know anyone who had an Aunt as fun as my Aunt Jackie. My friend Laura would come over and play with Jackie and me. She would stay overnight and Jackie would watch us. I asked Laura to recall those times with Aunt Jackie.

"Jackie was just always there. She was there helping your grand-mother, cleaning house. Kinda like a housekeeper in some ways. In other ways she was like a big sister, especially when she would come in the bedroom and play with us or show us her fan club collection. We knew Jackie long before we put people in categories or thought too deeply about anything. Jackie would show us her movie star magazines. She would lip sync to songs, and we asked her how she could do that. We were always respectful to Jackie though, we did see her as a grown up. I called her Aunt Jackie, too."

"I think Jackie saw you as a niece, too."

"Jackie was always very protective of me, maybe because I was so little."

"My Grandma Gregory (my dad's mom) always called you Laurie and Jackie would shake her head and correct her."

"I hated to be called Laurie and she knew it. She was this adult child person. We knew she was grown up, yet we played with her. We knew she was watching us, but in some ways we were watching her."

Jackie played many roles in the family at this time. She always played the role of the obedient daughter. She acted like a "house wife" with-out having a husband; doing household chores such as the dishes and dusting. She did not do heavy chores then like laundry or scrubbing floors. She had specific chores that were part of her routine. When my grandmother was alive, Jackie mostly helped her mother. She had a great deal of unstructured time which she spent looking through her movie magazines, listening to music, polishing her nails, and entertaining me and my friends.

Laura goes on to tell how she was compelled to do something special for Aunt Jackie.

"For some reason, I had a need to buy something for Jackie when we went up town. I think I felt bad because she could never go with us. I felt bad because she was always working and taking care of everyone. So I went to the dime store and bought her some dusting powder just because I thought she would like it. She put it on her dresser."

This quote represents the confusion with Jackie's identity in the family. Since Jackie was an adult she would not have walked uptown with us kids. Laura felt bad, because Jackie was an adult and because of that adult role Jackie did not go. She was also our playmate. As our playmate she would have walked uptown with us. As children we were confused by Jackie's role in the family.

At different times in life all people play various roles. Identity roles are not stagnant, but fluid. We knew and understood the roles our parents played and the roles of our grandparents, but Jackie was between two worlds. She acted more adult- like around her parents. When she was by herself with us children she would be silly. Historically, through a medical model perspective, individuals with disabilities have been defined by a specific set of attributes and their identity is assigned (Rapley, 2004, p.204). Shakespeare and Watson (2002) discuss the varying roles all people play, and at times people with disabilities identify themselves in different manners. Jackie, through her actions, displayed many roles, some of her choice and many which were placed on her. As children we had a narrow understanding of the fluidity of personality roles. My grandmother treated her as a forever child (Ferguson, Ferguson, & Taylor, 1992) in many ways, yet we were to treat her as an adult. Jackie would do something silly, not at all adult like, and we would be confused by her actions. An example discussed previously describes Jackie throwing the salad bowl in the air to toss the salad, and I was told not to always do what Aunt Jackie did. As children we were puzzled, but did notice that Jackie played more roles than the other adults in the household.

Jackie never disciplined me or told me what to do when I was young. There were four other adults in the house who would do that, so she did not have to play that role. This fact could also contribute to the idea that I saw her as an adult playmate, since she did not have to take on a disciplinarian role. Jackie also did what she was told to do, just like the children of the household. My grandmother (Mere) ruled the house. She parented my mother, Jackie, my grandfather, myself and my siblings. We knew never to cross Mere. My brother Tom said she would just give you a look and you knew you were in trouble. She had that kind of control over all of us, except my Dad. Analyzing this now, my Dad stood up to her. I think she admired that in him and saw him as an equal; the rest of us, including Jackie, did her bidding.

Even though Mere was strict, she had a sense of humor and I saw her fun side, too. Now I realize she was a very young grandmother. Children do not have a concept of age, so I never thought about the fact that she was in her forties. She would ride the roller coaster with me at the amusement park, she paid for and went with me to all my dance and baton lessons. My grandmother continued to have that sense of protectiveness, though. She insisted we have a cyclone fence put all around our yard. To keep me and my brothers in that yard, she bought us a swing set and slide. My grandfather built us a large wood sandbox, big enough for the whole neighborhood to play in. The fence was all around us, protecting us. The toys were the draw to keep us there. The instinct that she had to keep her children safe now expanded to her grandchildren.

We, her grandchildren, were from a different generation and we ventured out more than my grandmother would have liked. The gate on our fence was rarely locked, and typically was hanging open. Beyond the fence was the grassy alley that connected me to Laura and Debbie. As young girls we connected on the other side of the fence and those connections were rooted in friendship. The gate was open to the possibilities that lurked on the other side. Just on the other side of the fence is where I had the confrontation with the twins who called my Aunt Jackie "retarded". So, in reality, my grandmother could not keep us so safe after all.

Beyond the fence were also possibilities. Just on the other side were the homes of our friends, the path to school and uptown, the path that led us from our safety zone and gave us opportunities. Opportunities Jackie never had because there was always a fence. Jackie never went anywhere on her own. She could not drive and had problems with directionality and money, but she was perfectly capable of walking around the neighborhood. I wonder now if she wanted to go somewhere on her own or was she content watching her programs on TV, listening to music, and taking care of my grandmother? The more I seek to uncover, the more questions I have. We could venture out of the fence, but Jackie had to be invited to go somewhere in order to leave.

Changes

My grandmother passed away when I was ten years old. With my grandmother's death, our lives changed significantly. My grandmother had ruled the house and without her we were all a little freer in many ways, but there was a huge void in our lives. For as strict as Mere was, we always knew she was there to protect us, to make decisions for us. In many ways she provided a false sense of security. She could not protect us from all that hovered on the other side of the fence. There were now five children in my family. My sisters were babies when Mere passed away. My mom missed her mother. She had cared for her most of her life. To fill the void, she threw herself into volunteering at our parish, and worked a couple of nights a week singing at a piano bar. She never would have done that if my grandmother was alive, especially because it was one of the clubs where my great grandmother used to sing. I think this was an act of defiance on my mother's part. She could finally sing because she wanted to and where she wanted to, and the money helped support our family.

My grandfather drowned his sorrows in alcohol. Jackie would help him into bed when he would come home drunk. She'd say "Come on now

Daddy." and he would say "You're a good girl Jackie." as she brought him to his room. He always thought of her as his little girl. She never had the opportunity to grow up. Jackie worried about her dad. She would shake her head at him and her eyes would go back and forth. Whenever Jackie worried it always showed in her eyes. Her eyes would actually tremble, going quickly back and forth. I rarely saw Jackie cry, but especially in these times, her eyes were always moving.

Jackie missed her mother. She would tell me stories before we went to bed about things she and her "Momma" did together. Jackie's life was now so different. She had spent so much time taking care of and just being with her mother. She told me she missed making my grandma her Friday night highball. Jackie was proud of her drink mixing skills. She would proudly declare: "I make a mean highball. It is all how you stir it up." While she said that she would do a spinning dance. As we were roommates, I heard all the stories about Jackie and her mother. I was the one she confided in.

Not So Fun Anymore...

Right before my grandmother went into the hospital the final time, she had the bright idea to move bedrooms around. Jackie and I became roommates. At first this was not a bad situation, as I could stay up later in my room and read and Jackie would not tell on me. Within a short time, however, Jackie and I began to argue more like siblings. Her rituals and habits were beginning to bother me. We also had to share a double bed. The mattress was old and Jackie made a dent in the bed and I would roll into her. I did not want to be so close to her and she did not want me up close either. We would snap at each other daily. I also began to think all her questions were intrusive. This probably had more to do with me than her, as I was a preteen and everything was beginning to annoy me.

Jackie also would try to be a disciplinarian to my brothers. This attempt at pseudo parenting did not go well. My brother Tommy would dare her to come after him, or do crazy things like climb on the roof when my mom was not home. He would be yelling "come and get me" to her and would push Jackie emotionally to see if she would set limits.

My brother Ed would watch and just ignore Tommy's antics and Aunt Jackie as well. It seems to me now that Jackie was trying to act like a mom and it was not working. My grandmother had ruled the household and in regards to us kids, I wonder if Jackie felt she could take her place as a disciplinarian. Perhaps she also finally had an opportunity to act like an adult without her mother saying: "Jackie close your mouth," or "Jackie you can have a Pepsi now." Jackie was trying to exert this "adultness" on us, but we never saw her as a total adult.

Jackie was not so fun anymore to me and my siblings. She took on a housekeeper role and went about her business doing laundry, making our lunches, and dusting. My grandfather was drinking on a daily basis, Jackie seems like an afterthought from my perspective today. No one openly talked about my grandfather's drunkenness, my grandmother's death, or Jackie's feelings. We just lived. My grandparents had set the tone in the family not to talk about things. They had put up this fence to protect their own emotions and to protect Jackie. It created a culture of denial. This barrier did protect Jackie in that she did not think something was "wrong" with her, but it hindered her. She may not have known who she was and what role she was suppose to play.

My sister Colleen remembers Jackie as more of a sibling, not so much an adult. She said she just knew Jackie was more on a child level, yet Jackie took care of her. Colleen said she thought of Jackie as a big sister, even though she was her Aunt. She also mentioned that she rarely called her "Aunt Jackie" it was just "Jackie." Colleen is eight years younger than me and does not remember my grandmother, or when our Pa was living with us. As a child I was reminded to call Jackie, Aunt Jackie. Time went on, the years went by and it was now the 1970s. My little sisters were school age. My mother did not remind them to call Jackie, "Aunt Jackie" any more. Maybe losing that title also lost Jackie some respect as well.

Looking back now as an adult, at this point in time when I was around thirteen years old, I think I treated Jackie as some kind of a slave person. Her silly jokes were not so funny anymore and she would move my stuff or take bad phone messages. Jackie's appearance began to change as well. She would let her thin hair just hang, she no longer would fix it, so it looked stringy and dirty. My mom would have to remind her to take a bath or wipe off her mouth. She would wear dirty house-dresses, and never bothered to wear an apron anymore, so her stomach area would be wet or dirty from leaning by the sink. My mom was always saying "Didn't you have that dress on yesterday?" Jackie would pretend she did not hear her, and would walk away mumbling: "You aren't my mother." Other than family parties, trips to the movies or dinner with her Dad she rarely cared about her appearance. Without the strict guidelines set by her mother, Jackie did whatever she wanted to do. She once loved getting dressed up and always kept her nails polished, so not caring about her looks was uncharacteristic of the Jackie of my young childhood. The "old" Jackie was buried somewhere, possibly for self preservation as she was quietly coping with her own depression of losing her mom, her Dad's attention and her role as "Aunt" Jackie.

As a young teen, I was beginning to be embarrassed by her, not because she was disabled, but by the way she looked. As a teenager, my friends were always kind and respectful to Jackie. They would usually carry on conversations with her and listen to her silly jokes. I remember just wanting to get out of there; after all, I had heard all those jokes before.

My grandfather got remarried around this time. He moved out and in most ways he moved on, leaving Jackie. My mom would have to call and remind him to come and see her, take her someplace, or give my mom money for her clothes. He and his new wife did not have much time for Jackie. Jackie would get all excited when he did come by and she was thrilled when she got to stay at their house once in a while. Jackie still wanted to be Daddy's girl. They had been so close and now there was a new person in his life. There was not much room in this new life for Jackie.

At least, when my grandfather moved out, my parents and grandfather sat and talked with her about why she was going to continue living with us. This talk was a big step for the family that never talked about difficult situations before. In the conversation, Jackie expressed her reasons for wanting to continue living with us. She told my Pa she would miss the kids and that the house on Parkside was her home, and she wanted to stay with Doris and Art (my parents). Jackie had finally been included in a critical decision about her life. Jackie had always had the opportunity to choose basic things, like the clothes she wore, or if she wanted to go on vacation with us, or her programs on TV, but she never was consulted on anything important. Jackie finally had made an important choice for herself and voiced it well.

Guilt

Jackie almost died when I was in high school. She had an infection and slipped into a coma for days. My grandfather was there blubbering about his sweet Jackie, my mom hardly left the hospital, and I felt guilty. Being a teenager, it was all about me and I wanted a chance to tell her what she meant to me. My boyfriend at the time said I should hope Jackie got better so I could treat her better in the future. He said I should be nicer to her since she was *retarded*. I did not think of Jackie as retarded; she was my Aunt who at this time of my life was bugging me. I selfishly wanted her to get better, because I was feeling so guilty. I kept remembering how she was always so good to me when I was younger, and how at one time she was the coolest aunt around. I also realized I took advantage of her and treated her like a housekeeper sometimes and did not value her presence in my life. Jackie was just Jackie; after all, she had always been there. I needed a chance to make things better.

Jackie did come out of the coma. One day she just woke up and asked my mom who had been making the kids lunches; she was thinking of us. We were her life. I am not sure if it was maturity, getting my own bedroom, or true remorse, but Jackie was my Aunt Jackie again and I appreciated her presence (and her silly jokes) in my life.

Through the Years

The years go by and our family is changing. I married, my brothers went away to school and I had a family of my own. My parents moved from our home on Parkside Avenue to a new home. Along with them came Aunt Jackie and my dad's mom (Grandma Gregory) in the early stages of dementia. Aunt Jackie and Grandma Gregory acted like partners in crime. They ate whole bags of candy, got locked out of the house and called the fire department, and hid things rather than put them away. When my mom would ask them about what they were doing, Jackie would say again: "You are not my mother." Jackie never liked my mom telling her what to do. She had always accepted whatever her mother told her to do, because I suppose she played the role of the forever child with her mom. My mom was her sister, and Jackie did not like to be told what to do by her sister. As evidenced by some of the choices Jackie was making, she did need guidance, but this started a sense of rebellion in Jackie. "You're not my mother" were words she would say for many years to come. Grandma Gregory and Jackie were an interesting pair and like secretive children, got themselves into many situations. My sister Colleen (Jamee's mom) reflects on life with Grandma and Jackie

"For a while Grandma and Jackie were good for each other, they kept each other company. I think Jackie liked it that she was more "with it" than Grandma. She would tattle to Mom about something Grandma did. They were funny together."

My dad, who had served as the emotional stabilizer for our family, passed away. Jackie took on the role of comforter to my mom. She and my 5 year old daughter Amy would keep Mom company, singing songs and keeping her busy. There was now another generation of kids playing with Aunt Jackie. Amy loves telling Jackie stories.

"I thought Jackie was cool because she was an adult who liked to play with me. We would play games and she would read to me. We would sit on the swing in the backyard and make up stories about the cars that drove by, we would pretend they were being driven by Disney characters. When I started to read better than Jackie I think I started to think something was different about her, but it did not faze me too much because we had fun together. She did not like it when I told her she cheated at Sorry, though."

My kids loved their great Aunt Jackie and hung out with her. My son, Tim shares a Jackie memory:

"Mostly I remember going to club with her and her friends. I would play basketball with the guys there and sing with the people. I remember holding her hand in the parking lot, walking into club."

At age 58 in 1995, Jackie started to show signs of dementia. Little by little, she disappeared from us. At first she was forgetful and would leave water running, or forget where she put her hanky. Then she would get angry if her TV programs were changed. She always watched Archie Bunker at ten pm, when they moved the show from that time slot she was extremely upset. Jackie started to use foul language. Jackie had never even said "crap" before and she started talking back to my mom and using the "f" word. To provide a break for my mom, Jackie would often stay with me. At times she was herself, carrying on conversations, playing games with my kids, and then she would suddenly lapse into crying jags. Her crying was heart breaking, loud gulping sobs; this from the woman who rarely cried. One day she took off all her clothes in my office, with my eighth grade son, Tim and his friend sitting in the next room. Tim calmly handed her, her clothes and called for me. Jackie told me she did not understand why we told her to get dressed, because she was in her room and she was trying to get ready for bed. Jackie knew us sometimes and at others times was confused. She was frightened by walking up and down steps, noises, and weather. Her eyes were always trembling.

My mom was in denial and kept acting as if Jackie was not showing signs of dementia. Mom would get angry with her for forgetting things, and would try to correct Jackie or redirect her as if Jackie understood what she meant. Jackie would yell at my mom and my mom would get caught up in it and yell back. Mom would tell Jackie to go to her room; as if she was a child. All five of us children were now grown and married, and it was back to "Doris and Jackie." My mom now regrets how she treated Jackie during this time.

"I do not know why I treated Jackie that way; (starting to cry) I would never treat Jamee (her granddaughter with disabilities) like that. But to me she was my sister, it is not an excuse for my actions, I do not know why I would get so angry with her."

My mother had made a promise to her mother to always take care of her sister. With Jackie needing constant supervision, my mother was starting to realize that she could not continue to care for her sister. Lashing out at Jackie may have been the external signs of my mom's internal struggles. My mom had a difficult decision to make about Jackie's care and she did not want to have to make the decision.

When Jackie started turning on the stove and left water over-flowing, my mom finally realized she could not be left alone. Jackie was then enrolled in a day program with other adults with disabilities. A caregiver came and sat with her before and after the program until my mom got home from work. Jackie called the program "school" and she liked to fold clothes there. Jackie now required constant supervision, and while my mother inquired about community integrated living arrangements (CILA), she kept putting off making a final decision. After six months of my mother talking about making arrangements for Jackie, my sister Colleen, now a mother of a child with a disability, said she was going to call and inquire about Jackie's options. Colleen made the phone call and within a couple of weeks Jackie moved in with five other ladies, five miles from my mother's townhouse. Colleen was able to do what my mom could not force herself to do; let Jackie go to be taken care of by someone else.

Colleen talks about Jackie's CILA experience:

"You know it is too bad Mom did not do that sooner. Jackie would have enjoyed going places and being with people. She would have been a good housemate. I feel bad about that. I have mixed feelings about that whole situation with mom and all."

My mom had made a promise to her mother to take care of her sister. It was hard for her to let Jackie go. It was always Doris and Jackie, that is just how it was.

A Void in Our Lives

Jackie's health deteriorated within the next eight months. She forgot how to cough and kept choking on her food. She no longer knew us, though she remembered my mom and my daughter Amy the longest. She spent the last few weeks of life in a nursing home, on a feeding tube. Amy and I stopped in to see her, and she looked so scared. Her eyes were trembling. Fifteen year old, Amy held Jackie's hand and sang the song to

Jackie that Jackie sang to her as a five year old swinging on the backyard swing. Amy started to sing: "I played horsy down the street," and Jackie's eyes quit trembling, she looked straight at Amy as she sang the song. As Amy continued to sing, I went to the nurses' station and insisted they check on her. Her body was shutting down. Amy and I followed the ambulance to the hospital, calling my mom and siblings on the phone as we drove.

Fuzzy Socks and Heartfelt Good-byes.

The room is gloomy and a shadow is cast from the little bit of light coming from outside just peeking through the blinds. It is shortly after dawn of what looks to be the beginning of a cloudy, dreary day. We stare at the walls, the windows, the clock, anywhere, just so we do not stare at the reason we are sitting in a dark stuffy hospital room so early in the morning. My mom, my brother Tom, and sister Kathy have been sitting here with me since last night. The clock ticks the minutes away. It is an old fashioned round faced clock with with large black numbers. We hear every tick. Every time the minute hand moves, the sound is etched in our brain.

Tick.. Tick.. In between the ticks we hear her breaths, they are deep and rambling. Jackie has not opened her eyes since last evening. She looks so tiny laying there all tucked under the institutional cotton blanket. We hold our breath and wait. Sometimes we breath louder than Jackie, letting out a sigh or two. Tick..Tick.The doctor has told us it should not be much longer as all her organs are shutting down. We just wished Jackie would go peacefully into forever sleep. It is well past the time for her to leave us physically. She really had been gone from us for a few years, as Alzheimer's took over her mind and body. We rarely had glimpses of our Jackie in the past few months.

Mom, Kathy, Tom and I had shared stories throughout the night.

Kathy reminded my mom yet again that she and Colleen were raised by Jackie, since my parents were so busy volunteering at our school and church. Kathy teased my mom and said she owed everything to Jackie since Jackie did such a nice job of raising her. She also reminded my mom that Jackie would never have forgotten or left her alone when she was little. Kathy told the story about the time my mom forgot to pick her up at preschool.

"So I sit with my coat on, holding my little school bag, waiting by the door with the teacher for you to pick me up at the white house at the park. Kinda like today, I kept looking at the clock, not like I could tell time at 4 years old, but I knew you were really late. After awhile the teacher put me in her car and drove me to the park district office."

"Jackie, you never would have forgotten me. You always took care of me. You were always there when I came home from school, making me good TV dinners." Kathy is smiling in the direction of the bed.

"Oh Kathy, stop that, I only forgot you that one time." My mom is smiling with tears in her eyes and gazes at her sister as she tries to defend herself.

"Jackie sure loved you kids." We were talking in the past and in the present about Jackie, yet she was still in the room with us. The saying "hovering between life and death" really described the moments on that long night.

We sit quiet for awhile, lost in our own memories and thoughts of Jackie. Tick.. tick.. the swooshing sounds of the monitors and Jackie's raspy breaths seem to fill up the room. Tom starts to fidget, he has to talk, and break the eerie sound filled silence.

"I am not sure how much she loved me when I climbed out my of my bedroom window and ran around on the garage roof. Then when she told me to get back in, I dared her to come out get me."

"I do not think she said oh Tom, you're such a kidder that day," I chimed in.

"Shar, you weren't so perfect either, "Jackie, I told you not to write down that phone number, (Tom is imitating me with a girls voice) now I can't call my latest boyfriend."

"Well she never could write a phone number correctly. I kept telling her don't take a message. Just ask them to call back."

"Oh, Jackie how you messed up my teenage love life." I am laughing and crying at the same time.

My mom starts talking:

"And Art(my dad) was ready to kill you, Jackie. I think you messed up a big sale for him when you took the wrong information down for a potential client. You wrote the number down and it was missing a number. You kept arguing with him, telling him the number was correct. He kept trying to explain that a phone number had 7 numbers in it, not 6. He never was able to get a hold of the man. He was so angry. You just *had* to take messages."

My mom stops chuckling when she realizes she has said, "Art was going to *kill* you." My mom starts to cry, "Oh Jackie".

To try make my mom feel better somehow, I keep reminding her that Jackie will be with Daddy now and her parents, Mere and Pa.

My mom keeps saying, Oh Jackie... I never meant to get mad or angry with her. I loved her so much." It was always us Doris and Jackie... I hope she knows."

The swooshing sounds of the monitors, Jackie's raspy breaths,and the tick tick of the clock were the only sounds for what seemed like hours. Mom called my brother, Ed and sister, Colleen. Mom explained to them that it should not be much longer now. Did they want to come and say goodbye? Ed said he was ok since Jackie really wasn't there anymore. He was fine staying home and he told mom he loved her and Jackie. Colleen said she had Jenna,Jamee,and Jordan home and she had said her goodbyes to Jackie the night before when she came to see her in the emergency room. All five of us were definitely Jackie's kids.Mom said she would talk to them both when it was over. *Over;* another way to describe death.

The nurses come in and out. One nurse listens to her heart.

"It slowing down, not much longer now..."

We take a break and walk in the hall for a few minutes.

"They said that her heart is so strong," my mom says, "So many people with Down Syndrome have heart problems, but Jackie never did. Now I wish it would stop and just let her go."

We go back into the room and continue our vigil. Tick... tick ...her breath seems to get louder and deeper. We get close to her and hold her little hands, she looks so small and vulnerable. We wait and cry silent tears.

"Oh, Jackie."

"Love you."

"We will miss you."

"Say hi to Daddy."

"It's ok to go."

We whisper words of love and encouragement. It is her time. Tick.. Tick... a few breaths and Jackie is gone. We push the call button and a nurse comes in.

"Time of death 6:45"...so final and official.

Life is over in a single breath. How we will miss our Aunt Jackie. My grandmother was told to put her away when she was a baby. Children like Jackie would not live long. Life expectancy was three years old then. Jackie lived well beyond those expectations, all because those who loved her *had* expectations. Jackie was expected to live, just as she was expected to walk on time, speak clearly, read etc. etc. Expectation is an interesting word and even more interesting of a concept. I'm sure my grandparents did not know what to expect. After all there really wasn't anyone who could describe to them what life with Jackie would entail. I think because they did not have a developmental checklist of expectations for Jackie, she was able to surpass 1930 societal expectations for a *mongoloid, retarded* person.

Tom, Kathy, Mom and I walked out of the hospital making phone calls.

"She's gone." "Talk soon." "Thank you." "We will let you know when we go to make the arrangements." All typical—blah blah blah funeral type comments.

We were doing okay. Jackie had to be better off anywhere, but here. Her time was over. When someone I love leaves the earth, I am personally glad to believe in an afterlife. It is comforting to know that I will see, in some way, the people I love again. I will see Jackie again. Those last breaths and those last ticks of the clock did not mean the real end. I just kept thinking Jackie is able to live forever now. I do not wish that she will be in heaven as anyone other than her genuine self. I've heard people say that when someone with a disability dies, that the person will be perfect in heaven. I know people are trying to say something nice in a difficult time, but that means that there was something wrong with the person with the disability when they are here on earth.

I like to think heavenly Jackie will be the Aunt Jackie I knew when I was young. The spunky, playful Aunt Jackie who told silly jokes, loved to have her nails polished and wore pretty bracelets. Who knows maybe she is singing along with Mitch Miller in another place or she is dancing the Twist with Chubby Checker. Maybe she is mixing one of her "mean highballs" for her Momma. I just know that my personal idea of heaven has to include my Aunt Jackie.

The next couple of days were spent trying to catch up with life after spending the weekend at the hospital and planning a wake and funeral. I was just trying to get my life organized, in between writing words to a song for the funeral mass and thinking of "Jackie-isms" to go in the program. All the busy-ness was really a way to ignore, for a little while, the hurt that was within my heart. At least by planning the funeral, I could actually do something for Jackie.

As the day went on, I called my mom to ask what clothes she was bringing to the funeral home for Jackie. My mom said she had purchased a pretty pastel pink sweater for Jackie but Jackie had never worn it, because she became so ill shortly after, so Mom was going to bring that. I felt better knowing that Jackie was going to be cozy. Crazy, I know, but it gave me a sense of comfort.

Later in the evening I had to go to the store to pick up things for the family. The only store open by the time I got my life together was Walmart, so there I am going up and down the aisles at 11pm, trying to figure out what I need. As I am going through the store in a state of confusion, I think to myself we never discussed what shoes Jackie would wear. As of late Jackie had these really ugly orthopedic black shoes that she needed to wear. I knew my dancing Aunt Jackie would not want to go to heaven with ugly shoes. So I pull out the cell phone and call my mom. I knew it was ok to call so late, because I figured she was up going slightly crazy, too.

"I will find something for Jackie to where on her feet, ok?" I am telling my mom this in the shoe aisle.

"You will probably be better off with some slippers, because she has such short fat feet."

"I know, I will look and call you back."

I kept roaming around the store, it seemed like forever. Shoes? or slippers? or socks? Back and forth between aisles and departments. I finally settled on some pink fluffy slipper socks which would match with her sweater. I held them up to my cheek, they were cozy and warm. Perfect for Jackie. I called my mom back and told her what I had found. She laughed and said socks would be fine, since Jackie wasn't walking anywhere anyhow... Silly jokes seem to make the reality easier to bare.

Jackie left this world in style, in a pretty pink sweater, some comfy black slacks, and warm cozy socks. Her nails were polished in a shade to match her sweater and her wig was lookin' good. She even had a brand new hankie tucked in for safe keeping. Aunt Jackie was stylin' for the visitation. We were happy that Jackie looked so nice, since it was so long since she was able to care about her appearance. The florist even made a corsage to match her sweater. When he heard she was a lady with Down Syndrome, he wanted to do something just for her. She would have liked having a man give her a flower.

When I was a little girl Jackie and I had made up many silly songs. It was only fitting that I wrote words to a song to be sung at her funeral. My sisters, Colleen and Kathy and my daughter, Amy sang the song during the funeral Mass. Our family sings together for happy occasions. We were singing out and celebrating our Jackie. Singing in tribute helped ease the pain of our loss. We sang out in appreciation of the woman who helped all of us become the people we are today. We sang for the person who played with us, wiped our noses, chased us around, taught us how to play Sorry, but most of all who showered us with love. Kathy was really right when she said Jackie helped raise us.

As we walked out of church the bells rang out, signifying a job well done, a life fully lived. We love you Jackie. Enjoy your comfy socks!

Life Goes On...

I miss my Aunt Jackie. My child self misses games of war, playing Go Fish by throwing the cards in the air, yelling happy New Year on the front porch, playing Barbies and doing the twist. My adult self misses her presence in my life. Her calm demeanor when the world was falling apart around her, or coming to help me when I was a new mom. I miss her singing silly songs to my kids and I am sad that my younger nieces and nephews never had Aunt Jackie in their lives. As her family we miss her knock-knock jokes, her TV and Pepsi rituals, and the embarrassing moments.

Just last Christmas everyone was sitting around reminiscing and we began to swap "Jackie" stories. The stories were filled with laughter, some embarrassment and some "I can't believe she did that" moments. I heard everyone talking about an important member of our family. I gathered the stories, savoring the memories. For a portion of our lives we were not allowed to focus on Jackie's disability or say that she had a disability, nevertheless being a woman with Down Syndrome was part of her identity. We never discussed this while my Grandmother was alive and Jackie herself never called herself disabled, yet she did live as a person with a disability. Society, her parents and all of us tried to place her in constructs, which changed over the years. If Jackie had been born in another time, her life may have been quite different; many more opportunities would have been available to her.

For her time, she lived a full life. She had family who loved her, she went to school, her club, she went on trips, saw movies and plays, read books, and took care of people. She was needed and she knew we needed her. She lived when many other of her contempories with Down Syndrome did not have the opportunity. In retrospect, her lived experience could have been fuller or her opinion should have been more respected, but no one gets practice at life, we just live. My grandparents were not perfect, but they knew their Jackie was entitled to a life. We loved Jackie, a woman with Down Syndrome. She enhanced our lives, helped to form our personalities, and influenced our perspectives.

This is Jackie's story, it is my story. Jackie is at the root of this story; additional stories emerge as rhizomic offshoots representing life, friendship, families and disabilities. Oh...and yes, Jacqueline is indeed a nice name.

CHAPTER FOUR

Swingin' Chains and Trains

Chuck, 1961

Chuck and I grew up together. My lifelong friend Debbie is Chuck's older sister. Together, with our friend Laura we spent much time as children worrying about Chuck's preoccupation with trains. Chuck loves trains. As a child he would escape from his fenced in yard to go see the trains rush by three blocks away. His train adventures were well known throughout our neighborhood. If Chuck was able to figure out how to unlatch the gate to his yard, Debbie or Mr. or Mrs. E. would yell, "Chuck got out!" Some of us kids would run to my house to see if he was trying to sneak in to my house by going into our basement via an outdoor stair case. Mr. E. would hop on Mrs. E.'s old blue bike and start riding towards the train tracks with the rest of the kids running behind him.

Chuck always went one of two places. We would breathe a sigh of relief if we found him at my house, because the tracks were dangerous. We always worried that some day we would not make it in time and Chuck would get hit by a train. One time we could not find Chuck, and we knew the fast train was due to come through any minute. We ran as fast as we could down Central towards the tracks, yelling "Chuckie!" with tears running down our faces. We were so afraid he was going to get hit. Luckily Chuck moved slowly. His run was almost in slow motion; he would stick his back end out, hoist his arms up chest high and his whole body would twist as he would run. There was more back and forth action than there was forward motion. That day his lack of speed may have saved his life. Chuck's sister Debbie, Laura, and I caught up with him three houses away from the tracks. Debbie grabbed his arm and he sat down (obviously ticked off with us). Just then the train whizzed by. Debbie yelled at him: "See Chuck you could have been hurt!" She grabbed his one hand, Laura grabbed the other and I guarded him from behind, as we dragged him home. He kept turning around still looking for the train. Debbie kept pulling him forward, "Come on Chuck, let's go home."

Besides his passion for trains, Chuck likes chains. Since childhood Chuck has had a little chain he likes to twirl around. The "famous chain" is actually a pull chain from a light with a pen cap tied to the end. Chuck has two of these special chains; one for weekdays and one for weekends. He sits and relaxes by spinning his chain in the air, as he watches his programs on TV.

Chuck speaks, but for people who do not know him, it is sometimes difficult to decipher what he is trying to say. When I went to visit Chuck for an interview he proudly showed me his chains. Each chain is in a special pouch. He said, "weekend" to me, as he showed me the pouch that was on his dresser. This is the chain he uses only on the weekends and it is in a shiny leather pouch. Chuck even demonstrated how he swings his chain in the air. The chain is a much safer pastime than running to the train track. Chuck still enjoys watching the trains, but now he knows to stand far away as he watches them go by. Just as the Chuck's chain is linked together, or the tracks of the train need to be attached, Chuck, born 24 years after Jackie is a critical link in this generational story.

Chuck's Out!

I'm driving down 95th St., cruising along on a warm summer's day, jamming to the 70's on 7 on my XFM car radio. Not caring about who is looking at me, I am lost in my own car world. I am singing away :

"Saturday in the park, think it was the fourth of July." I notice that I am at Parkside. I can't help but to look down my old street.

"Oh there is my house. Hi, house" Singing out loud and now talking out loud to a house,(I have issues).

Some things just can't be helped.Whenever I am back in Oak Lawn and look towards my old house from 95th street, I always look up in sky and towering above I can see *my* tree. Funny, it has not been my tree in over 30 years, but I still claim it. It is a secure feeling to know it is still growing there, back in the neighborhood where all the roots were planted so many years before.

I look up and see my tree, "Hi tree", talking to yet another object. Tree is still growing,life is good. As I am driving toward Central Avenue, in the corner of my eye I catch this guy walking. I do a double take because he looks half naked, actually he *is* half naked. This chubby guy is strutting down the sidewalk shirtless, with his big belly sticking out, wearing only shorts, gym shoes, and large headphones. He looks to be singing out loud to himself. He must be caught up in this nice day, too.

I think to myself, "Crazy guy, not a good look" as I'm chuckling to myself in my car. I get to the corner and of course I hit a red light. I am stopped at the intersection of 95th and Central in the lane next to the sidewalk. It is my lucky day. I get an up close and personal look at the half naked man as he walks by my car.

"Oh my, it's Chuck!" I think about rolling the window down, honking, yelling, doing something, but he would never hear me. He is really into jammin' to his music and is pretty much oblivious to anything.

"Oh Crap, the light is changing, I gotta go." I start laughing in the car. It starts out as a little chuckle, but then as I am thinking about what I just saw. I am laughing hysterically to myself. Singing out loud, talking to myself, laughing by myself, (I need to get a grip).

How crazy, I rarely drive down 95th St. anymore and then the one time I do, I just happen to see Chuck. And I mean I **really** see Chuck. Actually more of Chuck than I wanted to see. He looked so happy though, and full of joy, strutting his stuff for all the world to see. Good for him. Interesting how my thoughts changed once I could relate to the man walking half naked. His happiness was contagious. I was still laughing.

I dug the cell phone out of my purse, (So much for safe driving) and called my mom. I just had to call someone who would "get it".

"Guess who I just saw ?"

"Chuck"

"So where are you? How is he?" My mom understands my bizarre travels and encounters. She was able to follow the conversation with ease. I did not even have to say a last name, Chuck is famous to us. We were now laughing together on the phone.

"Oops, sorry Mom gotta go, Oak Lawn cop, you know how they are." I click the phone off and continue singing to myself. Seeing Chuck had added to my enjoyment. I continued to give an enthusiastic concert in my car.

I started to sing to another song on the radio, but a little voice in my head kept saying, "Chuck Got Out! Chuck Got Out!". During our childhood we always worried when Chuck escaped from his yard. When Chuck would find a way to open the gate, "Chuck Got Out!" was our childhood battle cry.

Memories of Chuck came to the surface and I began to think about my childhood friend as I drove along. I was glad that Chuck was now able to be out on his own. Maybe he needed a bit of fashion advice, but I was pleased to see him so happy and independent, truly experiencing enjoyment. It really made my whole day, just that glimpse of his life. I was so happy he had the freedom to bask in the sunshine.

Most of Chuck's childhood he couldn't get out. When he was young he was restricted to the yard living on a busy intersection and having train tracks two blocks down. I felt bad, even as a child, that his world was so physically limited. His life outside the fence was totally dependent on us. If we were going uptown we would drag him, often literally, with us. If we decided to go to the park, he would be with us. There were a number of years by bringing Chuck with us, then Debbie would be able to come out with us. She would have to stay in the yard with Chuck, if we did not bring him with. I do not recall being upset with having to bring him with us. It was just how it was. He did slow us down when we went on our childhood adventures. Sometimes he preferred to sit on the ground. All of a sudden he would pull your hand down and plop himself, butt first, down on the sidewalk. Even though he did not talk much, he made it very clear that he had had enough. If we were on our way uptown to the store and he refused to get up, we would bribe him with promises of candy and ice cream. When he dropped to the ground on the way home, we would digress to threats.

"I'm going to tell Mom," Debbie would say. She would put her hands on her hips and peer down at him on the sidewalk.

"We can't bring you any more, if you do this."

Sometimes he actually rolled over, looked up at us with a smirk on his face, and acted as if he was going to lay down.

"You need to get up **now**, or I am telling Dad when he gets home!" Laura and I chimed in with "Yea" or "Come on Chuck, get up."

"Chuck you are going to be in big trouble!" Our voices would grow louder and more stern, as we would get tired of begging him and chastising him to get up. Sometimes we would get to the point of saying:

"Fine then you can just stay here, We are leaving you here, Bye Chuck." Being very dramatic little girls we would keep waving and saying "Bye,Bye, Chuckie" as we purposely stamped away, sneaking looks back the whole time. Mrs. E. would wring our necks if we ever really left him. We wouldn't have done that. We knew he was our responsibility, even at 8 years old, we knew he needed us.

The second we saw him make any move, we went back and pulled him up. Sometimes he got himself up and he would sneak up quietly coming up behind us grabbing one of our hands. To see Chuck walking around himself that day, stirred so many childhood memories that I spent the rest of the day driving in the car, making old movies in my head.

My mind kept replaying all the times with Chuck, Debbie and Laura, mini movies flashing by as I continued to make my way, driving around. I kept thinking of the times playing in the yard or pushing Chuck on his swing. On rainy days we played in the garage and every so often we walked over and gave Chuck a push on his swing which hung from the rafter. Sometimes we took turns with the swing, since there was just the one. Chuck was swinging, then without exchanging any words, he got off the swing and plopped down on the cement. There he sat cross-legged on the floor(We called it "Indian Style", then) and just watch or hum to himself while one of us took a turn.

Gentle, peaceful swinging... back and forth. Sometimes the only sounds were the creaking of the beam as the swing would move and the muffled sounds of traffic on 95th Street.

"Crick, Crick" "Crick, Crick" we were lulled into a peaceful trance. Other times we sang loudly to the rafters.

"Hey, hey we're the Monkees and we aren't foolin' around."

Chuck sang with gusto too,with words that only he could understand. It was fun when he joined in the craziness. In those fleeting childhood moments swinging in the garage,he had that same look of freedom, that I saw that day when grown up Chuck was strutting around. He was in some other zone and just looked really happy.

"Hey, Shar, go open the gate. I wanna come in and play with Chuckie."

My brother Tommy is at the back side of the fence, peering through the holes of the cyclone.

"Go away!" I typically found my younger brother very annoying.

"No, I'm going to come in and play with Chuck. Let me in."

I did not want him to come in. I wanted him to just go away. He never stayed for long and by the time I would go to the front gate, un-lock the two locks, open the gate, and lock everything up again;it really was not worth it. Tom would swing once or twice. Talk at Chuck for a bit. Say something annoying to me and then want to go back out. It was such a tiresome ritual to come in and out of the fence, so I thought, why bother? I never thought that Chuck might want to hang out with a boy close to his age once in a while. We girls acted as the gatekeepers. If you wanted to play with Chuck, we decided if you could. Sometimes Laura would let her brother Keith in, sometimes I would let Tom or Ed inside to play. We did not ask Chuck his opinion at all. We were very much in charge, and liked to exert our power.

We felt very empowered by helping Chuck. We knew he needed our help. We saw ourselves as his little helpers,but sometimes we acted like bossy mommas. We relished the control. It made us feel good to help him. We were patient with him, and we never pitied him. If anything, we had high expectations for him. We expected him to keep up when we were going places; to play along with our games of pretend. We encouraged him to talk to us. Often times Debbie would serve as a translator, since Chuck's speech was not clear.

As Chuck got older, we started to see more glimpses of his true personality. Once Chuck went to school, he started telling us what roles we could play in his pretend scenarios. We went along with his pretending to be male movie stars and TV personalities. He was THE MAN and we were commanded to be HIS GIRLS. He loved to act like *the* man in charge.

Sometimes he still let Debbie dress him up in her girly dress up clothes. He playfully strutted around, wiggling his butt and swinging a purse in the air. Chuck was all about the drama. There were times, too, when he refused to come out and play, and he would vehemently tell us so. We began to realize when Chuck said no, he meant it.

Chuck, as a 10 year old was exerting his own independence. All of our roles were changing. It was good that Chuck was coming into himself, because as Debbie, Laura and I were in upper grades;boys, cheerleading, school dances and social activities were a lot more fun than sitting on the garage floor and swinging with Chuck. Without our prodding him to come out and play,Chuck did become a bit more stagnant. He sat for hours in the TV room and watched TV, swinging his chain. Chuck was basically forgotten because everyone was so busy. We were busy coming into ourselves for sure. We were no longer his helpful playmates. As we reached our teens, we moved into a "be nice to Chuck mode." We did not share life moments any longer, we instead would say, "hello" exchange pleasantries.... and move on. We were kind, but removed. What is really wonderful though, is the fact that Chuck made his own friends from school, and then later from his work program. He did not need his bossy little momma friends any longer.

I do not "hang out" with Chuck as an adult. Other than formal type events,we really do not socialize together. There is still something very special, however, being with the people who knew you when. It is comforting spending time with those who knew you best when you were first exploring your little world. Chuck was part of my world. He was there when we were trying to act all grown up and he was there when we realized we were growing up. He was there swinging, observing, and becoming Chuck, right along with us. We never really noticed, as we lived our lives. Growing up kinda sneaks up on you. All of a sudden you are no longer children, or even teenagers, but full fledged grownups, having to do so called grown up things.

As I drove around that day thinking and reminiscing, I am envious of Chuck. He exuded such confidence and joy, as he strutted down the street. There he was, free of the fences, so obviously enjoying being himself.

"Chuck got out; how cool is that?"

Telling Chuck's Story

To portray Chuck's story, I spent time with Chuck and interviewed his parents, his only sister, Debbie and my friend Laura who grew up with Chuck. I was curious to know about the story of Chuck's birth. I knew this family forever, but we never talked *really* talked about Chuck. Chuck's parents shared their stories of the early years with their son with such honesty and passion. While the events took place over 45 years ago, they spoke with such clarity. I think they were relieved to actually discuss this time of their lives with someone who cared enough to ask. When I asked Mrs. E. about Chuck's birth, she shared the story of his diagnosis:

"When he was born the doctor didn't say anything. Then I took him to the family doctor for his first month check up. It was just me and Chuckie and Debbie, my husband wasn't with me. And I'd ask him questions, because something did not seem right. and he never...he never answered...he says don't compare them (to my oldest daughter Debbie). And uh when Chuckie was about 6 months old my husband was on vacation and he (Mr. E.) went with us to the doctor. We walked up there and the nurse went and took Debbie into another room and he (doctor) says he wanted to talk to us and he told us that Chuckie was Mongoloid. We did not know what that meant and he suggested that we should take him to Children's (Hospital)."

Mr. and Mrs. E. took their children home and tried to figure it out. What is Mongoloid? What does that mean? The doctor gave them a name, but no explanation, just that they should take Chuckie to see a specialist at a hospital. With Mr E. on vacation they went and told their own mothers that "something was wrong" with Chuck. Their mothers did not understand and said he did not look like anything was "wrong" with him. The use of the word "wrong" to describe disability is woven throughout the family stories. The fact that family members, who passionately love their relative with an intellectual disability, yet use the descriptor "wrong" serves as a testament to the social construction of disability. Jackie's family 30 years before had used the word "wrong" initially to describe her disability as well. The families have been programmed via a particular social view, that their relative does not have the attributes to be a contributing member of society.

They followed the doctor's suggestion and made an appointment with at the children's hospital. Mrs. E. tells about the appointment.

"We took him to be evaluated because Chuckie wasn't holding his head up. He wasn't sitting and he should have been... at 6 months, he should have been crawling, he wasn't. And I was concerned, and we went to see the doctor at Children's Memorial, and it was confirmed that Chuckie was Mongoloid, is what they called it. They didn't know if he would walk, whether he would be able to take care of himself, and he said there might be decisions to be made. That they would want us to put him in... (she looks away and cannot finish saying "institution" out loud). It's going to be up to us, and he said maybe you think and talk about it, and he might be too hard for us to handle, because they did not know the severity of his mental condition. He was supposed to be gone by the time he was 12 years old because of infections like measles or any of that. They did not know, twelve was the maximum, they thought."

The family was now even more confused; the doctor did not give any helpful advice. The professionals of the time were ill informed. Based on a medical model of disability (Corker & Shakespeare, 2002) doctors viewed disability as a sickness. Medical professionals defined these children by what they would not be able to accomplish, not what they could accomplish. In 1961 doctors did not have the information that Down Syndrome is a chromosomal disorder (Wright, 2004) nor did they have any accurate data about developmental milestones or longevity. The majority of children born with disabilities, especially intellectual disabilities such as "Mongoloid" (as Down Syndrome was referred to in 1961), were still living and dying in institutions (Rothman & Rothman, 2004). Society put up institutional fences and Chuck, just by virtue of being Chuck, was as an infant, locked inside. The E.'s brought Chuck to a hospital that specialized in children's health and pediatric illnesses. Laura, the mother of Jonathon, and Colleen, the mother of Jamee, went to the same hospital two decades later seeking answers, just as Mrs. E. did looking for information for how to help Chuck. These three mothers are connected through the bond of giving birth to a child with disabilities.

The doctor the E.'s consulted worked at the hospital which was considered cutting edge at the time, yet in comparison to what we now know about individuals with Down Syndrome, he provided them with little factual information. The doctor told them Chuck may never walk or talk, and that he did not know exactly what was in store for them. Similar information was shared with Jackie's parents two decades before. The doctor told them to talk it over and they had decisions to make, but he never gave them any exact information.

The E.'s knew sending Chuck "somewhere" was not an option, wherever that was, the doctor had never said directly, but they knew they wanted their son at home with them. Just as my grandparents had, the E.'s were beginning to resist the societal constructs of the time. Parents upon giving birth to a child with disabilities felt they were going on a journey, but were confused about where they were going (Wickham-Searl,

1992). Searching for answers, Mr. and Mrs. E. went back to the family doctor hoping they could talk.

"And when I went back to the family doctor, he just said …you treat him like you treat Debbie. Exactly the same way. So we did… We got him on the floor and exercised with him, my husband would do exercises with him. He had these bands and he would stretch Chuckie's muscles and his little legs, we put him in a baby walker when he could put some weight on his feet and we just kept working with him. We did it."

Mr E. was mostly listening up to this point in our conversation and just nodding, he finally spoke up:

"That was it. That is what we did. We were on our own. And he did start to walk."

While the doctor's advice was good advice, since it gave the E's the confidence to do what they felt was right for their son, they did not treat Chuck exactly like Debbie. They instead treated him "exactly like Chuck," and by being in tune with their child, they began doing exercises with him, and taking extra time to teach him new skills. I asked them if they ever saw any type of therapist such as an occupational therapist for suggestions to work with Chuck. Mr. E. said: "No, never" "Sharon, we did not know anything about those people in those days. We just did our best." Mrs E.'s voice was full of pride when she described how their work with Chuck led to improvement.

"We were on our own. Chuckie, by the time he was a year old, he was walking. Just putting him in the little walker and making him, and by the time he was 18 months old he was potty trained. And they did not think that would ever happen."

Mrs.E.'s pride about toilet training Chuck at 18 months of age was evident in her voice. Eighteen months is early even for a typically developing child. My grandmother bugged my mother about the correct age to toilet train my little sister, Colleen. I remember her making comments on how Jackie was trained by age two. As a 10 year old kid I did not care when babies should be trained, nor did I get the implications. One of the comments the doctors made to moms of children with disabilities when they were telling them to institutionalize their child was: "Your child will never walk, talk, or be toilet trained." So now I can understand why reaching the toilet training milestone was so very important.

Mrs. E. did not want Chuckie to being judged, or thought of as less, but I also believe she was fearful about being thought of as a "bad" mother. A good mother would have her child toilet trained in the proper time. Toilet training Chuck at a typical age was an accomplishment, for *both* Mrs. E. and Chuck. Mrs. E. was possibly proving to herself that she was a "good mother" and she would be able to parent a child with a disability successfully. The reality that Chuck could learn also impacted the decisions they were to make about his education.

An encounter with a neighbor helped Mrs E. make a decision about school.

"We lived in Chicago and there was another lady that lived around the block from us and she had a son, like Chuck. I had seen her pushing him in a stroller when I had Chuckie out. We really did not know each other, but seeing we both had, you know kids like,..... well she stopped and talked and she said she was going to put her Paulie in a school in the neighborhood. So she did. But then she found out it wasn't really school, it was like a bad babysitting service. She went to pick him up, and she said all he was…was sitting in the corner and nobody…with a bunch of kids…and nothing. No teachers, no nothing. And my husband and I would talk and just said we didn't want that for Chuckie. There has to be a better place, you know, for him to learn, he's learned to walk, he's learned to…you know, he was picking up stuff and we wanted it better".

The E.'s, in this short time, had already proven the doctors wrong. Chuck was learning, he was walking, toilet trained, and they were starting to hear him say words. Perhaps these revelations gave them the internal strength to want and demand more for their child. They were beginning to see the rhizomic possibilities and they were embarking on a journey to break down stereotypical fences. The school in Chicago had conditions similar to the institution exposed by Burton Blatt (1966) in *Christmas in Purgatory*. The E.'s wanted more for their son; they were on a journey to find it.

The search for a school for Chuck led them on a quest to find a home in the south suburbs, because they had heard of a school for children as they expressed it, "like Chuck". They wanted him to go to school; they saw that he was able to learn. In the least, they wanted him to learn to take care of himself. They felt he could be more self reliant given instruction.

Mr. and Mrs. E. discussed how they found Chuck's school. Mrs E. looked to her husband,

"How'd did it go, we heard of that other school, first?"

"We had heard of this Spring School, but we had not heard of Oak Valley. That school wasn't there at that particular time. And when we came out here (suburbs)…how old was he?"

"We came out here in 1965; he was four. We bought the house in 1965 and the school opened in 1968, Oak Valley opened in'68. Chuck went there when it opened."

The E.'s moved to their home on Central Avenue, which was next door to Laura's house and across the grassy alley from my home. Our neighborhood served as the root which grounded us and connected us to each other. Initially we were connected by proximity and similar cultural and religious backgrounds. As the rhizomic strands grew outward we were connected by the strings of friendship and disability; which have continued to entwine our lives for over forty years. The threads continue to grow and link our families to this day, connecting us intimately to each other for future generations. This rhizomic connection evolved because the E.'s moved to the suburbs seeking an education for Chuck.

"When we come out here, and like hubby says, we heard of Spring and then somehow we heard of Oak Valley through the grapevine when we visited Spring."

Parents of children with disabilities were starting to find each other. Children with disabilities were no longer in hiding (Trent, 1994). Parents were banding together forming relationships with the common goal of involving their children in society. Fences were still blocking their full access, but were not as high.

School Days

Chuck went to school at Oak Valley. The school was started by a group of parents who believed their handicapped (as disabilities were called then) children should go to school. In the late 1960s there were very few, if any, public school options available. Grass root organizations began to emerge to support people with disabilities. In the history of special education the sixties were known of as "the age of parent involvement" (Paul & Warnock, 1980). Many parents all over the country were finding ways to educate their children with disabilities. If schools were not available or did not offer programs designed to help their children, parents began starting their own schools. Oak Valley was started by a small group of parents typifying the era of parental involvement. Oak Valley School provided structured lessons and activities. The school was managed by a board of parents, and all parents were required to be involved financially and to help support the organization.

The E.'s main focus was for Chuck to be well cared for in a stimulating environment. They did not have clear academic goals for him, but knew he had the capacity to learn. They described Oak Valley as Chuck's home away from home. Van Manen (1990) explains the importance of home when discussing spatiality, explaining that "home reserves a very special space experience which has something to do with the fundamental sense of our being" (p.102). Home is the space in which a person can be himself. The E.'s felt Chuck was in a place where he could be himself. Parents in future generations such as Jonathon's parents in the 1980s would not be content with an educational program which did not reflect true academic expectations, but the E's were satisfied that Chuck was happy.

Oak Valley was managed by the parents and the E.'s were very involved in Chuck's school. They helped fundraise. As a child I helped out too, going door to door in the neighborhood with Debbie selling chances and ads for the annual fundraiser. Mr. E. was the janitor on Tuesday nights. All the families took turns cleaning the school, to keep the costs down. Chuck's sister Debbie recalls always being up at Oak Valley. She would go with her Dad on Tuesdays and her job was to wash the desktops. The E.'s found in Oak Valley an extended family and people they could trust to take good care of Chuck. In the Oak Valley family The E.'s found parents who understood their lived experience of having a child with a disability. The parents bonded, and together worked for the common good of their children. Perhaps if there had been a parent's group in Jackie's era, my grandparents may have not felt so isolated. My grandparents were very social and belonged to a number of organizations. They would have benefited emotionally by having other parents as friends who knew and understood their situation.

Eventually school was mandated for students with disabilities. The E.'s were happy at Oak Valley and the public school programs were in their infancy stages in the early 1970s. After many meetings, it was decided that the public school would give money to Oak Valley to support Chuck's education. As Mr. E. put it, "They gave Oak Valley the amount it cost them to educate a normal child." Every year they would go to a meeting at the local school to explain to the district representatives the reasons why Chuck needed to stay at Oak Valley. These were the days before individual education plans and multidisciplinary staffing (Friend, 2008). According to Mr. and Mrs. E. they had to fight the school district each year. In the mid 1970s, after the passage of Public Law 94-142, The Education for All Handicapped Children's Act of 1975, their school district joined with other districts and formed a co-op to teach the students with handicaps. This law would have a significant impact on Jonathon's and Jamee's school options in the future. The board approached the E.'s, wanting them to enroll Chuck in the co-op program. Mrs. E. told them that it would take a family tragedy for her to ever consider moving Chuck from his school.

When Chuck became high school age in 1976, mainstreaming was the trend in special education (Skrtic, 1995). According to Mr. and Mrs. E. the district superintendent sent a letter which indicated that Chuck should attend the local high school so he could be mainstreamed for some classes. Mainstreaming was a means to include students with disabilities with their general education peers (Turnbull & Turnbull, 1978, p. 149). Students could be mainstreamed for a single class or for most of the school day. Mainstreaming was a precursor to the inclusion policies which were in place in the 1990s for Jonathon and Jamee. The district representatives organized a meeting to discuss Chuck's educational options with his parents. Mr E. seemed to take over the conversation whenever school or medical topics came up. He told me his version of the mediation meeting.

"It ended up Sharon, that they told us, they protested. And they told us, this is what we are going to do. We are going to have a special meeting and you are going to present why he should go to Oak Valley and we are going to present why he should go to the public school system, and we are going to have a third party to be the objective mediator. He was going to make the final decision. Do you agree with that? Sure. Lo and behold, now they said Doctor so and so, and well that's okay. I am thinking it is a… (medical doctor) It was a Doctor from Summit School District. A Doctor of Education…from the next school district over."

Upon hearing her husband's recollection of the meeting, it brought memories back to the surface for momma bear, Mrs E. She now had her fightin' voice in full gear.

"And I told them, when they sent their letter, I said the only way Chuckie would be changed, would have to leave, is if hubby had to be transferred for work or death. 'Cause, otherwise he stays at Oak Valley and we'll have to fund…we'll have to do what we have to do to keep him there. Because he has his friends, and he started there when he was 6 years old, when the school opened in 1968. Oh, and what was the most important thing, and they had a workshop."

I was trying to ask another question. I kept trying to ask about the meeting but Mrs E. had something to say and she was telling me.

"So you had a meeting? How'd it go?" I was unsuccessfully trying to get more meeting details.

I told them, No way, (Nodding her head up and down with a determined look on her face) I told em, I was a tax paying citizen. I told them I would get my neighbors and get petitions. I would do whatever. (She takes a breath, it was as if all the frustration has been blown out with the breath). With a smile and slow nods of her head. Mrs. E. looked me right in the eye and said:

"It worked out, Chuck got to stay; they paid for it, bus and all.""Yea, (she looks up towards the ceiling and smiles) it all worked out." Mr E. was looking at Mrs and encouraging her as she spoke, he added:

"You know it's funny, they said they have all these programs, and at the end when he was 21 we had a meeting, and they could not help us with anything for after high school. We were on our own. So good thing we had Chuck in Oak Valley they had a workshop and work for Chuck. The high school had no idea about what he could do next."

The conversation with the E.'s about Chuck's school and their expectations for placement, as well as their meetings with the school district is revealing on many levels. The E.'s knew the spatiality of Oak Valley. The lived space of Oak Valley served as a safe place for Chuck. Oak Valley was what the family knew. It was not only Chuck's lived space but the family's lived space. The family was invested in Oak Valley; they thought of it as Chuck's home away from home, so they would not be open to going to a new program. Oak Valley also had a continuum of programs for Chuck. Chuck could attend the work shop at Oak Valley upon graduation, and the organization was starting to build homes in the community for their graduates. It is critical to consider the temporality of this story. In the mid 1970s a workshop with real work for individuals with disabilities was progressive (Friend, 2008). Chuck would be able to go to a work environment and receive a paycheck. Today, many individuals with disabilities and their family members consider workshops oppressive, keeping people with disabilities separated from the community (TASH, 2009, p. 44). Neither Jonathon or Jamee and their families are even considering a work shop program. Jonathon is completing college and Jamee, with the support of her family,is looking for community based activities. The E.'s, in the early 1970s, did not view the workshop as a fence but as a rhizomic possibility, a place that Chuck could go in the future, and still feel at home.

Debbie and Chuck

It was always Debbie and Chuck, just as in Jackie's story it was always Doris and Jackie. As children if we wanted to play with Debbie we would go inside the fenced yard and Chuck would be there, even if he was not playing the same games we were playing, he was always near. Mrs. E. kept Debbie and Chuck in her sight at all times. Whenever I went in the yard I always felt her presence. Although I did not understand what I was feeling at the time, I now know I could feel Mrs. E.'s protectiveness hovering over her children. The other parents in the neighborhood were never right around us, but Mrs. E. was. She was nice, she would give us cookies and Kool-Aid in shiny metal cups, and she would always invite the children in the neighborhood in for lunch and even breakfast if they showed up early. Mrs. E. made us feel welcome in the yard. We were fenced in along with Debbie and Chuck, but the atmosphere was pleasant for us as young children, so we stayed and played. Again, this scenario represented a separate but safe place. Possibly, Mrs. E. made us feel welcome; so we would come back to play with Debbie and Chuck. She was facilitating socialization for her children by opening the gate to let us in, yet simultaneously protecting them. Resistance is a genre of pushing and pulling (Gabel, 2005, p. 8). Resistance Theory recognizes the social constructs placed on people with disabilities, by opening the gates and disregarding the oppressive fences. Resistance "pulls people into disabled people's way of seeing" (Gabel & Peters, 2004, p. 595). Mrs. E. was unconsciously negotiating an understanding of disability. She was orchestrating companionship for Chuck, pulling us in, and helping us understand that Chuck could be our friend. While she was assisting us to look at Chuck, a disabled individual, as a person first, something kept pulling her back. She would push out; but the fence (her fear and protectiveness) kept reining her in.

If we did venture out of the yard, Chuck was with us. We always knew to hold his hand. He typically liked to walk up town with us. A few times a week Debbie, Chuck and I did grocery shopping for our mothers, especially when it was warm out. Our families did not own two cars and Mrs. E. did not drive, so we were frequently at the store. It was common for older siblings to watch younger siblings, so we did not think too deeply about Chuck being with us. It was the life we knew. As children we did not analyze our reality or question why we lived as we did.

Our spatiality was a protective environment. We were protected by the safety found in the grassy alley that connected our yards, the fences that surrounded our properties, and the protective aura of my grandmother and Mrs. E.

I asked Debbie her recollections of growing up with Chuck.

"We played together, he let me dress him up, we played hide and seek in the yard, we would cook with the Easy Bake Oven, we would play... it was, (long pause) he's my brother. I did not think about anything, he was just Chuck. Maybe we were different kind of kids...we took care of our brothers and sisters, that was how it was, we watched out for everybody."

It was the 1960s, and we lived in a neighborhood where those who dwelled in our two block radius had very similar experiences. We were all Catholic, we all went to the local Catholic school, and walked there en mass on a daily basis. With the exception of the E.'s, all of the families had five or more children. An older sibling, bringing younger siblings with them to the store, park, or school was a common occurrence. For Debbie to have Chuck by her side, in many ways, helped her be like everyone else. Laura usually had her sister Mary with her, I had my brother Ed or my sister Colleen with me. We would all go to the E.'s and play "house" or "school", or all of us would go "up town". All of our mothers knew each other. In warm weather the doors were always open and we were always in the "earshot" of one of our many mothers, who were not afraid to discipline any of us if necessary. The neighborhood served as the taproot of our experiences with all of us connected through the rhizomic strands of mothering protectiveness. In some regards we had a collective experience, one that included Chuck.

Whenever I have looked at research on the subject of siblings having a brother or sister with a disability, I have read that siblings are *made* to feel responsible for their less abled sister or brother. Much of the literature has very negative connotations and I was curious as to Debbie's feelings about always being with Chuck. I asked her directly if she felt she had to be responsible for Chuck.

"I don't know, I don't think that it was so much Chuck, but my mom bringing my cousins into the household. (Over the years Debbie's mom took care of three nephews that her sisters were not able to care for). Chuck was pretty self reliant, he was not aggressive. You'd tell him to do something, he would usually do it. It wasn't like we had to watch him 'cause he'd get into something, it was when my Aunts started leaving their babies with us. I was more the babies' babysitter than I was Chuck's. He loved anything he was included in… and he did not cry if he wasn't."

Debbie uses the words, "leaving the babies with us". Her vocal tone sounded comtemplative and sad as she discussed the cousins coming in and out of her life. One little cousin was there three years, and three others lived with the E.'s for months and months at a time. Compared to babies that came and went, living with Chuck was easy for Debbie. It was her "normal" experience. Debbie never said she resented having to stay in her yard or watch Chuck. She did seem to resent the burden of having to watch the cousins.

As adults we have talked, and Debbie resents that the aunts took advantage of her mother. The reality is that Mrs. E. put herself out there to be the consummate mother. Motherhood defines Mrs. E. She never worked outside the home. All her social relationships revolve around Oak Valley. Her idea of an evening out is dinner at the local snack shop with Mr. E. and Chuck. Vacations are spent on a farm referred to as "down home" in southern Illinois. Mrs. E. has never ventured from her comfort zone. Her lived experience has a direct effect on the life she has constructed for Chuck.

Just as my grandparents never discussed Jackie's disability, Debbie's family really never spoke about it either. We were still a guarded society in the 60's. Parents never discussed anything considered "adult business" with kids. Debbie talked about the lack of communication.

"No, we really didn't talk about it. Why? I guess because it was just our life, really, I knew he went to a special school. Really…. we never talked about it. Now as adults yea, my mom will say he has Downs, my Dad actually said he's (Chuck) *retarded* recently. That sounded so strange, we never said that. I was surprised, I think that is derogatory, I do, even my children were surprised he said that. We were like, Wow!... I can't believe he said that and that's just recent, he never said anything before."

As I listened to the E.'s and Debbie share their experiences about life with Chuck. Mr. E. and Debbie are more grounded in the reality of the situation. Using a term like "retarded" to describe his beloved child Chuck, Mr. E. may be trying to force his family to look at life more realistically. Mr. and Mrs. E. are in their seventies. Mr. E. survived a massive heart attack and heart surgery. He has had to face his personal mortality. The E.'s have to deal with their mortality and Chuck's future. Mr. E., in a "shocking" manner is trying to get the family to look at the reality of life and death.

S.:   Did you ever feel like you had to prove something because you had Chuck, or felt left out?

D.:   No, not really, my parents did a good thing keeping things balanced; maybe because I'm a girl, he's a boy. I had my dress up stuff. I was not embarrassed when people came over. He never did anything crazy, Lots of time he was in his own little world, just sitting. I almost think with the babies and all that he was even a little over looked because he was very content.

S.:   So growing up with Chuck, did it impact you in any specific ways?

D.:   It made me more compassionate, just the simple stuff everyone has feelings, even if people can't express them; it's that... how would you feel if someone did that to you? Like, just because a person can't express it, he still knows if you are angry or if you say something. People know when they are being left out, even with my own kids, I tell them not to leave any one out, and no one wants to be excluded, because they are different, no matter.

Many siblings of people with disabilities, express that having a loved one with a disability impacted them in positive ways (Strohm, 2005). Siblings of people with disabilities describe themselves as being more empathetic, kind or patient because they shared their lived space with a person with disabilities (Connors & Stalker, 2003). Debbie shares such feelings.

S.: Since we are looking back, what do you think are the best things your parents did for Chuck?

D.: Mostly that they disciplined him, if he did something wrong, he got in trouble. If he had a tantrum when he was a child he would get a spankin' or go to his room. Because of that, he can go anywhere. He is easy to be around for the most part. They had expectations for how he should act. Because of that he has a full life.

King Chuck

I enter the King's domain (aka the living room at Chuck's sister Debbie's home) to go get my customary hug. There is a family birthday party happening and I have yet to speak to Chuck. My old friend is sitting quietly on the floor. Chuck is in his element. People come in and out to spend time greeting the king, it is as if he is holding court. He sits and waits until someone comes to talk to him. Different people file in and out of the room to speak with King Chuck. As his royal subjects approach, he will hug or kiss the girls and women and the males will receive a warm hello. The king is definitely in control. Chuck relates to the whole king idea. He often compares himself to Elvis, and will pose in a suggestive manner saying he is *the* king. When he sees me enter the room, he gets up to say hello. After the my hug, I sit down on the footstool next to Chuck as he sits back on the floor. We will now catch up on his latest news. This is pretty much our routine at every family get together held at Debbie's home.

"What's new Chuck?"

"What exciting thing is happening in your life?" I quickly rattle off a couple of questions.

Chuck pats his stomach and says, "New Diet."

Chuck is always on a diet either real or Chuck created. When we were kids he was on the fried chicken and soda diet or the ice cream diet. He vehemently declared that he could only eat specific foods. He tried to convince us that the doctor said he had to be on special diets. Sometimes Chuck has very real diets. He has had some heart trouble and is supposed to watch his calories and cholesterol etc.

"So what is the diet you are on?

"Is this a doctor diet ?" I always seem to ask Chuck multiple questions at once.

"Did he put you on this diet?"

He nods the affirmative, dramatically puts his hands on either side of his stomach and loudly says "yes" answering all my questions. Mrs. E. must have been listening in the other room and yelled out:

"You know you're supposed to be watching what you eat, son."

After hearing his mom, he just nods and looks down, dismissing the interruption. I can feel the tension, so I bring up a new topic.

"So Chuck, are you still seeing Lee?

A big grin comes across his face and he starts to giggle like a girl. I laugh as Chuck does his best Lee imitation. Lee is always smiling and has this contagious giggle. I think Chuck enjoys her happy disposition. The women in his family are not the giggly types. Chuck's mom is very matter-of-fact and I do not think I've ever seen her have an all out laugh attack. Chuck's sister Debbie is usually busy when he is in her company, so I'm guessing there is not much joking around these days. It seems his girlfriend Lee encourages Chuck to be his silly self. He really enjoys her refreshing spirit.

I had seen Chuck and Lee together years ago when I worked at a school where they were on a cleaning crew. One day I saw the two of them in the hallway, they were poking each other and looking into each other's eyes and laughing. Chuck was trying with limited success to stifle his laugh, while Lee was totally out-of-control; giggling loudly. I heard a woman's voice tell them harshly:

"You two are lucky that you are even together." "You need to get away from each other and get back to work!" (Ouch)

I did not see the supervisor because I was in my classroom by then, but everyone along the hall heard her reprimand Chuck and Lee. Chuck usually picked up the trash in my room on Fridays. He was typically by himself, and I would tease him about Lee when he came by. After hearing the job coach, I felt bad because I had encouraged Chuck's flirting in the past.

Chuck then came into my classroom to empty the trash, Lee must have gone to another classroom as he was alone. I noticed he was really upset. His chin was almost on his chest. He did not want to look in my eyes. I certainly was not going to get my typical sideways hug hello.

"Chuck are you okay?"

"Trrubbb mmm Lee," Chuck was mumbling.

I felt so bad when I had to ask him to repeat what he was saying. In fact it took three times for me to understand.

"I'm in trouble. She yelled at me and Lee."

I finally realized what he was saying. I felt terrible for him. The work place issues pose an interesting dilemma. Chuck and Lee are adults, yet when the job coach redirected them, they were treated like naughty children. Granted, teasing and giggling with one's significant other is not appropriate in the work place, however if a supervisor saw this in a typical work environment, she might talk to the worker privately, or perhaps write them up. Were Chuck and Lee scolded like little kids because they have an intellectual disability? As Chuck left my class I heard the job coach talking at Chuck and Lee. Loudly again, with that condescending tone she said:

"I trained both of you and I expect more from you."

I was teaching so I could not leave my class, but it really bothered me. I asked my classroom assistant to close the door to my room, hoping the woman would get the hint that she was being really loud.

The following Friday, Chuck came to empty the trash and he was by himself with the job coach. I was by the door putting things away in a closet as he walked in. I was in the mood for making a point, so I said hello to the female job coach and I put my arms out and wrapped Chuck in a big hug.

"Oh, Chuck it is so good to see you!"

I was gushing with enthusiasm. Chuck was a bit taken back by my over zealous greeting. I had been seeing him every Friday for months, but he politely patted my back and said:

"Hi Sharon."

He looked at the job coach and said,

"Old friend."

I explained to the job coach that Chuck and I were family friends. I also let her know that I knew his Mom, Dad, and sister. I told coach what a great job Chuck did with the janitorial duties. The coach just stood there. I think she thought I was a bit over the top. I purposely made an issue that day, and made sure I mentioned Chuck's parents. Chuck's Mom and Dad have been supporters and workers at Oak Valley for years. Rumor had it that you do not want to mess with Chuck's mom. Other people I worked with would say, "Oh, you know the family, don't want to get on the mom's bad side." But they would also say how hard the family worked for the good of the organization and that Chuck was a great guy. Even Mrs. E had said in the interviews:

"You don't want to mess with Marlene," when she was describing how she advocated for Chuck when necessary. Mrs. E can definitely turn into a mama bear protecting her cub when the need arises and her growl is pretty powerful. Since the job coach acted all important yelling at Chuck and Lee, I figured some name dropping would not hurt anything. It was my own little way of letting the job coach know that I had Chuck's back.

The whole job coach business brings to the surface something I think deeply about, especially as I work with organizations which support adults with disabilities in their work and home environments. Chuck is an adult. He needs a certain degree of assistance with some life issues due to his intellectual disability, but he is an adult. Most people in his life do not treat him like an adult very often. He is mostly told what to do, by his mom, dad, sister, job coaches, etc. etc. He is this child- adult expected to play a particular role. Sometimes Chuck enjoys that role. In fact he milks it for all it's worth. He will sit at the table while his mom makes a plate of food, or he will say he can't do something he is totally capable of doing, because then someone will do it for him. At other times however,you can tell he so wants to be an adult and enjoys expressing his opinion and exerting some control over his world.

Living at home, in the bedroom of his childhood, following the same routine he's been doing for years does keep Chuck a forever child in many ways. Every so often rebellious Chuck will do something to remind people he's an adult with his own opinions and he can do as he wishes.

Returning to the scene of the party.....It is time to eat. Chuck joins the rest of the us in the kitchen. Mrs.E was busy telling him what he wanted to eat like all moms tend to do:

"There's chicken."

"Did you get a roll, Chuck?"

Chuck mumbles and continues in the food line. He then looks up and sees my teenage daughter is in line getting food. He sets his plate down and gives Amy a big hug. He has a big grin on his face. I notice that Mrs E. is not grinning.

"Chuck, let Amy get her food." Chuck gives a little additional pat to Amy in pure rebellion. He goes even further and finds a seat next to Amy for dinner. Chuck continued to smile and tease with Amy all through dinner.

After we sing happy birthday and have cake, the attendees split up. Some people are in the living room, some are helping clean up. Conversation goes on and everyone is just milling around. Chuck quietly moves away from the group back into the living room. He retreats back to his personal kingdom where he can sit in peace and be the king or the adult he would like to be.

Chuck's Life

Chuck lives at home with his parents, and everyday he takes the van to his work at Oak Valley. He gets himself up in the morning and goes about his daily routine, shaving, dressing, taking his medication, having breakfast prepared by his mom. He knows when the van is going to come and watches out the window for it to arrive. Once at work he has a variety of jobs in the workshop. He is also on a janitorial crew, cleaning at two schools in the community on a weekly basis. During the Christmas holidays he works at a department store passing out boxes. The store manger has requested Chuck year after year. He has held a variety of temporary jobs in the community over the years. Chuck is one of the old timers at Oak Valley. He has been there from the beginning and that carries with it a certain level of respect in itself. Everyone knows Chuck, and he has been given jobs which require good judgment and organization.

I spent time observing Chuck at work. He is very independent in the work setting and carries himself like the adult that he is. His shoulders are straight back. He stands tall and his walk is almost a strut. When he passes the supervisors he gives them a nod of his head as a greeting. Chuck is currently the lead crew member on a job line. The job consisted of pens being packaged in a zip-lock bag. Oak Valley Work Center has a contract for packaging pens with a commercial office supply company. When the workers finished the packaging step of the job, the bags of pens were placed in a bin. When the bin was full, Chuck inspected the packages, placed them in a box and sealed the box. He then carried the box over to the docking area. Chuck talked in easy banter with co-workers from time to time. He teased one of the men when he was not keeping up, saying "go, go, go" and gesturing with his arms to move forward. He smiled as he is talked and the gentleman he was coaching smiled back.

I told Chuck I saw him teasing with his co-worker, and he smiled and said: "Joe, crazy." I asked if he and Joe were buddies. Chuck nodded, made a big arm gesture, and said, "Way back." Chuck and Joe are both long term members of the Oak Valley family, and were classmates back in the late sixties.

A Full Life

Debbie described Chuck as having a full life. As citizens of the world there are particular attributes which constitute a full life. As a phenomenologist, I am compelled to "go back to the things themselves" (Husserl, 1970, p. 252). I sought to uncover the everyday experience of Chuck at work by venturing into his lived space (Van Manen, 1990). I particularly wanted to engage in close observation to look for evidence of a full life. Van Manen reminds me to remain as close as possible to the situation, while retaining a hermeneutic alertness to the situation at hand so I am able to reflect on the meaning of the situation (p.69). A full life includes friendship, autonomy, self respect, decision making, communicating, and employment to name a few.

While the spatiality of a workshop is limiting in itself; fencing Chuck off from the community, I saw signs of a "full life" within its walls. Chuck has a sense of self respect at work. He is autonomous in the work setting, navigating his environment with a sense of dignity. He knows his role as the man in charge of a work line. He carries himself in an erect manner, much straighter than the relaxed posture he exhibits hanging out in his bedroom at home. I took this body language as a symbol of Chuck's self respect. Chuck has friends at work. Joe looked to be a true friend, as evident by the familiarity of the exchanges between the two men. Most of the supervisors, while not intimate friends of Chuck, greeted him in a manner that was indicative of co-workers rather than supervisors. Chuck can make independent decisions at work. He looks over the inventory and does product quality tests. He is employed and understands what it means to get paid for his work. The pay is not equal to what a person would make in a factory in the community, but Chuck does receive some compensation for his work. The workshop is much like the fenced in yard of Chuck's childhood, keeping him safe, but giving him autonomy within the walls.

While his speech is not always clear, Chuck gets his point across. He also uses gestures and will act something out if he sees you do not understand his speech. Chuck is also very aware of his rights at work, and will not tolerate unfair treatment. He tries to let others know when he is unhappy about work situations.

Chuck has his job, parties with Debbie and her family, and he also has an active social life. The social activities mostly revolve around Oak Valley. He is part of the Oak Valley Players, an acting troupe. He impersonated Elvis Presley a couple of years ago and according to Debbie, "he brought down the house." Chuck showed me his Elvis picture in his room. After playing Elvis on stage he is now a true admirer. He also bowls weekly and over the years he has been involved in Special Olympics. Chuck follows the White Sox and Chicago Bears and showed me the pennants from his favorite teams. Of all the items he showed me, he clearly treasures the photos of his girlfriend Lee more than anything else.

Chuck Loves Lee

In all the interviews I had with the people in Chuck's life, everyone shared, "Chuck loves Lee." Chuck told me: "Lee is my girl, I love Lee," as he showed me the pictures of the two of them together. Then he said "tickle." I had no clue what he meant and that must have been evident on my face, because he started to imitate a girl laughing. Mrs. E. said "Oh that is his nickname for Lee because she is always laughing like when you tickle someone." Chuck told me he calls Lee on the phone, by acting out making a phone call. I had worked at the school where Chuck and Lee were on a cleaning crew together, and Chuck is right, Lee is always laughing. Mr. E. said Chuck "staked his claim" years ago, when Lee first came to Oak Valley after a brain injury from a car accident. They have been a couple now for about 15 years. Chuck tells me Lee is pretty and others would agree, she is a beautiful young woman, always smiling and laughing. The two of them appear content with their relationship which consists of laughing on the phone and having dinner with family once in awhile. They are always together at all of the Oak Valley gatherings where everyone is aware that Chuck loves Lee.

Mrs. E. says Chuck loves Lee, yet she controls the boundaries of the relationship. Chuck and Lee are never left alone. Their dating consists of phone calls and dinners with each other's families. The relationship with Lee has been added to Chuck's controlled routine. He does not appear to push the boundaries set by his parents as it pertains to his relationship with Lee. The family looks at their relationship as "cute". They know Chuck loves Lee, but they do not consider it adult love; having set parameters to Chuck and Lee's relationship. This situation is much like parents setting up controlled play dates with young children. The E.'s are constructing a protective fence again, treating Chuck at 47 years of age as an ever-child. Again, one has to reflect on how their viewpoints come from a particular time and place, and much of their perceptions about disability remain rooted in the 1960s.

Routine

Chuck is a man of routines and rituals. He does certain things at certain times in his own way. He watches the old reruns on TV and knows what times his shows are on. Exactly one minute before the time of the show is when he turns the TV on, not five minutes, but one minute exactly. He enjoys his shows and sits in his room swinging his chain, watching TV and appears to enjoy the solitude. Debbie recalled how she visited the E.'s one day with her children and as soon as she got in the door Chuck wanted to know when she was leaving. All the noise and activity bothered his routine. Debbie told him that he hurt her feelings and according to Debbie, "he got an earful" from his mother about how his sister could come whenever she pleased, so that stopped his complaining.

Chuck clears the table after family meals, but for the most part his mother still takes care of him. Mrs. E. does the cooking, cleaning and his laundry. He has very definite ideas about what is woman's work. He likes predictability in his life and needs to know if there are going to be changes in his daily schedule.

When Mrs. E. decided 47 years ago that she was going to take her son home and give him a life within their family unit, she took on the role of the forever mother. A role she does not want to relinquish. This is a common element in the generational experience of disability. The construct of disability is determined between the relationship between the definer and the defined (Bogdan & Taylor, 1989, p.136). Mrs. E defines herself as "Chuck's mother" and he plays the role in her concept as "my son."

The Future

Debbie worries about Chuck's routines and how his lack of flexibility will affect his future. She is concerned because her parents have not made financial or legal provisions for Chuck. The idea of having to take all of this on herself is frightening for Debbie. She worries because her parents are now in their seventies and have medical issues of their own.

"I'm worried… I'm scared that they have not made any real provisions for him. That scares the hell out of me. Maybe they think they'll still outlive him. At first they thought he would only live 'til like twelve, maybe that is still in their mind. Maybe they don't want to face it. But I don't have the patience, because he is still childlike, yet he is a man. For instance, we were at the house in Southern Illinois, and I said, "Come let's make your bed Chuck", and he told me he did not have to, that he is a man and that is woman's work. I tend to treat him like one of my kids, but he is so much older. It's hard because even now he will mumble under his breath at me and say "Don't tell me what to do". That is one thing I wish my parents had done different was to have him do some chores. He could be helping them. My mom still does so much."

Debbie continued to talk about her concerns…

"It will be hard, because I will have to take over the mom role in his life, and he knows I am not his mother. I am his sister, and he does not think he has to listen to me. He does not like having his routine messed up. My life is not routine, it is anything but routine."

As Debbie spoke I thought of the situation between my mother and Aunt Jackie. I recalled Jackie telling my mom "you are not my mother."

Chuck was basically expressing the same concept to Debbie. It was usual for both Jackie and Chuck as adults to still be mothered by their mothers, but they did not want their siblings telling them what to do. Debbie is worried about the future. Whatever the future brings, she knows she will in some way be responsible for Chuck. The E.'s, seeing Chuck as a child, have never sat down and discussed Chuck's future options with him. Just as Jackie was never consulted when she had to leave school, Chuck is not being included in the decisions that impact "his" life. Debbie asked me to try to talk with her parents about Chuck's future, thinking they may take my opinion as a professional in the field.

Forever Parents

I had this weird feeling in my stomach as I drove into the driveway. I do not think I had ever driven into the E's driveway before. They had left the gate open for me, so I pulled in. I kept self talking as I drove in.

"Ok, Shar you can do this."

Mr. E. was coming from the back to greet me. I got out of my car and smiled.

"Hi there, Sharon, can I help you with anything?"

"No, I am good, thanks," as I grabbed my bag.

Just hearing Mr. E's voice and seeing him smile put me in a good place and all the worries seemed to slip away for a moment. As I walked to the back door, and looked around it felt like I was in a time warp, everything looked the same as it did in the 70's. I had to fight back the urge to yell out "Yo Debbie" as I stepped up on the back stoop. The self talking started again in my head.

"Oh Debbie, I am not sure if can talk to them about Chuck's future. I am not sure how this will go, why would they listen to me?"

I was excited about getting more information for our story. When I called and talked to Mrs. E. and explained my ideas for writing this story, she was really eager to participate. The E's, I know are proud of me. They are pleased that I went into a field of work that revolved around supporting people with disabilities. I'm sure at times they still see me as a freckled faced, redheaded little girl that played in their yard. Sometimes, honestly, I still feel like that little girl, and go back there to our little fenced in world in my heart. On this day however, I was going to have to be all grown up and tackle some difficult questions. Debbie was hoping I could ask them directly about their plans for Chuck's future if something should happen to them. She said they were always evasive when she tried to ask them about specifics for Chuck.

"I will try Debbie, if it works out." I was having conversations with Debbie in my head.

Talking about the hard stuff is difficult especially when you are trying to be all smart and adult-like with the people who use to clean up your skinned knees or called your mom when you got in trouble. Even if I summoned the courage to bring up hard subjects like Chuck's future, will they *really* hear me?

So I sat at the table, conducted the interview and I looked out the picture window towards 95th Street. Sometimes I caught my reflection and the refection of Mr. and Mrs. E. in the window, it was surreal watching us as we talked, it was as if I was not really there, but watching from some other place. I became so immersed in their stories. The interview process really got away from me. I found their back-and-forth banter about Chuck interesting, and almost musical. It had this back and forth rhythm. Mrs E. talked and then almost on beat she asked Mr. for confirmation.

"Isn't that right Cho?" she'd ask.

He started to answer and she finished what he was saying. It was hard to conduct the interview because I kept getting caught up in the conversation. It was entertaining and revealing. Sometimes it wasn't the exact words, but how they cut each other off or spoke together or said the same things at once. Listening to the recordings of the interviews later, I had to replay it over and over to get the exact words about their plans for Chuck's future.

"So Chuck will live at a home through Oak Valley if you cannot care for him any longer?"

I asked with trepidation. I was slightly afraid that Mrs. E. would soon be calling my mother to tell her I was naughty.

"Oh yeah, we are on that list, you know they fixed up the 40 bed." Mrs. E. started telling me about the fundraising they had been involved in and talked about the remodeling at one of the current intermediate care facilities at Oak Valley. As she was talking and going off-topic, Mr. E. kept talking quietly in the background.

"Mmmm... I wonder what is happening with that housing," Mr E. was saying to himself. He kept talking while Mrs. E was talking louder about current happenings at Oak Valley. Mr E. finally caught a small break in the talking and said:

"We were on a list for Chuck to live in a house, but you know, come to think about it, Sharon, we haven't heard a thing about that in a long time." He looked straight in the eyes of Mrs E. and asked:

"Have we?"

It was as if the question had never been asked. Mrs. E. kept talking about other happenings at Oak Valley. I think she purposely wanted to act as if she had not heard what Mr. E. had asked.

As time went on and we talked, more feelings and insecurities were uncovered.

"You know Sharon, they never thought he would live long and look he's 47 years old. You never know, you just never know." Mrs. E. was talking to me, but kept looking away. Possibly she was looking into her own heart and seeing Chuck grow older in her mind. Or maybe she was remembering the moment she was told Chuck was Mongoloid so many years before.

"They told me he would not live till.... what did they say Cho, 30?" "Chuck has had heart problems."(Mr. never got the chance to answer)

"He's doing okay now isn't he?"I asked.

"Oh yeah we watch him, but I do think or thought we would live longer than him." She looks away again and her voice grows quiet.

"Just thought he'd go ahead of us."

There were moments as I was listening to the playback that I just cried. It was really heart-wrenching. I can understand that it is hard to prepare for your child's future when somewhere deep inside, you do not believe you need to make such preparations. This is the child that was suppose to have died years ago.

What could I say to really change their minds or have them make additional preparations for Chuck's future? Chuck had been living on borrowed time to them for over 20 years. I am not the parent of a child with a disability, nor can I ever fully understand how a parent who has a child born with a disability feels. I would never presume that I know better than they do, as they are making decisions about their child or adult child with a disability. I *am* a parent however, and while my children were not born with disabilities, I can understand the feeling parents have when they cannot control what is happening with their child.

There are times as a parent when you feel so helpless and so insecure in the role. I have been wearing my "mom hat" now for over 30 years. I have three grown children. I am now Grandma Sharon to three little ones. Over the years I have faced some very scary circumstances. There were times when I was really frightened and worried that my child was not going to be okay. I have lived through my children struggling with eating disorders, back injuries, broken hearts, operations and car accidents. I think about those moments and the hurt that was in my heart. In those moments of despair, I felt scared, worried, and most of all helpless. I could not get things in control. Parents are suppose to know what to do, we are suppose to be in control, it is our job to support our children. Parents just want their children to be happy, to find joy. When your child is hurting emotionally or physically it is just so difficult. As parents we want to fix it, make it all better, kiss the boo-boo and make it go away. If the issues our children face could only be fixed by putting on the "Hello Kitty" or "Batman" band aide, what peace we would feel. Oh, if life was only that easy. The E's just want Chuck to be happy; they continue to try to fix things for their little boy.

I know how out of control I have felt as a parent at times. There have been moments when I was so filled with guilt because I wondered if I did something wrong or if my parenting, or lack there of, caused my child's difficulties. If I am feeling this way about my so called *normal* kids, I cannot even fathom the issues tugging at the hearts of parents who have children born with disabilities.

Parents with children who are disabled may feel that hurt or frustration constantly. I only experienced that hurt in moments when I felt I could not "fix it" for my kids. When I listened to Laura, Chuck's parents and my sister Colleen describe their lives with their children, I could feel the tension at times, the worry in their voices. Sometimes it was not the actual words they said but more *how* they said it or the tone. They talked about their child with a quivering voice, or with a scared or faraway look in their eyes. At times anger was just below the surface of their words.

Debbie worries about Chuck's life situation especially if something should happen to her parents. What if they are physically no longer able to care for him? What if her Dad has a fatal heart attack? He has had one already. Mrs. E. can hardly walk, how long will she be able to care for Chuck or herself, for that matter? Debbie is not Chuck's parent, but as his only sibling she knows Chuck's care will ultimately fall on her. In fact, she is expected to take care of Chuck. This is rarely discussed with her parents,but she knows she must. She does not know if they have anything exactly in place for him for his future, at least nothing legal, or written down. She shared that when she asked about it, her mom says,"It is fine." or "It is all set." The trouble with"fine" or Chuck being "all set," is that it not been has not been thoroughly explained to Debbie, the one who will be ultimately responsible for the future plans. Debbie has not seen anything specific in writing, which is also worrisome for her. Deb and Chuck's parents are part of a different generation. As people in their 70's, they keep much information about themselves *to* themselves. They only share when absolutely necessary. Debbie does not need to know about the plans now because Chuck is with them and everything is *fine.*

It is not always easy to talk about the hard stuff. Knowing that your child with a disability may outlive you or their siblings and wondering if someone will love them like you do, is scary. I wonder if Mr and Mrs E. worry about the basic things that bring joy to Chuck. Will someone care about his routines? Who will see that he wears his favorite clothes? Will someone know that Chuck likes to watch reruns at 3:45 each day? Who will fix his chain properly if it breaks? The E.'s have always put Chuck's needs before their own. They know their man- child intimately and had lived with the fear that he would have a short life. Now it seems they fear him living a long life, possibly without them.

Just recently I saw my friend Debbie in the hallway of the school where she works. I told her I was writing additional stories for this book and I inquired about Chuck. She said like many individuals with Down Syndrome in their 50s, he is now in the early stages of Alzheimer's. She said he is doing okay. I started to think about the interviews I had with her parents. Alzheimer's or not, Chuck could still outlive his parents who are in their mid 70's. Jackie exhibited symptoms for about eight years before she passed away. I had to keep my big mouth closed and not say anything to Deb about how difficult it could get in the future. We had watched Jackie slip away from us into her own Alzheimer's world. My heart felt sad for them, and I said a silent prayer that Chuck would not have the difficulties Jackie went through.

Debbie continued up dating me on Chuck's life:

"So yeah, Chuck is learning how to make Alzheimer's work for him," she explained.

"We were together over the holidays, and my mom asked him to do something and he ignored her.

"A little while later my mom said:"Chuck, I told you to go do that for me."

"Chuck pointed to his head and said, "Sorry, forgot it's my Alzheimer's."

No matter how much or how little the E's want to parent Chuck, he still finds a way to be in control. I walked away laughing to myself. I never thought I'd be laughing about a person with Down Syndrome and Alzheimer's, but it was just such a "Chuck" moment. Proving once again, that in many ways, he can handle things for himself. The E's may see the forever child Chuck, but he sees himself as the man.

Future Concerns

Debbie can articulate her worries about Chuck and his future. When she speaks in generalities about Chuck, it is of a simplistic nature. She said Chuck was always Chuck, he is her brother, and life was good. She said she never was ridiculed for being his sister and in many ways she never thought about him having a disability. Now she is compelled to contemplate about what the future may hold for both her and Chuck. It is obvious that Chuck is a person with Down Syndrome. Debbie did not have to think about it because it was her lived experience. Disability was always present, but time and again the people closest to the situation do not see it as such, they see the person they love and somehow separate disability from the person. I contend to authentically acknowledge "Chuck" or "Jackie" we must embrace them as individuals with disabilities. It is as much a part of their entity as my identity as a 50 plus year old white woman. As much as I know and understand this, I too fall into the "Jackie was just Jackie" or "Chuck is Chuck" mode. Could it be that we love them so much and want them to be seen for themselves, not their disability? Or are we at some level in denial ourselves? Their presence in our lives was a gift, an interesting gift, but a gift none the less.

God's Gift

Mr. and Mrs. E. believe Chuck has been a gift to them. They never wanted pity. They are happy that he has surpassed anyone's expectations for him.

"There are people every once in awhile that say, "Oh, I'm sorry for you." Mr.E. shared. Mrs E. had something to say about that:

"I've heard that, "Oh I feel so sorry for you."And I say, "Please, don't feel sorry for me. He can walk, he can see, he can hear, I says…he's not able to talk clearly but there are a lot of people in worse condition than Chuckie is." I said that's who needs the(help, pity?)...not Chuckie... Chuckie's fine. Ah... Chuckie's special, and God gave him to us, and God gives special kids to... ah, special people. He's Chuck."

Chuck is his parent's son, he is Debbie's brother. He is a man with likes and dislikes. He enjoys routine, old TV programs, trains and Elvis Presley. He loves Lee, his parents, sister, and his nieces and nephews. While his life has been one of rhizomic possibilities it has also been a life full of fences. The fences of society were ever present putting him in a particular social category of "retarded" by virtue of his being a person with Down Syndrome. The family put up fences to keep him physically and emotionally safe, by viewing him as a forever child. Chuck's life is full and busy. He surpassed all the doctors' expectations for his future. It is difficult to know if his life is complete or if it truly is the life he has chosen to lead. The choice has never been posed to him. He has been given many things; a safe home, school, responsibility at work and much love, but the critical choices have always been made for him. As Chuck sits and swings his chain, I wish I could fully see the world he sees or find out what he wants for his life. I do know his family is important to him and it is evident that he loves them, just as they love him. The family did the best they could with the tools and information they were given. This is Chuck's story, but it is also his family's story entwined like the root structure of the rhizome, joined and nurtured with love. My childhood friend, Chuck, is the second link in this generational *chain*.

CHAPTER FIVE

A Pirate's Tale

Jonathon, 1986

Jonathon says he is a pirate, chidingly, but a pirate all the same. He has a wallet with a skull and crossbones on it. When I asked him if he had an affinity for pirates, he laughed. He said that is how the students at the Newman Center on his college campus think of him, as a pirate. Jonathon explains: "They do not realize I think of myself as that too, with the one eye, an eye patch without a patch. When I say that to them, they say, okay now we get it." Jonathon is blind in one eye and wears a prosthesis so in a way he does have an eye patch. He also identifies with pirates because they are masters at their craft. I found this whole pirate subject interesting and I sent Jon an e-mail requesting further clarification about his identification with pirates. He wrote back:

> I like pirates since to me they represent the ultimate in manipulating. Just think about what they have to do in order to achieve something that they want to accomplish. This can be applied to me since I have to modify some things I do in daily life such as minding my left hand when I have to do something new that I've never done before, therefore, my left hand does exactly what my right hand does until I master the new task..Up until I master the task, I have to continuously modify and/or change what I'm doing. Until I find a way that works for me. I'm a master manipulator.

I asked Jonathon if I could share this concept with his mother and he said fine, so when interviewing his mom, I shared with her how Jonathon identifies with pirates. She laughed and said, "that is because a cute girl said he looked like Johnny Depp." Johnny Depp is famous for his role as a pirate in the contemporary movie, *Pirates of the Caribbean*. I would propose that the real reason for Jonathon's pirate fascination, may lie somewhere in between. No matter the particular reason, vanity or inspiration, Jonathon identifies with pirates, and this is Jonathon's story.

Of the three individuals with disabilities that I interviewed, Jonathon was the only person who could verbally answer my questions in a typical manner. Jonathon (at the time of our first interview) is a 22 year old, credit earning college student, short and slight in stature with sandy brown hair, a mustache, and sparse beard. He wears square preppy glasses and has a style of his own. He is very put together with a blazer, rock t-shirt, jeans and Converse gym shoes. He has a unique style that is him, and he wears it well. In the beginning of the interview it was obvious that he was nervous, and initially spoke loud looking down at the tape recorder, but after a few questions he became more relaxed and the conversation flowed with easy banter. Jonathon has his own opinions and perspective on life, which came across loud and clear, as his story came to fruition. To understand the person, Jonathon, I asked about his world, his interests, and background (Van Manen, 1990, p.102). I started by asking him just to tell me a little about himself.

S.:   So tell me about yourself, what you like to do?

Jonathon/
Jon: Well, uh I'm Jon. I'm in college, and in clinical lab science at NIU (Northern Illinois University). I tried respiratory, but I didn't like it... (Long pause) So I went to DeKalb. Uhh (pause) I like video games, working on the computer, and stuff. Studying...I like to go to school...I like to learn. I like to go to the Newman Center.

S.:   So tell me about the Newman Center. (I could sense a change in his demeanor when he said Newman Center, and felt this might give me an opening)

Jon: My favorite part at school is that I got involved in the Newman Center. It is a Catholic student center, but anyone can join. Anyone can join the chaos which is Newman. Yea... they have pizza every Wednesday night, but you have to go to church first, but they kinda get you... but it's really cool there because they don't judge you, they just accept you for who you are, it's not like... I don't like you... you look different. So I won't talk to you. Everyone goes... its good.

I found it interesting that on the second question, without any prompting from me, Jonathon discusses people judging others because they "look different." He appeared relieved, by his voice and demeanor, that the people he has met at Newman so far are not judgmental. He said, "They accept you for who you are." Often time's people with disabilities are fenced out of social situations because they look or act different. Jonathon has found a social group where the young people are open to knowing all people, not just people who look or act in a particular manner. Jonathon's ability to meet people at the center is representative of the existential of lived body or corporality. When a person meets another, they are first meeting bodily. This meeting is an uncovering. Jonathon was taking a risk to open himself to friendship. Van Manen (1990) tells us that this meeting is "both revealing and concealing at the same time"(p.103). Having friends is critical to an individual's emotional and psychological well being. The following quote represents relationality.

S.:   So you have found good friends there?

Jon: That won't backstab you. I'm going to umm every third Thursday to a homeless shelter and serve food up there. But before we go there, we make everything by scratch. I enjoy cooking... yea and the last two times it was meatloaf and mashed potatoes. So we made those and I have a retreat, which is NIK, and I'm a member of it. I'm part of the team that is involved with planning the whole retreat. I like the retreat because it's student led, student run, so that's kind of cool.

Jonathon is excited about his involvement in Newman Center, and was eager to tell me about the activities he has joined at the center. His experience at Newman is representative of possibilities. Through the acceptance he has found there, Jonathon is open to rhizomic connections. He is connecting to other people, and is becoming more confident. He is now able to talk other college students and enjoys being with friends. The entire time he spoke, he was smiling, and would look off and nod his head up and down. Having the autonomy to lead the retreat and the confidence to take on a leadership role is a significant step for Jonathon, who has not put himself "out there" in the past. Newman is a safe place for Jonathon. With a supportive emotional climate he is able to join in and also reach out to help others. Jonathon was searching for the communal; "a social sense of purpose for his life" (Van Manen, 1990, p.105). The spatiality of Newman has assisted him in this quest.

S.:   So is this the first time you've taken on a responsibility role.

Jon: Yea, in high school I didn't get involved in anything like that. I wouldn't because I was like shy and timid. Newman opened me up.... (Pause) on spring break I'm going to West Virginia to help other people, with all other volunteers to build houses and clean-up stuff.

S.:   That's great, like Habitat for Humanity?

Jon: Yea, that stuff, yea, and that's good.

Jonathon revealed that Newman has opened him emotionally to opportunity. He now has the confidence to go beyond his personal fence of shyness. He is breaking down fences and opening himself to opportunities.

Living Independently
Jonathon is living independently for the first time at age twenty-two.

S.:   So how do you like living on your own?

Jon: I like it a lot.It's more relaxed and I can go to the store, whenever I want. I feel comfortable there. Me getting out of the respiratory program and then we did not sell the house at Northern after Melissa (his older sister) graduated. I am glad to be away from this house (his childhood home, where the interview occurred). It all worked out. I am more comfortable driving the country roads, it's not so congested. And people are friendlier there than here. Everyone's like…. Ah… Hi, how's it going? I am not a city person, I want to blend in, but stand out…a little.

Jonathon finds pleasure in basic things like going out to the store and having neighbors who say hello. His family home is located in a busy south suburb of Chicago. Jonathon prefers the atmosphere around his college, which is located in a farming area. Jonathon drives with special mirrors to compensate for his lack of peripheral vision. The crowded nature, and stop and go traffic in his home community, makes him nervous. He much prefers to drive where it is less crowded. He is in a comfortable place both physically and psychologically. He has found a home space where he is safe to be himself. As human beings we long for a safe lived space. Lived space is the existential theme of "finding oneself at home" (Van Manen, 1990, p.102). Home is not as much a physical place as much as it is a feeling. A sense of comfort and safety comes over people when they find themselves "at home". The comment, "I want to blend in, but stand out, a little" is reflective of resistance; the safety of blending in while simultaneously having the courage to stand out.

Self Description

S.: Describing yourself, what do you think are your best attributes?

Jon: I'm anal, (laughs). I really have to get stuff done before it's actually due. And uh, I'm trustworthy and calm and I listen to people. But I want improve on being more social, and just... like... talking to people. It's better now, but I still need to.

Jonathon has broken down his personal barriers of getting to know people, and now that the fence is down he wants to venture out, beyond the shadows of the fence. He wants to step out to unknown areas and put himself out there to be more social and talkative. Jon realizes the significant steps he has taken and how far he has come, but knows he needs to push farther and be open to possibilities.

Jonathon and I carried on a conversation and discussed our interests and comfort zones. We talked of professions and school. I told him about my role as a special educator and professor in the field of education, and how I have evolved to have a disability studies (DSE, 1, 2008) approach to special education practices. We then began to discuss what it means to have a disability.

S.: Has anyone ever asked you if you have a disability? What do you say?

Jon: No, they are amazed that I am what I am now. People don't know... but then they're amazed.

S.: So do you think you have a disability?

Jon: Everyone has a disability. But it's not... but if they choose to think of it as a disability than more power to them, but it's not.(pause) Once I get to know people, I might tell them that I'm blind in one eye. And the comment I get is. You don't look blind, and that my eye looks normal. They are like... WOW. Sometimes I'll tell them if I need to, because of the fine motor stuff. My one hand mirrors the other hand, I need to practice something, and then it slowly fades away when I can do it.

S.:   That is pretty amazing.

Jon: Yea, I have to tell my hand not to do what the other one is doing.

Jonathon dispels a medical model of disability (Scully, 2002). He does not view his differences as something to be fixed, but instead a part of his identity. Jon separates having a disability from a disabling condition. Pity or self pity is oppressive. Jonathon believes if a person thinks their condition is disabling, it will become disabling; he chooses not to think in that manner. It is Jonathon's choice as to how he sees himself, and he has the right to determine his own level of success (Phillips, 1993). Jonathon does not want to be an inspirational disabled person (Shapiro, 1993), but he is intrigued about how his own body is able to function. Jonathon is blind in one eye, his eye never formed in utero. He also has agenesis of the corpus callosum; which means he is missing the connective tissue of the brain. The two hemispheres of Jonathon's brain are not connected. He demonstrated to me how both his hands do the same thing at the same time, when he is not focusing; then he focused, and only one hand moved and the other hand was still. Sitting at the table watching Jon's brain work was interesting to me, and I expressed that amazement. I was not looking at Jon as an inspirational "super crip" (Shapiro, 1993, p.16), but I was admiring the beauty of how his brain works; it was an aesthetic experience. Gabel (2005) describes the aesthetic as "a coming to know or understand" (p.34). I was coming to understand the beauty of Jonathon.

Jonathon's lived experience is representative of resistance. Resistance

Theory looks at the whole picture, not one side or another, but the entire experience of disability. According to Gabel, (2005, p. 8) "it opens up possibilities and blurs boundaries, while it avoids the construction of abstract or rigid models of disability." Jonathon is embracing who he is and dispelling any constructs society may place upon him.

Early Years

The circumstances around Jonathon's birth in the summer of 1986, are relevant in coming to understand the adult Jonathon of 2009. According to Van Manen (1990), "the temporal dimensions of past, present, and future constitute the horizons of a person's temporal landscape" (p. 104). To understand the present, I asked Jonathon about his past.

S.:	So have your parents ever told you about when you were born?
Jon:	Umm... That they wouldn't think that I'd live. That they thought I was the miracle baby. No doctors or health-care specialists thought I would survive, but they kept referring to me as a wonder child.
S.:	So you feel like a wonder child?
Jon:	I feel like a normal person, because it's part of my life. It's who I am.

Jonathon repeatedly dispels any construct which puts him in the category of "surpassing all odds." He did surpass the professionals' expectations, but Jonathon has not let the "wonder child" persona define him.

A Mother's Perspective

Obviously Jonathon does not remember the circumstances of his birth. He only knows what people have shared with him about those times. Jonathon's mom, Laura, provides her version about the temporality surrounding Jonathon's birth.

S.: Tell me what you remember when Jonathon was born?

(Laura/Jonathon's

Mother) L: Right after he was born, just the microphthalmia (missing an eye). Then they told me everything was fine. But I had a C-section, and after they sedated me, and then they must've done... like the MRI. I was out of it and they couldn't do a transplant for the eye because it was like spaghetti noodles there. And it would not work. The doctor for Jonathon was going away for some seminar, and he was in a hurry and he told me from the hallway, "Your son is really sick, if he makes it, he'll be a vegetable, then he left. And I remember I was still paralyzed on the bottom from the C-section. And I couldn't move, and I was stuck in the room. So I called my grandmother, and it turned out that my cousin was the head nurse in the OB Department. So she (the cousin) hurried out, and got me into a private room. Then my OB came in, and he got everything together for me, he got a neurologist, a surgeon and did everything. The doctor that should have been taking care of it, just left. Later then, I got a bill from him. I called his wife, who was his receptionist, and I said, I'm not going to pay for this and she said, "He lived didn't he?" I never paid the bill.

Much like the mothers of Jackie and Chuck, Laura was looking to the doctor to provide her with information and an explanation about her child. A doctor, not knowing or not having access to the correct information, is reminiscent of the physicians in the stories of Jackie and Chuck. One would think parents of children born with a disability in the 1980s, would not be treated in a similar fashion as babies born in the 1930s. The doctor did not have prior knowledge about Jonathon's situation, so rather than working through it with the family, he called Laura's baby a vegetable, and physically walked away. Fortunately, Laura had a caring obstetrician and a family member who happened to be in the right place, at the right time to help initiate a plan of action.

It's a Boy!

We came in from Timmy's baseball game. I noticed the answering machine was blinking. I hit the button and the sounds of "it's a boy" rang throughout the house.

"Whoo hoo Tim, Amy,... Laura and Steve had a baby boy today," I yell out to the kids.

"You gonna call them, mom?" Tim asked.

"I will call as soon as I get a chance to talk to her. We are going to have to go shopping for a gift."

I got busy that day and did not get a chance to call Laura at the hospital until the following day.

"Hi Laura, congratulations, a boy. How is everything?" I was talking all excited and did not even realize at first that Laura hardly responded.

"Hi Sharon." She sounded so quiet. It finally hit me-something does not seem right.

"Are you feeling ok? Is the baby fine?"

"I'm ok, but something is not right with the baby, anyway they are running tests."

"Tests for..?" My heart was already hurting for my friend, something appeared to be wrong. Laura's voice seemed so distant and quiet and even trembled as she spoke. This was not the voice of a new mom celebrating the birth of a child.

"So what kinda tests are they doing?"

"Well his one eye did not form right for some reason."

"What?"

"Yeah, its like the eye is not there, so they are running tests to see what else is wrong or why."

"So do you know anything yet?"

"I do not think they know, but it does not seem good. Oh I don't know. It could be something wrong with his brain."

"Oh Laura, anything I can do-you need anything?"

"I don't know."

"Where's Steve? Is he there?"

"Not now." Laura stopped talking.

I was so worried for Laura, the baby did not have an eye, never heard of anything like that. How scary.

"Want me to come see you?"

"No, there is not much going on-I'll be ok."

Laura always was the leader in our little friendship trio. Laura was the one who took charge. Debbie and I went along because Laura always seemed to have it all together. She just knew about everything. Now she was alone in her hospital room and she did not know everything. Her life was out of control. She had no real answers or reasons about her baby boy. I was sitting home with my two healthy kids and I could not do anything to help my friend. I felt guilty, holding the phone in my hand. My two kids were fine, why did this happen to Laura?

"So Laur, you sure there isn't anything I can do?"

"No, I'll call you."

"Really, I want to help." I kept trying to think of what to say.

"There's nothing really. I'm going to go. I'm going to see if anything is happening."

"Oh Laura, what did you name him?"

"His name is Jonathon." She almost started to cry. "I'll talk to you, bye."

I just started pacing back and forth. What is going on God? Our friend Debbie (Chuck's sister) had just lost one of her twin sons. Brian had been sitting in his high chair and went into some sort of seizure and died later, at 2 years old. We still did not know the final autopsy results as to what happened with Brian and now Laura's Jonathon. I didn't get it. There was nothing I could do for my friend, but pray.

Laura is very private in many ways. She has this quiet determination and just does what she needs to do, I am, however, the talkative "out there" type and I selfishly wanted to do something for my friend. I knew I needed to let her deal with whatever was happening in her way, but I felt so useless,helpless, and guilty. Why was this happening to my friends?

Laura actually knew a bit more than she told me on the phone. She just couldn't repeat everything again.

The neurological tests showed that he was missing part of his brain. The doctors did not have any answers, because they did not have much experience with his condition.

I called Laura back the next day. She told me she was going home from the hospital

"Oh, is the baby going home, too or does he have to stay longer?"

"No, Jonathon's going home too. There is nothing they can do."

"What? Nothing? What do you mean?"

"We're going to get him baptized at home. We're trying to work it out. We have families coming over."

"Can I help?"

"No, I just have to do this."

I hung up the phone and the tears poured down my eyes. What was happening? I don't get this at all. Sending him home. Why aren't the doctors doing anything?

I called Debbie, which also was difficult. She was still grieving her own baby and I did not even know what to say, but I needed to talk.

"Hey Deb. So you heard about Jonathon?"

"Oh Sharon. I can't believe it. I just know though I would take Brian living here with me, no matter what was wrong. Even if he couldn't see or walk or talk at least he would be here. So Laura will just love him."

"I guess they're having a Baptism at the house. If you talk to her call me, ok?"

Debbie said, "Yeah, you too. If you talk to her call me."

"Yeah, I don't want to bug her."

"Me either. Talk soon."

"Hey Deb, take care ok?"

"I'm ok, Shar. I just worried for Laura."

"Yeah, me too."

The weekend passed and I did not hear anything more. No news was good news, I guessed. So I called Laura and Steve's house. Steve answered.

"Hi Shar, we are doing alright. Jonathon is eating, taking a bottle. So far so good."

"Is it ok if I come by to see him and you guys?"

"I'm sure that's fine. I'm here. Melissa's playing, Laura's laying down, but I'm sure thats fine."

I was so nervous to go see Laura. What was I going to say? I wanted to be happy for my friend. A birth is a joyous occasion, at least it should be. But who knows if Jonathon will even live? The whole situation was so sad. His birth still should be celebrated so I did what I normally do when someone has a baby, I went shopping.

The kids and I went shopping for a present for baby Jonathon. They helped pick out a sleeper and an outfit and Tim insisted we get him a "boy" toy. After the mall I drove to my parents and dropped the kids off to play with Aunt Jackie. I didn't think I should bring them the first time I visited. Amy at three and Tim at seven years old were way too busy and active. It would be better if I went alone.

I drove to Laura and Steve's house. In my head I rehearsed what to say, my mind kept racing. It was just so upsetting. I drove up to their house. Parked the car. I hesitantly knocked on the door. I didn't want to ring the bell or knock too loud. I have this unfortunate habit of being loud or doing something stupid when I am nervous, so I kept self checking, and self talking.

"Calm down Sharon, be quiet Sharon, don't knock too hard Sharon," (Knocking on the door).

Steve answered. He was smiling. Phew. What a relief.

150

"Hi Shar. Come on in."

Jonathon was sleeping in a bassinet in the family room. I looked in and saw a sweet baby boy all swaddled in a blue blanket. I could barely see him but saw his little patches of light brown hair.

"Awe Steve-congratulations."

"I'll go up and get Laura. She's laying down."

I kept looking at the sweet miracle in front of me. He looked fine. Sweet little baby. I could see his little facial features and was trying to figure out who he looked like. I tried to remember what his sister Melissa looked like when she was born. I kept myself occupied looking at some gifts that were on the table. After a bit Steve came back down.

"Laura must have fallen asleep, Shar. I think she probably needs to rest. Its been a rough couple of days."

"Don't worry Steve. I'm glad she's resting. I just wanted to bring the gift over and meet baby Jonathon."

Steve and I continued to make small talk, back and forth for about ten minutes.

"Let me see if she's up yet, just in case." Steve went upstairs and quickly returned. "Still sleeping, sorry."

"Im going to get going. The kids are with Jackie anyway so I don't want to leave them too long."

I gave Steve a hug. "Make sure you call if you guys need anything, ok, please? Tell Laura he is sweet. She can call me when she wants to talk."

I drove back to my parents, wondering what would be in store for my friends and their little boy. How long would Jonathon live? How would Laura deal with this? How do you prepare yourself for the death of your child when you have just welcomed him to the world? Tears came to my eyes as I was driving.

I got to my parents house. I walked in the door and was hit immediately with the reality of my life.

"Mom, Timmy was mean to me. He was mean, wasn't he Jackie?" Amy, always full of drama, couldn't wait a second to tattle on her brother.

"Mom, it wasn't me, it was her, she kept singing in my face." Tim made a face and walked away from his sister.

"Were they ok Jackie?"

"Oh, they were just silly."

"Come on you two. I gave both of my kids a hug. Amy saw that I was upset. Are you ok Mommy? Did you see the baby?"

"I'm ok Amy. Yes, he's a cute baby."

"Did he like the presents?"

"I'm sure he'll like them."

I wondered if he would ever play with the toy bat and ball Tim insisted we give him. Would he even get to wear the clothes? As a mom, I couldn't even think what Laura was going through.

Days went by and Jonathon was still here. Any day I did not hear from Laura was a good day. She continued to go to doctors to find answers, but mostly she just lived. Whatever amount of time she had with Jonathon was going to be good. He was going to be good. He was going to live his best life no matter how long his life would be. Laura, with her determination and practical approach, lived each day at a time.

Days turned into weeks, weeks turned into months. Laura and I would talk about the doctors' suggestions and therapies. She was really busy with toddler Melissa and baby Jonathon. I was so happy that he seemed to be thriving in spite of or despite missing part of his brain. I had never heard of agenisis of the corpus collosum, until Jonathon was born. One more issue to worry about when a baby was born. Debbie received Brian's autopsy results and his death was the result of brain tumors, and now Jonathon with his brain issues. Interesting coincidence that both boys had something wrong with their brain.

Laura was busy being the mom of a child with medical issues and I was busy teaching high school special ed and running around with my two kids. Life continued as it does and I received a surprise. Surprised is putting it mildly for how I felt.

After Debbie and Laura's situations with their boys, Dave and I felt we were blessed to have two healthy kids. I had a job I loved and we felt that our family of four was good. We pretty much had the idea we should leave well enough alone. At work, I noticed I was feeling really queasy, especially in the lunch room on hamburger or gyros days. My hair was acting weird too, it would not curl and kept standing straight up. My teacher friends at work kept teasing me and saying I was pregnant and in denial. I denied that I was in denial. Dave and I had gone on a cruise for winter school break and Scott,one of my guy friends at school kept whistling the Love Boat theme whenever he saw me in the hall. His wife was pregnant so he felt that he was an expert on pregnancy signs.

"Sure right.. we have two healthy kids. I can't be pregnant. It is not in the plans. I had wanted a whole bunch of kids when we first married, but not anymore. With all that had happened in life lately;Debbie's Brian, Laura's Jonathon, my Dad was really sick, a friends marriage was falling apart, a good friend of mine had two miscarriages, but **we** were fine." I was always thinking about being pregnant, but kept doing self talk and did not want to admit it.

We wanted to leave things the way they were. We did not want to do anything to destroy our personal safety zone. My husband,Dave and I were trying to tread softly. I finally could not deny things any longer. I picked the kids up from the sitter after work and stopped at Cavette's the local drug store. I needed encouragement to follow through with the pregnancy test, so I drove to my mom's house. Jackie was amazed that I had to pee on a stick. The kids were busy watching cartoons, but just having my Aunt Jackie there helped. Surprise(not really) the EPT test said that I was pregnant. Jackie was grinning ear to ear and waving her hanky around. I called Dave to confirm what we really had known.

I settled into being pregnant and was actually happy that our family was expanding. My sister Colleen and brother in law Bob (Jamee's parent's) had their first baby, Jenna and it would be nice to have cousins close in age. My Dad was sick with heart and liver failure at 55 years old and kept reminding me, to value life and rejoice in the new life I was carrying.

One day I stopped over at my parents on my way home from work. I went upstairs to say hi to my Dad. He was sitting at his drawing table working on a plan for work. I was exhausted, hot and sweating, after a full day at school without air conditioning. The school year was coming to a close and I was sad that I was going to be leaving my teaching job.

I loved my students and was working a great school with good friends. I wanted to talk to my Dad about my feelings, he was always the one to talk things out with. Before I even had a chance to talk, my Dad happened to notice how much my belly had expanded and when I adjusted my jeans he saw the new purple stretch marks on my baby belly.

"Awe honey, how are you doing?", he held out his arms.

I fell into his arms, crying. He just held me.

"How can you be so sad with this baby coming and Tim and Amy and Dave? Sharon, I am so glad to have each day. I open my eyes in the morning and just thank God for another day. You have your life ahead of you, life is a gift. It will work out. You will think back and wonder why you were ever upset about this." My dad always knew what to say to me. I never even told him my concerns, they seemed irrelevant after his advice.

I had this feeling I was going to have a boy. The kids helped pick out a name, Ryan Patrick. We did not even pick out a girl's name. With Laura's and Debbie's situation, I was a bit scared of what my baby's health situation would be, but I put it out of my mind. I really did not dwell on worrying the rest of the pregnancy. My husband does not like to talk about things that bother him. His way of dealing with tragedy, is to work hard and remain calm. He was silent through Brian's death and Jonathon's birth. He was physically there but emotionally in a "tucked in" place. He felt for his friends Keith (Debbie's husband) and Steve, but he never discussed his concerns with me. He kept his feelings to himself.

The entire time I was pregnant, Dave was worrying. He believed in his heart that the connection Laura and Debbie and I shared had an influence on the health of our baby. I had to go to the hospital twice toward the end of the pregnancy with hemorrhaging. The doctors did not have exact answers with why this was occurring, but the baby was ok.

The doctor decided I would stay in the hospital until the baby came. The second day I was there my labor started. It started and progressed fast. The nurses got me on the cart as I tried to breath through the pain. They ran the cart to the delivery room. My doctor casually strolled in brief case in hand. He took one look at me flying by and the look of terror behind Dave's surgical mask.

"Oh I better hurry, looks like we are having a baby now," (I'm thinking, 'ya think? Get this kid out!).

The delivery of Ryan was my easiest. I was not worried, I just knew whatever the situation, we would deal with it. I saw Laura and Debbie deal with whatever life had put before them, I just knew it would be okay somehow.

Dave must have been really worried. As Ryan was born, he was gripping my hand, squeezing it hard.

"It will be alright, Shar."

"I know, hun."

The doctor didn't need forceps or a vacuum or anything like they used when I had Tim and Amy. With a couple of pushes and Dave tightly gripping my hand, Ryan was born. The doctor held held him up for us to see. For some reason I had the shakes and I was struggling to get a good look at him. "So Sharon and Dave, meet your baby boy. He's perfect." The doctor was looking proud of his accomplishment.

Dave looked at our son and seemed to breathe a sigh of relief.

"Oh Shar, he has two eyes."

The doctor looked at me and made a questioning face. I just smiled. I understood.

A Baptism of Reality

Laura continued to discuss Jonathon's hospital stay, and described an instinctive urge that swelled within her soul. She somehow "knew" she had to forcefully advocate for her son. Laura, like Mrs. E. and my grandmother, felt the need to fight for her son. In the literature pertaining to the family members of children with disabilities, the word "fight" is prevalent (Berube, 2004; Ferguson, 2003; Gans, 2007; Spiegel& van den Pol, 1993; Strohm, 2005).

L.:   I remember this fight thing was immediate. I had birth announcements, and I said, we have him for now, so we'll just fill these out, the birth announcements. So we sent those out and we went to get him baptized at the hospital and the priest there said unless we know he's going to die, there is no sense doing this. And the nurse told him we don't know. So he said I'm not doing it. So then a nurse came in, and said, "I can do a conditional baptism." Anyways, we didn't want that. So Steve (Laura's husband/ Jonathon's father) went over to St. Julie's (their church) to see the priest. Jonathon was released that day. We just didn't know, we called the family to come over and we had a Baptism. The priest came about a half-hour after Jonathon got home.

Laura was fighting an institution, just as my grandmother had to "fight" at the meeting at the rectory fifty years previously. A conditional baptism performed by a nurse was not good enough for Laura and Steve's son, he deserved a true baptism. Steve knocked at another rectory door, and the priest came to baptize Jonathon as soon as he came home from the hospital. The family did not know if Jonathon was going to live to see another day, but on this day they knew he was being baptized in the protective circle of his immediate and extended family. Laura and Steve found a way to get what they felt their child needed, at least for this day.

Jonathon was alive and since no one was aware of his prognosis, Laura began to seek ways to work with Jonathon. In the early months of his life it was obvious he needed extra support. He had trouble breathing and swallowing, his hands and legs would move together, and he could not hold his head up. Decisions needed to be made about therapies, medical specialists, and a prosthesis for his eye. Laura describes these times:

L.:   Then my cousin got me in touch with Blue Hill (an infant program for children with disabilities). He started there at about three months. And a little later on, there was a girl from high school who had a son with Down Syndrome, and she knew about Good Samaritan (Another program for infants with disabilities). Their program was three days a week and then eventually five days a week. A bus would actually come and get him.

S.:   At some point did anyone say this child is not going to die?

L.:   No, Never. They kinda said at the hospital, you're taking him home to die. You know it's weird even if he sleeps long, even now; I go and check on him. I remember putting him in all his outfits and taking pictures of him, so I just… we thought he was going to die. I just kept changing his clothes and putting him in different things. To show he had a longer life than maybe he really did.

S.:   So you were creating memories?

L.:   Yes, that's what I really did.

Dressing Jonathon in a variety of outfits, and taking pictures was an example of resistance. Laura was fighting against the realization that her son could die at any time, yet she was desperately trying to live in the moment. Voicing the fact that she still checks on 22 year old Jonathon when he sleeps too long, indicates her profound fear that her son could be taken from her in a moment. Those fears are now buried deep inside, yet still exist. The existential of temporality is representative of not just clock time, but subjective time. Van Manen (1990) explains "the temporal dimensions of the past, present and future constitute the horizons of a person's temporal landscape (p. 104).The past emotional experience of almost losing her son ties Laura's past to the present.

Mothering and Fighting

The next part of the conversation with Laura describes how, at first, everything just seemed overwhelming to her. Within hours of his birth, she came to the realization that she was going to do everything she could to help her son. Darling (1979) refers to this realization and questioning experience as parental entrepreneurship. Laura was acting as an entrepreneur, negotiating and finding her way. She was rejecting what did not feel right to her and embraced solutions that actually applied to Jonathon.

L.: I was really down when we first got home, and then we had got into a different pediatrician. I had just an awful headache and I couldn't function. I remember the doctor told Steve you need to worry about your wife more than you need to worry about your son. Your wife's bad… Then I thought pull yourself up, you'll get him in a program, you will do whatever you can. So I decided that was what I was going to do, and my sister said, you can't change someone's IQ. And I said I don't care. I am going to do everything I can. I am going to quit working and I am going to do everything I can to get this kid where he needs to be. I just went about in my OCD way and bombarded him, and I think that is why it is what it is. I thought to myself, don't tell me what I can't do. It was like, I'll show you… and I became like a fighter.

Laura was fighting for Jonathon, and at this early stage in his life, she was fighting against the stereotypes typically assigned to people with brain damage. Her own sister tried to tell her that a person's IQ cannot be changed. Just as my grandmother and Mrs. E. did not believe the doctors when they were told their children would never walk or talk, Laura believed Jonathon would improve. She took it as a personal challenge to be sure that he did.

L.:   And I remember going to Loyola and the doctor
        saying, why bother getting his eye done…and I said
        you're treating my son like a piece of meat. He's my
        son, so respect him. I said to him, you're no prize
        yourself. He did stop and give me a look, but he
        changed his attitude. For that to come out of my
        mouth was major.

The doctor actually expressed that Jonathon did not need prosthesis because he was severely disabled and he might die. A similar attitude had been expressed by the professionals in the past when they advised parents to institutionalize their children since they would not live long anyway (Castles, 2004). The doctor felt that it was not necessary to go through the "trouble" to make an eye for Jonathon. This professional had assigned an identity to a two week old baby. As Goode (1984) indicates, identities are socially produced and depend on the context on which people are viewed. The doctor looked at Jonathon, and did not see a baby, he saw a disability. He was defining Jonathon as a "non person" (Goffman, 1963). Laura had to demonstrate resistance and break down another fence; that of the oppressive attitude of the doctor. Laura actually told the doctor off in an insulting manner. Through this confrontation, the physician realized Laura meant business, and he made Jonathon's prosthesis. Getting her son what he needed, and deserved as a human being, was Laura's main objective, and she succeeded.

Laura said she got to the point with all the specialists that she said, "Don't tell me what you think it is, and just tell me when you really know." She only wanted to know what they were sure of and what she could actually work on. The professionals wanted discussion and she wanted action. A tension existed between the opposing viewpoints. She explained: "You can't have a pity party. You can have one for a day or two…Ah, I think I had one for about five days. I was so depressed. It was either you or Debbie that came over, and I said, "Steve, (her husband) I can't get out of bed."

S.:	It was me. Steve introduced me to baby Jonathon.
L.:	I was probably postpartum. I really thought the worse for Jonathon. I thought I will carry him and then we'll get a wheelchair. We will take it one day at a time and we'll do whatever we have to do.

Like many mothers after giving birth to a child with disabilities Laura felt overwhelmed. She did not get the opportunity to be joyful about giving birth. From the time Jonathon was born she had to figure out an action plan. Wickham-Searl (1992) describes the life changes after giving birth to a child with disabilities as a "journey along an unknown path" (p. 13). Laura was trying desperately to find her way so she could find and navigate a life path that that made sense to her for Jonathon.

Jonathon's life was full of doctors, treatments, and therapies. He had a developmental specialist, occupational therapists, physical therapists, neurologist and orthopedic doctor, to name some of the professionals who impacted his life. He was now a toddler, attending therapeutic services daily, plus private therapy, and he was showing signs of improvement, both physically and intellectually. Since he had already surpassed other children with agenesis of the corpus callosum, the professionals told Laura "to keep doing whatever you are doing, because it is working."

Laura and I discussed Jonathon's progress throughout his toddler years. He could walk with difficulty, he could see with his one eye, with the support of glasses. He could talk, but had some articulation difficulties, and "reading" the social nuances related to communicating. His fine motor coordination was very poor, and his one hand was always mimicking the other. At this time, Jonathon's personality was evolving and his likes and dislikes were becoming apparent. As a very young child he loved to "hang out" in the kitchen with Laura, and he always had a book in his hand. He would look at books over and over again, he especially enjoyed cookbooks with colored photos of food.

S.:	So life went on....

L.: I think I realized things would get better 'cause he started reading. He loved books and he liked to cook, so we would cook together, and then he suddenly started reading the recipes. Everyone said he must have the books memorized, but then he started reading the recipes, you don't memorize that. He started reading at three or four years old. He was about three when he was reading the recipe to me. Everyone is like… no way, but he was reading recipes to me….. Then I started thinking, holy shit!... This kid is smart.

With the realization that Jonathon could read, Laura knew he would be able to accomplish academic tasks. She said discovering his ability to read was a turning point for her. It gave her a sense of relief. After negotiating the path of "unknowns," she finally had something concrete to grasp. She "knew" for a fact that Jonathon could read and follow written directions. Rhizomic connections were being made by a boy missing the connective area of his brain. Laura was always forward thinking, but now her "gut feelings" that Jonathon could learn were coming into fruition. Having grown up with Chuck and Jackie, Laura realized that people with disabilities could accomplish much. The connections of the past, her friendship with Chuck, and love of my Aunt Jackie propelled Laura forward.

Answers and Questions

Laura felt the realization that Jonathon had a medical condition of brain damage almost at of the moment of birth attributed to his progress. At three weeks old he received therapeutic intervention. As discussed, the first few months of his life was filled with doctors, evaluations, eating and swallowing difficulties, and overall controlled chaos.

Laura tells her version of life as she knew it then.

L.: It helped because we knew something was not right from beginning. So we started doing things right away. We didn't know exactly, but he had a medical diagnosis; agenesis of the corpus callosum. Loyola (hospital) had not seen a case. So we went to Children's (hospital) and Children's had seen three cases, and they were all girls and they were severely retarded. But the doctor said, he'll be fine, if he's retarded, he's retarded, Are you going to love him any less? So what. He's going to be fine. Bring him back in a year, take him home and treat him like you treat your daughter. Then in second grade, she said, you don't have to bring him here anymore. Invite me to his wedding.

S.:   She was the right person at the right time.

L.:   Yes, she said, it is what it is. You're doing the right thing. So we kept doing what we were doing.

Laura was aware she did not love Jonathon any less than her daughter Melissa, but it gave her affirmation to hear she was moving in the right direction from a professional. Just as Mrs. E. was told by her family doctor to treat Chuck like her daughter Debbie, Laura was told to treat Jonathon like his sister. The reality was that both of the mothers were going to love Chuck and Jonathon as their other child, but by no means would the mothers be able to treat their children the same.

Jonathon needed scores of intervention and therapeutic support in order to function in the world, and Laura's daughter did not require those supports as a young child. In fact, Laura told me how Melissa's schedule revolved around Jonathon. Laura chose Melissa's preschool because it had the times which were congruent to Jonathon's school and therapy schedules. Laura and her husband Steve had to purposely set aside time for Melissa, and make sure they were not ignoring her needs. Melissa spent much time going to doctors and therapists with Laura and Jonathon; waiting. Since Melissa was young, she was not sure what exactly she was waiting for, but that she had to be patient and wait. Laura said she was sure to enroll Melissa in activities without Jonathon so Melissa could be "Melissa" instead of "Jonathon's sister."

Hastings, Beck, & Hill (2005) conducted studies and determined that siblings of children with disabilities may exhibit more emotional and social adjustment issues than children without siblings with disabilities. Laura and Steve were consciously working at giving Melissa attention so she had the autonomy to pursue her own interests, and not have personal difficulties because she had a sibling with a disability. At times, the fences constructed to deal with the disability experience were found inside the lived family space. Laura and Steve needed to keep both of their children safe, yet inspire them to be open to the possibilities on the other side of the fence.

School Time

Jonathon was in a school type program from infancy. As an infant, he attended early intervention with his mother and then, at age two, he rode a bus to the program. Jackie, born in the thirties, and Chuck born in the sixties, did not have the benefit of programs for early intervention, since such programs did not exist when they were babies. My grandparents and the E.'s realized their children needed additional assistance to reach developmental milestones. Stretching Chuck using elastic bands, and teaching Jackie to walk and balance, using ties and a belt for support, reflect their personally constructed early intervention programs. After Laura visited many preschool programs for general and special education, it was decided with the support of the school district, that Jonathan would attend a local commercial preschool with his peers. While at preschool, he received the assistance of an adult paraprofessional. This unique program funded by his local public school also included physical, occupational and speech pathology services. Laura was learning quickly how to operate in the maze of special education.

By virtue of the special education laws passed while Chuck was in high school in the 1970s, in 1992, Jonathon reaped the benefits resulting from those laws. Jon had the opportunity to attend school with his peers, and have the support of an individual education plan (IEP), so he could obtain the supports he needed to fully participate in school. Jonathon's school district promoted inclusion for students with disabilities, and Jonathon, like Jackie 50 years before, spent his elementary school years in the general education classroom. Laura discusses Jonathon's adventures in Kindergarten.

S.:   So tell me about his early school experiences.

L.:   I remember him going to kindergarten, and his teacher thought *she* was all good because *she* was taking on the special ed. student. But then it was almost like she was pissed because the kid that could read was the one with the IEP. And he was reading, *really* reading, but his fine motor skills were bad. And she couldn't deal with that. And she'd say things like: "You just sit there until you get that boot on". He spent most of his time trying to do things he could not physically do, instead of school work. So finally I had enough and I said to her: Would you tell a kid with no feet to go out and run? He cannot put his boots on. He can't do it. Do you understand?"

S.:   And she couldn't?

L.:   Well… no, so then I started volunteering, and I would get her to focus on what he *could* do. She would act like he wasn't trying. I got to the point when I thought,… you may think you know my son, but I know him better than anyone else. And it is what it is. I just started going to school.

The teacher was working from a medical model perspective (Peters, 1999) which has oppressive consequences. She was going to "fix" Jonathon and was driven to make him conform. His kindergarten teacher was not looking at what Jonathon was able to achieve, but instead was focussing on what he could not do. This situation is reflective of a deficit model perspective (Harry&Klinger, 2007). Laura, again, is displaying resistance, and is fighting for her child's rights in the school setting.

Jonathon's School Reality

Jonathon was not eager to discuss his elementary years in school. He did not talk about the academic expectations, and answered in a vague manner. Jon appeared anxious, and looked away when I said: "Let's talk about elementary school." Perhaps elementary school was not a positive lived experience for him.

S.: So tell me about school, beginning with elementary school.

Jon: I just went to school in…. and well, I just went to school, but I really didn't have any… I had friends. But I was shy… and it was kind of from first grade until today. I'm getting more open.

Jonathon could only tell me, "he went to school." I thought about Jackie showing me her school pictures and naming all her classmates. I felt that Jackie actually had a more positive childhood school experience than Jonathon. Jackie was in her 20s when she told me about her school pictures, not much older than Jonathon, yet it was obvious to me that the feelings Jonathon had about elementary school were still raw and something he was uncomfortable talking about. He started to say he did not have any friends, then caught himself, instead he said he was shy, possibly, he is blaming himself for not having friends, or he was embarrassed by his need for support. Jonathon was included in school. He was an active member of Indian Guides with boys from his neighborhood, yet it does not appear that he had a good friend or group of friends. Bogdan and Taylor (1982) purport that being "in" the community is not the same as being "of" the community. Jonathon was included in school, yet he did not have relationality with the other students. Jon suggested that his shyness impacted his school relationships. Jonathon's shyness served as an internal fence separating him from his peers.

Based on Jonathon's body language and demeanor, I surmised that Jonathon did not want to discuss his elementary years. I had prior knowledge that he had been involved in some high school activities which he enjoyed, and felt that I could use this prior knowledge as an entry into Jon's story about his high school experience.

S.: So how was high school, what were things you were involved with there? I know you were involved in band.

Jon: I was in band and culinary arts club and um… everything in high school was organized by adults, not students…so I went along.

S.: So did you get pulled out of class for anything?

Jon: Yea, for disability testing and to take tests and stuff. Most the times I was included in high school. They wanted to hold me back, but I just said, screw you guys… they wanted me to…um. They thought I wasn't ready for anatomy and physiology, but I said that is a field I'm getting into, so that why not take it in high school, if I can do it?

S.: So how did you do?

Jon: I did it. I got A's in it. And it seemed like they were mad at me. But whatever, I did it. High school was hard because for all my teen years I was in the back and a leg brace. And that really cut down on my social life. Because I had to be in it 12 hours a day.

Jonathon has again provided a reason why he did not have a social life after school. The full body brace he wore for his severe scoliosis was necessary so he would not have to undergo spinal surgery, but it served as a fence to his social freedom. Jonathon's timid nature during the school day and wearing a brace during his free time, contributed to his lack of social opportunities.

Beginning to control his destiny, Jonathon began to advocate for himself regarding course work. Jonathon's sense of pride and determination was evident when he said, "whatever; I did it." The "pirate" took control over took the ship of low expectations placed on him by the counselor.

Now that Jonathon seemed more relaxed, and even proud about his school accomplishments, I continued with questions pertaining to his school experiences.

S.:   What was your favorite part of school?

Jon: I like learning the stuff and certain teachers have different styles. They might give out note packets or use PowerPoint. I liked that approach. The worst part was teachers underestimating my power and saying you are not allowed to do that. I had to fight for what I wanted.

Jonathon expressed his anger at teacher's underestimating him, and limiting him. Some of the high school teachers were employing socially constructed opinion as they looked at Jonathon, as his kindergarten teacher did ten years previous. The teachers were trying to define Jonathon and he wanted the opportunity to define himself.

S.:   So what about your classmates?

Jon: Some were nice and some were not so nice… some were indifferent. Once in a while they would say stuff out loud. In the beginning of high school I was in class with…um… where everyone had disabilities in there, too and they grouped on me. But the funny part was that they had the same disabilities. So… I didn't understand that. (Jonathan switches to the type of class he was in, and appears more comfortable talking about the logistics rather than the students) I was in a smaller classes first, then resource. I was like "no"…, so they moved me to a half-hour resource/lunch. Then some teachers were so nice and said, "Just go to lunch." I was speaking up. My mom had to speak for me sometimes, but not a lot. And I finally said to them (special education teachers), I will come to you when I need help, you don't have to come to me.

Jonathon, as a 15 year old high school sophomore in 2002, wanted to control his own life. He felt he should be able to ask for support when he needed it, and the rest of time he should have the opportunity to try to do the school work on his own. He clearly did not like being in a separate program for students with disabilities. Being in the freshman special education center at his high school was disabling for him, and he kept finding ways to get out. He was also being bullied by the other students in the program which he could not understand. Since his classmates had disabilities themselves, he thought they would have been more empathetic.

I asked Laura for her thoughts on Jonathon's high school experience.

S.:   So how did high school go for Jonathon? He appeared uncomfortable talking about it at times.

L.:   Jonathon has his quirks. People would pick on him. When Jonathon walks, he keeps his eyes down, and so he's an easy target. People will pick on people when they know they can. It was the people who had worse issues. Kind of like the man who comes home and kicks his dog. They would try to bring Jonathon down to pull themselves up.

S.:   A special ed. pecking order?

L.:   Yea, kind of like that. At the time… maybe he should not have been in that freshman thing. But at the time it was the best option. It was good for him, but he was also thrown in with a lot of people with issues. He was stuck with them all day and then there were parents going in to fight their kids' battles still.

S.:   And you quit fighting?

L.:   I quit in about the middle grades, unless it was something to do with academics, and it wasn't just Jonathon. Basically, junior high was good, except for the PE teacher. He wanted him in PE. Yea right, put the kid with no balance, low vision, asthma and eye hand coordination issues in a gym class. I don't know why the guy wanted him in PE. He was pretty intense about it.

Laura was able to clarify the situation with Jonathon's experience in high school. She expressed to me that the Freshman Center was an academic support classroom, and was the best option available when Jonathon entered high school. The high school that Jonathon attended had over four thousand students. Laura thought at the time that attending the Freshman Center would provide necessary support as Jonathon negotiated this large populous high school for the first time. In retrospect, she thinks that being picked on and not feeling comfortable in his surroundings was not beneficial for Jonathon. During his freshman year, he was clearly unhappy in school. She did say that after a while, Jonathon began to advocate for himself. He wanted the chance to prove he did not require such a restrictive environment. Jonathon was employing self-determination practices which would continue to serve him well in the future (Algozzine, Browder, Karoven, Test & Wood, 2001).

The Theory of Blah Blah Blah

"Hey you, yea I'm talking to you." The kid gave Jon a little discrete shove.

Jonathon just wanted to get in the door of school. He wanted to go about his routine and blend in. Rather than acknowledge the kid from his English class, he kept his eyes down and just kept walking. Inside his head he was doing some major self talk.

"I'm not going to answer him, I'm tired of them saying stuff to me. Figures I have to be in class with them. I do not need to be in Freshman Center with THEM."

Jonathon was shy in high school. He just wanted to be left alone. Because of his physical issues he had a great deal of stuff going on. It was difficult for him to navigate through the halls of his public high school of over 4,5000 students. He had to find his way despite being blind in one eye, lacking some motor planning and difficulties with peripheral vision. Jonathon also had to really concentrate so both of his hands would not do the same thing at once. When he was nervous or was not concentrating both of his hands could be moving around.

The best way for him to survive the school day was to blend into the walls. If he could be an inanimate object, all the better. The focus was to be as unnoticeable as the desks in the classrooms. Jon did not want to have to explain himself, or answer to anyone.

"Just let me get to class on time for once without being stopped or being pushed."

The feelings and issues went on day after day.

"Mom, I hate that I have to be in those classes."

Jonathon was home after school and was getting some help from his mom, Laura with his back brace. Bad enough that every day at school he had to put up with all the social teenage crap and then he came in the door and from the time he got home until the next morning,he had to wear a large back brace for his scoliosis.

No one at school knew about his back brace."Good thing those guys did not know." Jon told me during our interviews, but he would not share much about what really occurred at school.

Jon's mom explained to me during the interviews that when he went to the local high school, they had just started a Freshman Center, developed to support any student who may have issues with transitioning to such a large school. The students in the freshman center may have had adjustment issues, needed English language support, or benefitted from smaller or remedial classes, but they were definitely not all special education students.

The students had a core group of teachers, were in classes with less students and had study hall/tutoring support. Jonathon felt that it was a punishment to be in those classes. He wanted to prove to everyone that he didn't need to be in special ed or the freshman center or whatever they called it. It did not matter to him that it really was not special ed; it separated him and he did not have access to all the courses he wanted to take. He hated being labeled. The other kids in the classes with him really had more academic issues than he did, yet they picked on him and bullied him. During our talks, Jonathon did not share any of this with me. He mom, Laura, had to fill in the gaps about his high school social and educational experience.

Jon did however have very specific feelings regarding his academic choices. Late in his sophomore year, Jonathon looked over the course offerings for junior year. Jonathon wanted to enroll in an anatomy and physiology course. He went to his advisor with his ideas.

"So I go in and she says "I don't believe you are ready for that level of a science course". She had this nicey voice, but she thought I was too stupid or something. So I said, "I'm going into science in college so why can't I take this in high school. I met the prerequisites and it is what I am signing up for."

"She finally gave in and signed my schedule. Good thing, cause they wanted to hold me back. I think I said screw them (to myself), screw them all. I can do this." Jonathon's voice grew louder as he told the story and he was very forthright in telling me his feelings about the anatomy course.

Jonathon kept referring to *them*. He only had the meeting with one advisor, but to him she represented everyone who doubted what he could do. There was one, middle aged, woman counselor sitting at a desk, but she represented the school who did not want a special ed student, the kindergarten teacher who kept insisting he could not go out to play until he could tie his shoes or the 8th grade gym teacher who insisted he run laps with asthma, uneven gate and all. He was going to show <u>them</u>. Anyone who had doubted him in the past or had put unnecessary, unrealistic expectations on him; he would show them.

"How did you do in the class?" I was afraid to ask.

"Well I showed them. I got an A. I think they were mad at it though."

"Who was mad?" I still wasn't sure who "they" were so I thought I would ask.

"You know, all of them, the special ed people, the counselor, the advisor, all of them."

I couldn't help but to think that he also meant the guys that made fun of him or pushed him around when no one was looking. Jonathon had this chance to prove he was "smart." He secretly may have been proving it to himself.

"Teachers, I think underestimate my power. I can do the school work. It makes me mad, I can control my destiny, I can do the work." Jon was feeling more comfortable sharing his feelings. Telling me he received an A in the course, seemed to give him the confidence to tell me more about his school experiences, past and present.

"So you did not need any special education help?"

"Nah, not really. I had an IEP, but I was in control, if I needed help I would get it. It was like, leave me alone. When I need something, I'll ask you."

"So you don't focus on your disabilities, or do you not see yourself as having any disabilities?" I found it so interesting to hear Jonathon's perception of disability.

I had uncovered in our conversations that Jonathon does not like to dwell on the special ed/disability aspect of his schooling, so I wanted to push him to speak about issues that were a bit out of his conversational comfort zone. I was eager to hear more about his ideas and wanted to understand his personal experience of disability. Jonathon, once comfortable, was open to giving his opinions. He did tell me (as he talked about his school experiences) that he never really talked to anyone about the school "stuff". Jon may not have verbalized how he felt, but he had a plan. I came to realize, he also had a strong sense of self. Whether he realized it or not, he also had an interesting concept of disability.

Jonathon does not think people should focus on disability. Help, assistance, support, should simply be given if someone needs it.

"People want to focus on the disability all the time, instead of just giving you something when you need it. They like to stereotype, if you *have* this disability then you must be *like* this, you must *need* this. It is not that way, it should not be that way, that's stereotyping."

Jonathon looked me directly in the eye and pointedly said:

"You know they say he has **blah blah blah,** so all people with **blah blah blah** need **blah blah blah,** oh and we must treat him **blah blah blah,** and he will stay **blah blah blah.**"

I have studied many theories of disability, but Jonathon's theory cuts to the chase and says it all in simple terms. If you label someone disabled they will be categorized, treated a specific way and will be given what someone else "thinks" they need or deserve. Jonathon believes in the power of the individual. He believed in his own power to take control, to not only take the anatomy and physiology class, but to receive an A. With determination and the knowledge that he could do it, he charted his own future course. Those of us in teaching professions talk about self-determination and we diligently work to set goals for the future for the students in special education, but often it is about us, what we think they need, not about what they want or need.

Jonathon said his theory is based on giving the person the power.

"My theory is to let them try. Maybe he will need help, maybe he won't. It's ok to need help, but just let them try."

As he was explaining his theory, it was a personal plea as well. Jonathon just wanted a chance to try, he wanted a chance to do what he wanted and needed to do. He did not want to fulfill someone else's expectations, he had expectations for himself. He really did not care if they understood his desires, as much as he wanted them to give him the chance to do it for himself.

What I found refreshing about Jonathon is that he is so matter of fact. All his life he has needed help of some sort. He has depended on doctors, therapists and family members to help him with some of his medical and physical needs. If someone needs help for a legitimate reason they should get it. It is not a big deal. As he says, "it is what it is, and so what."

He does not believe that people should be labeled.

"Once you are labeled, then comes all these expectations. The expectations can help or hurt."

Jonathan also gave a warning about labels to anyone that works with students who have been labeled:

"You better be careful with those labels, those expectations you put on kids, you may not want to do that, you don't want to do that unless you want some cranky parents mad at you."

I told Laura, his mom, about the cranky parent suggestion and she laughed and said,

"I think he was talking about me. I was one of those cranky parents when people had unrealistic expectations."

I remembered Laura creatively telling the kindergarten teacher off-asking her if she would make a child who had no feet put on boots. Or when she told off the neurologist who originally did not think Jonathon needed a prothesis in for his eye socket because he would not live long. He said in front of baby Jonathon that it was a waste of time and money to provide Jonathon with a fake eye.

Laura let him know her feelings:

"You know you are no prize yourself, That is my child, not some piece of meat. You treat him like you would your own child!"

The doctor then wrote out the referral for them to an ocularist for the prothesis and kept his mouth quiet. Mmmm wonder where Jonathon gets some of his feisty spirit?

Laura had expectations for Jonathon as a young child and as the years went by she encouraged him to find himself. As he came to his own realization of what he was capable of doing, he realized he had to take on the fight. His mom did not need to fight for him any longer, he could do it himself.

Jonathon may not have stated it in words, but insisting on taking the anatomy class in high school was a personal battle for him. A battle he fought and won, not for the nay sayers, but for himself.

I shared Jonathon's story with graduate students in a family and disability course that I teach. I asked them for feedback at the end of the course and requested that the students tell me a specific element from the course content that impacted their understanding of disability.

A student, Lori shared:

"Isn't is all about what Jonathon said, it's all really about blah blah blah- we educators try to make students do blah blah, so they will be blah blah blah. We need to listen to Jonathon's advice and not have rigid expectations for what we want for them, but learn to listen and understand. I now have a better understanding about disability and its based on blah blah blah, thanks to Jonathon."

Marching On

Jonathon was involved in marching band in high school. For an individual with gait and vision issues this proved to be very challenging and interesting, to say the least. Jonathon had to remember fifteen different formations and simultaneously play his instrument. In his freshman band season he was given schematics to follow, and he would memorize the various formations. In his second year in band, the director only gave out little slips of paper with the formations and the steps had to be counted out without a diagram. Jonathon realized that the section leader had the schematics. He explains: "I was like, come here, let me see that, give me a copy of that...I asked for help."

The band gave Jon an honors grade, club membership, but mostly a social group and self-confidence. Band was an activity he would not have been able to join when he was younger. Through hard work, asking for help when he needed it, and keeping a schedule in place, he was able to participate. His band mates never knew that as soon as he got home from band he had breathing treatments, dinner, and exercises, and then he was in a body cast for the next twelve hours. As Jonathon shared with me, it put a deep dent in any social life outside of school. The band meant more to him than anyone knew. Jonathon said: "The band was like a breath of fresh air for me, like Newman is now."

Newman Center is Jonathon's refuge in the college experience. It is there that he has found self-worth, and has been given the opportunity to take on leadership roles. He has reaped the benefits from having a true friend. I asked Jonathon about his friends at the Newman Center.

S.:   So you have found friends at the Newman Center?

Jon: Yea, people are just nice. I had a good friend I got to
           know. We played video games together. We met on
           retreat, and we got together and played video games
           and watched movies together after the retreat... She
           liked science fiction, it was kinda creepy, she'd call
           and say come watch this movie with me and I'd go
           and there would be giant rats or something. I was
           watching it for like half an hour and I told her...
           that's enough. All this stuff is crazy! She graduated,
           that made me a little sad, but there will be a new
           group in February.

Jonathon's confidence has grown because of the positive experiences at Newman Center. He found a true friend. Another human being sought him out because she enjoyed his company. Although his friend graduated and is no longer close by, Jonathon is now open to making new friends. He is beginning to be "of the community" (Bogdan & Taylor, 1982) at 22 years old.

Looking Back; Moving Forward

Jonathan and I discussed the factors that have led him to be the person he is today. He is walking, talking, driving, on the Dean's list at his college, and is living and thriving on his own. As a young adult, he realizes his parents had a great deal of influence on the person he has become. He explained: "My parents had a lot of influence on me, because my dad is a hard worker, and that plays off on me. My mom always has to get everything done, done, done, and that plays off on me. It is a powerful combination." I asked him to tell me more about his parent's influence and how he has surpassed anyone's expectations.

S.:   So your parents had a big influence on your achievements...

Jon: Yea, My parents were in defiance, they believed... like you never know, the truth is you never know.

S.:   So did you ever think deeply about that, that no one at first expected you to live?

Jon: Yea, I think about it. Up in De Kalb at church one day, they were like... it's kinda amazing really who we all are...it was like wow, and that really made me think.

S.:   So you do not focus on your disabilities?

Jon: No, people I know want to focus on the disability instead of just what you need. It's like stereotyping... it's like he has blah, blah, blah so he must need blah, blah, blah. We have to treat him blah, blah, blah. And my theory is let him try. Maybe he will need help and maybe he won't. And labels... with labels comes expectations, and you don't want to do that unless you want some cranky parents mad at you.

Jonathon understands that people with disabilities often are victims of stereotypical labels assigned to them by people in society. Jackie and

Chuck were victims of "blah, blah, blah" as Jonathon so eloquently stated. People looked at them and assigned a particular set of descriptors to define them. There is a rhizomic connective strand that unites Jonathon to Jackie and Chuck, they are all people who defied the odds and did not give in to the stereotype. Jonathon is able to express this defiance in his own voice.

Jonathon has a very matter of fact approach to his abilities. Over and over again he says, "It is what it is." He uses support when he needs it, and if he does not require support, he is not afraid to let people know. Currently, in his college setting, he has extra time allowed for tests and the use of a calculator for all math work. Jonathon shared with me that he cannot perform mathematical equations at all. He does not even know 6 x 3 if you ask him, but he can solve any equation, even algebraic, when given a calculator. He said scan tron tests are still a problem for him, so someone will input his answers for him. Jon also wanted me to know that he is getting better at scan tron tests and he may be able to do them on his own soon.

With Jonathon everything is planned. He researched the expectations for many careers in the health care field before he found one that best suited him. He is currently dually enrolled at a junior college and a major university taking course work in clinical laboratory science. Jonathon hopes to be a medical researcher. He always goes beyond the expectations in his course work. If a professor mentions a movie or book in class, he will go and watch the movie or read the book. He loves to learn. He has set particular educational and social goals for himself. Both he and his mom shared with me that he had two main goals this year; to live on his own and to become more social. He has flourished living on his own, so this semester he is focusing on his socialization goal.

Jonathon is very eager to learn. He has a variety of interests; enjoying the computer, old time photography, the intricacy of cells and diseases, and posting quirky things he has discovered on his Face Book page. He gets very consumed in particular concepts. Laura said in many ways he is almost like a genius, consumed by things he finds interesting. She said he is the opposite of "what they expected at first." It is like he operates on a different plane. She explained "His interests are pretty out there. I do not think of him having a disability, but then his interests are so out there, that he is almost too smart, but that is like a disability too. Most people are not interested...I'm not interested, that does not help the social situations."

Disability is not a term the family ever embraced. Laura said, "We never allowed that term disability cause there was not going to be a pity party, and if you think you have a disability, you'll have one. He was always on an IEP. It was there to get him what he needed. Even now he gets support for what he needs, he doesn't take advantage." Laura's entire philosophy is steeped in normalcy. Life is what you make it. Like Laura and Jonathon say, "it is what it is."

My grandmother, Mrs. E. and Laura are all mothers who took on the fight for their children. These three strong women are rhizomically connected through viewpoints, determination, and dispelling the stereotypes that were placed on their children. As a child, Laura was connected to my grandmother; she affectionately called her Mere, just as we did as her grandchildren. She was in and out of our house throughout her childhood and had a comfortable connection with my grandmother and Jackie. Laura spent much time playing at Debbie's and Chuck's house, as well as being supervised by Mrs. E. Laura and I were always bringing our little sisters places with us. Just as my mom took her sister Jackie to school or to the store in the 1940's, Laura took her little sister Mary up town with us, and I would bring my little sister Colleen. Laura often held Colleen's hand walking up town as a child, and as adults 20 years later, she held Colleen's hand once again as she gave Colleen advice about therapists and programs for Jamee. Laura, as the mother of Jonathon, is a thread in the rhizomic connective strand of four mothers linked generationally through disability. Jonathon, the self proclaimed pirate, has benefited because of the determined strength of his mother, Laura.

Jonathon is a pirate as he steers across the sea of life. He is a master manipulator not only in controlling his right and left hand, but manipulating and adjusting to whatever life has thrown in his way. Just as a pirate has his weapons to fend off enemies with whom he comes in contact, Jonathon has pulled out his weapons when necessary to ward off his adversaries. The enemy was disguised as disability labels, or social expectations, or mean classmates, but Jonathon took them on in his own pirate way. The pirate lives.

The Pirate Lives

The pirate is still navigating the high seas of life as only a pirate can. Two years after the initial interviews with Jonathon much has changed in his life. The pirate, Jonathon, has mastered the turbulence of the sea of life. He has ridden the waves and is now coasting on a new life level. Life is much like the eb & flow of the ocean;the ups and downs, high tides and low tides. Jonathon has faced some treacherous waters, but utilizing his self-proclaimed pirate skills, he has emerged to find himself on a different level. He is embarking on a whole new phase in his life, one he has created through his tremendous determination and strong will.

Jonathon is currently completing his clinical experiences for his degree. In May of 2012, he will graduate with a bachelors degree in Clinical Laboratory Science. One of his hospital clinical sites has even contacted him for an interview to continue to work in the hospital lab upon graduation. With Jonathon's degree in this area of medical science, he could apply to medical school if he chooses. This is the same "special ed" student who was almost kept out of anatomy class in high school.

Laura, Jonathon's mom, provides me with regular updates on his latest accomplishments. She is obviously proud of her son, yet she maintains the same matter of fact attitude that has sustained her throughout Jonathan's childhood and now his young adulthood. Jonathon is an accomplished pirate, but Laura has been a great captain, quietly, but forcefully steering the ship of Jonathon's young life. Letting him jump into the high waves, but being there to encourage him when he begins to go under. She pushed him,but she also let him know it was okay to ask for a life jacket, if he needed one.

Laura has a message for those who tried to curtail Jon's dream:

"This just goes to show you that nobody can tell you what you can or cannot do. People can control their own lives."

If Jonathon has listened to the advice of the so-called experts, he never would be the person he is today. His life is steeped in opportunity. His prospects for the future are positive, but most importantly, he has made the choices for himself.

As Laura reflects on the past she has some additional advice for those who think they know:

"What educators and other professionals need to remember is that they themselves don't know what the future holds."

Laura shared that parents want and need information, but the information should be real, not someone's opinion. For some reason many professionals seem to be compelled to share the worst possible scenario with parents in regards to their child with a disability. Such professionals were the ones who sent Jonathon home to die as an infant or said he would never walk or talk; the teacher who insisted he had to tie his shoe her way, or the counselor that did not want him to enroll in the high school anatomy class. Laura continued:

"Facts are important for parents to know when they are based on realism or can offer true options. Give me information that I can do something with, the rest keep to yourself."

"So what should I tell them in the conclusion, Laura?" I was interested to hear her feelings now that this journey we have been on is ending as far as this version of our story. I love when Laura shares her thoughts.

"Remind everyone that they should not give parents such bleak outlooks, sometimes all a parent wants to know is that their child is happy and their child is doing everything they are capable of."

Jonathon is living on his own, in a home by himself. He enjoys his independence and while he had a roommate in the past, he relishes having his own domain now. He continues to be involved in a church social group, but has changed groups. The group he is involved with now, is more open and welcoming. Some of the members of his former Christian group became judgmental and dictative. Some of the "well meaning" Christians from the first group started telling Jonathan how he should act, who he should talk to and what he should believe. Jonathon told me,

"You know how I was going to Egypt with my dad, these girls from the group,they told me my fascination with the pyramids and Egypt was sinful."

"Really?" I was thinking the girls were crazy and judgmental. How ridiculous!

"Yeah, they said it was sinful and against the church because my interest was like worshipping false gods. Those girls were stalking me, just because I'm interested in ancient history. I had to get away from those crazy people."

Jonathon now socializes with a Universal Christian group which embraces individuality and acknowledges that everyone has qualities to contribute. They are not telling Jon what to do. For now this works for him and keeps him socially involved. He can continue to help others but within a group more aligned to his personal philosophy. Jonathon does not need anyone to tell him what he should do or think. He has worked at being an independent person and enjoys being part of a group which understands and embraces independent thinking.

Jonathon's spirit has helped him become the man he is. The pirate in him led him on many adventures. With Laura navigating the ship (with emotional support from her husband, Steve) with her strong common sense, Jon was able to manipulate the situation at hand to make things work for him. I know Jonathon and his parents will be so proud when he walks across the stage to receive his degree. I can imagine Jonathon thinking "I showed them." and Laura saying "It is what it is."; her favorite line. I personally think whatever Jonathon was able to accomplish himself, Laura would have been proud.

The pirate does not just live, he thrives. His life is still ahead of him. I'm looking forward to watching it unfold.

CHAPTER SIX

Home Girl

Jamee,1991

Jamee loves her home. She enjoys the routine of her life and the warmth of her comfy couch. As a person with a limited vocabulary, Jamee does have her words which frequent her repertoire, which she extols loud and clear. Jamee loudly bellows "home" when she has had enough shopping in the mall, is ready to leave a birthday party or has had enough at school. She will also say "home" with a more demanding style when she wants someone else to go home. If she wants to get on with her life and she thinks a person may be interfering with her routine, she has no problem telling that person, whether it be her grandmother, a favorite cousin, or her sister's friend to go "home." Home is her sanctuary. She enjoys cuddling on the couch before bed every night with her mom, or sitting at the end of the kitchen table reading her teen magazines, working on a puzzle, or listening to her CD player. Home is Jamee's lived space. It is the place where she is comfortable, protected and loved. Van Manen (1990, p.102) tells us that "home reserves a very special place experience, which has something to do with the fundamental sense of our being." Home is where Jamee shows her authentic self. Her temporal landscape, rooted in her comfortable surroundings, provides her with a grounded perspective on life. Jamee is a home girl and this is her story.

Rhizomic Links

By virtue of her year of birth in 1991 and her place in this connective rhizome, Jamee has reaped the benefits of the rich soil which has been watered by the experiences of those who have come before her in time. Once upon a time there were three young girls living in the 1960's who were linked by proximity, friendship and disability. These three girls; Laura, Debbie, and Sharon (me) are connected intricately with Jamee via the offshoots of the rhizomic experiences that have connected our lives through the generations. Jamee is the great- granddaughter of Dorothy, the courageous mother of Jackie who was determined to defy the social constructs of disability imposed on her in the late 1930s.

Stubborn will power and steadfast determination flows through the blood of Dorothy's granddaughter Colleen, the mother of Jamee, as she advocates for choices for her daughter. Colleen never knew our grandmother Dorothy (Mere), she was only 2 years old when she passed away, but when I look at my sister, Jamee's mother, I see my grandmother's sense of control, strong will, and dominance. There is also an eerie aesthetic connection between Colleen and my grandmother. Colleen is the only one in our family to look like Mere. She resembles my grandmother more than my mother or any of the other grandchildren. Both Colleen and Mere having green eyes, dark hair, left-handedness, and similar facial characteristics and body structure. It is almost as if Colleen had some predisposition to be Dorothy in another time to raise a child with a disability.

Colleen, Jamee's mother, walked up town with Laura, Debbie, Chuck, and I as a young child. We shared lived space and temporality as we encountered our childhood world. Colleen played in Chuck's yard and shared swing time with him. Growing up as Jackie's niece, and sharing personal space with Jackie for over 20 years, gave Colleen an understanding of living with and loving a person with an intellectual disability. Laura, who held Colleen's hand on many of our uptown walks or pushed baby Colleen around in her stroller with me, is now intimately connected with Colleen, one mother to another mother, both having a child with a disability. By giving birth to Jonathon four years previous to Jamee, Laura has been very helpful to Colleen, providing her with the names of orthopedic specialists and programs to support Jamee. Three girls, three families connected through the generations and still growing; continuing the rhizomic connections established between the fences of our youth.

Waiting; Waiting For What?

"I don't know Aunt Sharon, all I remember from when I was little about Jamee was waiting."

I am interviewing my niece, Jenna, Jamee's older sister and she is trying to pull words from her heart to come out of her mouth.

"I don't know, this is so hard. People don't usually ask me about Jamee like this."

Jenna starts to cry and she takes small breaths trying to stop herself.

"It's ok Jen, do you want to stop?" I feel bad that I am causing so much emotion.

"No, I can do this."

(Deep breath) "So I remember sitting in the waiting rooms at the doctor's offices, I think, or maybe therapy sessions. It all blends together."

"It was probably both, your mom was taking Jamee all over trying to get answers." I was talking in an effort to help Jenna calm.

"I was always waiting. I had my bag of stuff. Books, dolls, games, scraps of paper I would bring my bag, take stuff out and play by myself."

"I remember your bags, we teased you about becoming a bag lady. You always were with Jamee and you always had a bag over you shoulder."

"My bags, Jamee and waiting, it's not just a memory, it's a feeling. Waiting, just waiting, waiting for what, I don't know."

Waiting, not knowing, scared, unsure, questions... This was the life of my sister, her husband and Jenna. From the minute Jamee was born, the family was in a state of "wait".

Jenna was four when Jamee was born, while she really did not understand what worries her parents may have had about Jamee, Jenna felt something was bothering her parents. There was this aura of uncertainty which hung over the family, something that could be felt, but difficult to specifically name. Jenna felt it, and her parents, Colleen and Bob, were living it.

As soon as Jamee was born, Colleen noticed that her baby was very shaky. Jamee kept trembling. Her Apgar scores were in the normal range, but Colleen wondered to herself why Jamee was trembling.

The nurses cleaned baby Jamee and wrapped her tightly in white and blue hospital blanket. Like any new mother Colleen unwrapped the tightly wrapped child so she could take a good look at her second daughter. Once Jamee was unwrapped, Colleen noticed that her tiny hands were turned in and the wrists were facing up and Jamee's little fingers were hanging from her wrists in a weird manner and shaking. Her right hand was even more turned in than her left. It was as if her little fingers were bellowing in the breeze, just hanging there gently moving back and forth.

When the nurse came back to check mom and baby, Colleen showed the nurse Jamee's hands. The nurse looked at her charts and told Colleen that the family general practitioner, Dr. Tom, was called when Jamee was born. The nurse explained that she was sure he would be in to give baby a thorough check up. Colleen waited anxiously to hear what the doctor would say about her daughter. Dr. Tom entered Colleen's hospital room and congratulated her about the birth of her daughter. He then sat down and talked with her about Jamee's examination. He talked about her muscle tone, and her reactions. He had certainly taken note of her shaky hands. At the end of his verbal checklist of what he noticed, he said

"Based on my years of taking care of babies I think she may have Cerebral Palsy. Let's watch her and we can talk at her office visit next week."

He was speaking in a calm, comforting tone, but Colleen was no longer caring how he was talking but what said.

Dr. Tom left and she was in her hospital room all alone crying and her OB, Dr. Ray, came in.

"What's wrong Colleen. Are you in pain?"

Colleen was crying more, caught her breath and said, "Dr. Tom just left and said Jamee has cerebral palsy."

"That's ridiculous, you can't just diagnose that so easily. Let me get a pediatrician over." Dr. Ray said, "I'm going to contact Dr. Wu, and don't worry, ok? We'll figure this out."

Shortly after that conversation occurred, at the hospital, Colleen called me at home.

"Shar, Dr. Tom said Jamee has CP, you know how her hands were shaking..." but I cut her off.

"What? He's crazy. How can he say that so quick, you have to look at a lot of things to determine CP." (I was talking louder and fast; not sympathetic, but ticked off).

"I know, I know. Dr. Ray just came in and he said he shouldn't have said that, He's getting a pediatrician in to check her out."

Colleen still sounded like she was crying.

"Col, it will be ok, you'll see. She looked good expect for her hands, there must be a reason for that. Want me to come up there?"

"No, it'll be ok. I'm going to the nursery. I just need to see her, then I'll see when Dr. Wu, the pediatrician will come to check her over."

I hung up and was fuming at Dr. Tom. He was our family doctor, he should know better. He had taken care of my parents and was good with my dad until his death. He met me at the office at 11pm at night when my son, Tim, had a high fever as a baby. He had diagnosed a birth defect in my husband and recommended treatment that basically saved his life. But no one can mess with my little sister. His saying Jamee had CP felt personal, it felt as if he had hurt our family. I was too full of anger to think straight. Rather than think clearly about Jamee's physical issues, I focused my energy at being pissed of at the doctor. It was definitely a "kill the messenger" moment.

Dr. Wu came in to look at Jamee, Colleen was right there when he looked her over. He did not think she had cerebral palsy but recommended that Colleen and Bob take Jamee to Children's Hospital in downtown Chicago so they could look at her hands.

Colleen felt better but still wondered why Jamee was so shaky. She called for an orthopedic appointment at Children's Hospital. They had an opening in two weeks. Colleen wished she could get in sooner to get answers.

Colleen did not realize at that time that she would be spending the rest of her life waiting. Life with Jamee **was** and **is** a series of waiting.

Jenna had said, "Waiting for what? I don't know?"

The waiting was and is different depending on the circumstance at the moment. After waiting for the test results from Children's Hospital, it was determined that physically Jamee's hands and wrists were fine. The orthopedic specialists concluded that her hands may have been turned in and shaky because her hands were "tucked in" in utero. So Colleen accepted their expert opinion. The waiting for answers was over for a couple of months.

Colleen and the immediate family began to notice that Jamee was not developing typically. She had a sweet smile but was very complacent during daytime hours. At night she would cry and let out loud screams as if she was in pain. Night after night, Colleen paced back and forth holding her baby in her arms and crying with Jamee. Jamee started throwing up all her formula; she would drink and it would fly out.

Dr. Wu determined it was reflux and sent Colleen to a pediatric gastroenterologist to treat the acid reflux condition. Colleen waited to find answers to cure her baby's pain. Colleen also told Dr. Wu that Jamee seemed different from her sister. She explained that she did not move around and didn't try to grab things.

He said to Colleen, "Oh mommy all children are different. Jamee's fine."

Colleen knew something was not fine.

"But I was 23 years old and they made me think it was me. I knew, I felt it, they thought I was this stupid, young mother. I was starting to think I was crazy."

At 7 months, Jamee still was behind on all milestones, she wasn't sitting up, and she was still shakey at times. So finally Dr. Wu suggested an MRI of her brain. Colleen didn't want to have a poor diagnosis for her daughter, but she remembered Laura had a son with a brain condition, maybe Jamee had one, too. At the very least now, possibly the doctor would believe her, if there was physical proof, and Jamee could get some help.

Colleen and Bob nervously waited for the results of the test. The neurologist called with results.

"Great news mom, every thing looks normal." Colleen did not know what to think.

"I thought I'm losing it. I've taken her to all these specialists and no one has answers. They are suppose to know; they are the professionals. I tried to trust them, but Jamee needed something, she needed help, something was wrong."

Colleen waited for Jamee's twelve month physical and approached Dr. Wu again. Jamee did not crawl and could not roll over. Dr. Wu now said Jamee exhibited "failure to thrive" and was malnourished due to all the reflux issues.

Jamee was referred to Easter Seals for physical therapy sessions. Bob brought the paperwork for insurance to cover Jamee's therapy and waited for reimbursement. Jamee was denied coverage for therapy because "failure to thrive; possibly developmentally disabled" did not match their diagnostic codes for insurance coverage.

"Jamee was getting older and I knew she needed help. As a mother you want to do what is best for your child, I was losin' it, someone needed to figure this out."

For nine months more, Colleen, baby Jamee and big sister Jenna went to more specialists to get answers, help, services, therapy; just to get something.

Colleen brought Jamee to a new pediatric gastroenterologist who questioned Colleen about Jamee's previous treatment for reflux. He explained that her reflux was chronic and that she should have had surgery at 6 months old which would have corrected the condition. Colleen showed him all the paperwork from the past hospitalization and treatments Jamee had been through.

Jamee, at 19 months, had a surgical procedure called a nissen fundoplication which basically wrapped her esophagus around the stomach so she would no longer throw up her food. In surgery the doctor noted that her esophagus was full of scarring from the first 19 months of her life living with acid reflux. When Colleen heard this it made her sad, angry and frustrated that her poor baby girl had been through so much pain.

"It wasn't like I didn't tell them. I kept taking her to doctors. I knew something wasn't right."

The new gastroenterologist discussed Jamee's "diagnostic" issues with Colleen. Colleen told him how Jamee was often denied services and insurance coverage because she did not have a disability diagnosis.

The doctor suggested since Jamee was in the hospital anyway, recovering from the surgery, if Colleen would like he would call in a developmental diagnostician to evaluate Jamee.

After a full diagnostic review it was determined that Jamee had the attributes of a child with Cerebral Palsy.

Colleen had waited for 19 months to get answers so that Jamee could get help. She had waited for months yet she had received an answer the day after Jamee was born.

Dr Tom, the family's general practitioner, had correctly diagnosed Jamee's "condition" shortly after birth.

We all had so much anger with Dr. Tom; we had felt he made a rash decision. Colleen initially disregarded what he said because the general consensus from the other doctors and nurses at the hospital when Jamee was born was to get a more learned opinion. Since she wanted to do the right thing, she sought advice from professionals. Colleen received opinions from a pediatrician, a pediatric gastroenterologist, a pediatric neurologist and an orthopedic specialist from Children's Hospital. She just wanted to do the best for her child.

"I went to them because I was told they were the best." Colleen shakes her head remembering Jamee's early months.

"I wish I knew then, what I know now. We should have listened to Dr. Tom, I guess. Maybe Jamee would have had help sooner. You do your best though, (as a mom), that's all you can do. Sometimes the professionals don't have all the answers."

Colleen continued:

"I get what Jenna said, waiting for what? We had no idea what to think or what we wanted, we just wanted someone to help Jamee. It's been a waiting game since she has been born. We still wait, just now we aren't waiting for what to call her disability, but we are still waiting for whatever Jamee needs next."

"We are always waiting."

Answers

As a young adult, Jenna is still patient and very worried about her sister. These feelings are temporally grounded in her personality and were fostered as a six year old big sister waiting for "something" to be revealed about her little sister. The worries and waiting continued and Colleen relied on the expertise of a mom (Laura) who understood and knew of resources to help Jamee.

Upon hearing of Colleen's frustration about doctors without answers at a family party, Laura told Colleen to take Jamee see Doctor T., a world renowned children's orthopedic specialist with a wonderful supportive demeanor. Jonathon was being treated by Dr. T. at the time and Laura was pleased with his expertise and compassion. The roots established as children between Colleen and Laura now led to possibilities for Jamee. Jamee was to see Dr. T. and he held the key to the door of services for Jamee.

Dr. T. (orthopedic doctor) said because of Jamee's low muscle tone and physical attributes, as well as the results provided by the evaluation conducted by the developmental specialist, Jamee would qualify for services under the diagnostic category of cerebral palsy. Jamee required a named disability and cerebral palsy served as a key to unlock the gates for therapeutic services and insurance support.

As much as Colleen dislikes labels and always refers to Jamee as Jamee, not by any descriptive attributes, she desperately needed a medical diagnosis for Jamee to receive therapy and early education services. The medical model of disability (Trent, 1994) dominates all social service agencies, and people, even 18 month old Jamee, must be coded correctly in order to receive the services they require for the necessities of life. Dr. T. was willing to put a diagnostic name on a piece of paper and Jamee reaped the benefits.

The world of social institutions, such as the medical community, service providers and insurance companies, is difficult to navigate. There is constant struggle as the parents of children with disabilities try to go forward, but keep hitting their heads against the fences of bureaucracy. Professionals have the privileged role of serving as the gate keepers, by virtue of their knowledge and position in society. The parents and the people with disabilities are truly the ones with the knowledge. They are immersed in the corporality and spatiality of the lived experience of disability, but are frequently locked out of the process. Children with disabilities do not always receive the support they deserve because of who is making the decisions. Colleen, Laura, Mrs. E, and my grandmother often had to convince the gatekeepers to listen to them. Many of the so-called professionals turned a deaf ear to their demands. Jamee was young at this time of her story. Colleen, as her mother, was relieved to have Dr. T. open the gate of support, but there would be more fences and closed gates in the future.

Colleen recalled Dr. T. telling her "Momma who we have here is Jamee; we just do whatever we have to do to take care of her." Dr. T. was a connective strand of the rhizome added by Laura which linked the families. As time went on, it was Dr. T. who reminded Colleen she could not do it all. He told her to get babysitters and spend time with her husband. The entire family was supported by Dr. T. as Jamee went through surgeries. He was especially reassuring to Colleen and Bob telling them frequently of the wonderful job they were doing parenting Jamee. Dr. T. even convinced Colleen into taking Jenna (Jamee's older sister) on vacation all by herself. He told Colleen that siblings need time with their parents to be themselves not someone's brother or sister. I again link the present to the past and wish my grandmother and Mrs. E. had a Dr. T. in their lives.

Colleen felt all the concerns and worries she felt were medically based in the early 1990s, when Jamee was a toddler. I personally recall

192

more details of those times than Colleen. She may have tucked them into an emotional place she does not want to return to. I spent many days with Colleen and Jamee, visiting doctors and sitting in hospitals. When I would tell Colleen what I remembered with specific details during our conversations, she would reply "yea" that's right," but she did not expand on my revelations or make any additional comments. Colleen may choose to not remember those times, because she prefers to live in the temporality of present. She has never been a person who dwells on the past. Colleen is very much "into" today and the future. This could be for self preservation or it could be a personality trait. Having this attribute seems to help her negotiate the maze of scheduling for Jamee and living a life focusing on rhizomic possibilities of the future, rather than the negative aspects of the past.

Colleen said at some point Jamee had another MRI which showed a thinning of the brain stem. The doctors felt that this factor attributed to Jamee's motor and intelligence difficulties. She said it was "on her" to look for answers, but it was still medical. Colleen explains: "It was all medical then, we thought maybe Jamee would catch up, if we found the right information, she would be able to and no one said anything else. It was easier then, we were kind of going with the flow, but she was getting older and not catching up." Bob (her husband/ Jamee's Dad) was not sure about Jamee having a disability. There is a lack of research regarding fathers' reactions to having a child with a disability. However, fathers such as Michael Berube'(1996) and Philip Ferguson (2003) have written about their lived experiences raising a child with a disability. Research, however, does indicate that fathers have a more difficult time than mothers asserting their involvement with their child and professionals. The grief or uncertainty faced by a father is often times unexplained or not expressed (Herbert& Carpenter, 1997; Hornby, 1991; Rodrique et al., 1992). Forced by societal expectations, Fathers must act as strong silent protectors remaining competent in a crisis situation (Carpenter, 2005; Tolston, 1977). With his quiet uncertainty, Bob may have taken on a silent protector role.

"I couldn't help it", Colleen shared.

"I just took over… with all the medical stuff."

I heard Colleen say the words, "I just took over." I had heard Laura say almost the very same words when she described how she went about seeking support for Jonathon. This again demonstrates the connective strands linking mother to mother as they confront disability. Colleen also discussed her husband Bob not thinking Jamee had a disability. She said he was unsure because no one had provided exact information about the nature of her disability. Bob thought with therapy and getting the proper nutrition (since her reflux problems were now remedied) she would begin to catch up and start reaching developmental milestones. Colleen said she was not sure either, because they saw Jamee improving physically and she was trying to talk. Colleen and Bob were not so much denying Jamee's disability as much as they were looking at possibilities, always looking to support their daughter in her growth.

Colleen also revealed something very interesting by saying, "You are at the mercy of people who you "think" know more than you do."

"You are at their mercy, because you just do not know, and they make you doubt yourself. They are suppose to know."

A point of view exists in society whereby certain professional people such as medical doctors are thought to have all the answers. Colleen went seeking answers from these learned individuals and was instead coming to understand that they did not have the solutions after all.

At two and a half years old Jamee was enrolled in an early childhood program.

"I am not sure how we found Joe Henry (an organization for children and adults with disabilities) but just when she was around two, we went together… I went with her, and then she went to the toddlers program herself. She loved that. It was a good place for her, just for part of the day." Colleen smiled during the recollection of Jamee's first opportunity to go to preschool.

In 1994, two and a half year old, Jamee is beginning to be social. She enjoyed the opportunity to go to school, sharing lived space with other children. Jamee's personality was becoming apparent. She was always smiling when she was around people. "Hi" was one of her first clearly articulated words and she would say it loud and clear, hoping to receive a response.

Jenna recalls at that point she and Jamee played together.

"Mom and I would put Jamee in the stroller, I was what... 6...7 years old... and we lived in town then... and we'd go for walks... We'd go to Budnick's to buy things and look in windows. I liked to take her for walks. We mostly went to the library at least twice a week. I liked books... I'm not sure if she liked them as much as me, but I liked to read to her. I'd take her down the block to the library up the elevator and we'd sit in the corner... and I'd read out loud to her. She'd sit and listen...I'd read her all kinds of books. There the two of us were, tucked in the corner all by ourselves, behind the big shelves, me and Jamee reading books".

Colleen shared similar memories:

"I remember when Jenna was little she would walk all over with her; they'd go to town and to the library. Sometimes Jenna's girlfriends would go with them. They met new girls at the library and, and then they would come and go to the library with them, too. And Jamee was starting to move more then. She and Jenna would play up in Jenna's bedroom, and Jamee would crawl, sit and play. They would play for hours with Jenna doing all the talking and Jamee happy to be with her."

Jenna, like Doris and Debbie, was often with her younger sibling. There is a difference in that Jenna asked to take Jamee with her. The situation was different with Doris and Jackie and Debbie and Chuck, they were told to take their siblings with them, and then it became a matter of fact, where they went, their siblings went, too. Both Jenna and Colleen displayed a happy reflexive demeanor when they talked about Jenna and Jamee's excursions to the library and the stores down the block. Colleen and I began to discuss topics more serious in nature.

"So you were beginning to realize the extent of her disabilities... how did that make you feel? I was interested to hear Colleen's insights.

Colleen, struggling to answer.

"(Silence)... well... I wasn't into... you know... It wasn't how this could happen to me... I didn't ask why... I didn't ask why this happened to me, to Jamee. Maybe it was... (Silence) normal, having Jackie and Chuckie, too in my life and around. I used to play with Chuckie and swing on his swing... you know the one in the garage? ... You know it always was... and being with them... it wasn't like I didn't know... so it wasn't this... how did this happen to me kind of crap? It just... is."

Colleen was very matter of fact as she talked about her feelings, pausing to gather her thoughts, but very to the point. Parents react in a myriad of ways when they realize that their child has a disability. Some theorists propose that parents go through the classic stages of grief; denial, blame, fear, guilt, mourning, withdrawal, rejection, and acceptance (Prout & Prout, 2000). Others dismiss this as too simplistic, and the reactions of parents are as varied as the parents themselves (Stoneman & Gavidia-Payne, 2006). None of the parents in this story went through the classic grief stages. They all faced the reality of having a child with a disability differently, but none of them got caught up in grief for long or kept asking "why me?" My grandparents, the E.'s, Laura and Steve, and Colleen and Bob, all sought answers about their children, but all of them were forward thinking. The rhizome symbolizes linkages. The families are generationally connected by connective rhizomic strands dwelling on possibilities for their children.

School Time

Colleen and I entered into a conversation about Jamee's school years. At three years old Jamee entered an early childhood program at her local public school. She then attended the public school near her home for kindergarten and the primary grades as well.

"Again, you are at the mercy of people you know, um, think more than you do and you trust them. But she had a good early childhood program and good kindergarten and then they tried to include her in first grade and that didn't work. I didn't care what they labeled her for school. I hate that word retarded, though. I just wanted her to get what she needed."

Auntie Special Education Teacher (me) leapt into action at this point. I spent time with Colleen at IEP meetings, special meetings to determine why the teachers were not following Jamee's academic plan, and observing in the classroom and her resource program. The special education director proudly showed me how Jamee was "pushed in" with the 1st grade. I sat in the back of the class to observe. The class stood for the Pledge of Allegiance and the teacher said "Jamee start the pledge." Jamee pushed the flag icon on her Dynovox (communication device) and the programmed robotic voice said the pledge with the class.

The remainder of the morning Jamee sat in the back corner of the room with her one on one assistant. An oral reading lesson took place and each student orally read a short passage. While they read, Jamee played with animals and her assistant showed her some pictures. By the end of the 50 minute reading period, the toy animals and picture book were no longer of interest to Jamee. She let out some moaning sounds, and the assistant tried to calm her down, to no avail. Jamee began to pound her one hand on the desk and with the other she was pulling her hair. The Dynovox, Jamee's communication device was placed on the counter out of her reach.

The Dynovox was Jamee's means to communicate her wants and needs. It was also to serve as an educational support and was to have her reading words programmed into the device for her to participate in class work. By not providing access to her communication device, Jamee was not able to participate in class. Without the benefit of communication, Jamee was being fenced out of her education while sitting bodily in the class. Jamee was physically included, but the teachers did not have the understanding or training for her to really be included.

Despite the laws for access to equal education for students with disabilities developed when Chuck was in school, and reauthorized to be more inclusive while Jonathon was in elementary school, Dowling (2008) uncovered that many schools still had difficulty providing a learning situation to include all students, especially students with significant disabilities. In 1997, Jamee, at six years old, was considered "profoundly retarded" based on her school's IQ test, and "multiply impaired" because of her physical, motor and language difficulties. Jamee's school staff did not know or understand how to work with students with significant disabilities. The director of special education for the district at the time did not have an educational background. She had been trained as a school psychologist and her area of expertise was working with children with behavior difficulties. Jamee also had three special education teachers in one school year. The district was attempting to facilitate an inclusion program without training or a solid knowledge base pertaining to inclusionary practices. Jamee was a victim of their lack of understanding.

I had never seen Jamee this frustrated, not even when she was physically in a body cast. It was reported by school personnel that Jamee was trying to hit herself and bite herself. This was not the Jamee everyone saw in her home setting. The only way anyone could tell Jamee was bothered by something at home, would be when she would say "owe" or "no." School was not a comfortable place for Jamee. No matter how many meetings were held, the personnel at the local school could not find ways to teach Jamee, or include her so she was *truly* included. Colleen discusses the school situation.

"They called it inclusion, but she really wasn't included. She was physically with her class and the kids were nice to her, but they treated her carefully like... and she wasn't invited to anyone's birthday parties, she knew the other kids to see them, but she was with her assistant, separated mostly. Then it was meetings, phone calls, consulting with a lawyer, more meetings, more phone calls, tours of other programs and they finally let her go to school at Well Spring then. But it was a fight... and we tried to work it out. But in the end, it was better for her to be where the teachers and therapists knew what to do with her."

All of the back and forth with the school district took over two years. Colleen and Bob philosophically wanted Jamee in the community and at the local school, but Jamee was regressing instead of progressing. Much like the E.'s had looked for a school for Chuck in the 1960s, Colleen and Bob began to visit co-op programs and private schools for children with disabilities. They found Well Spring, which had been founded in the 1960s by a group of parents just as Chuck's school, Oak Valley. After Jamee had a negative school experience for three years, her parents were seeking an atmosphere where Jamee could have the spatiality of "at homeness" (Van Manen, 1990, p.102). They wanted to find a school program where the staff knew how to relate to Jamee's needs, provide her with choices and encourage her to communicate. With the financial support of the local school district, Jamee entered Well Spring as a third grader and she has remained at the school since then. Jamee is now a 12th grader and is still progressing academically, socially, and physically in her school setting.

School is now a stimulating place for Jamee. She has therapy sessions, reading, math, and vocational classes. Jamee uses the Dynovox to answer questions and complete her assignments. She touches picture symbols on a computer screen for all of her lessons. Her entire classroom is adapted so she can be an engaged learner. She has friends at school and like her Great Aunt Jackie, loves to name all the people in her class photo and yearbook. Jamee has been to prom, dances, and has been part of the pep club for her school's basketball games. She enjoys both the academic and social activities at school.

Home Girl at Home

Jamee is a young lady of few oral words, but much action. The best way to get an understanding of her lived experience was for me to share in the experience. I followed Jamee at school, "hung out" with her at home, and drove with her sister Jenna to one of Jamee's physical therapy sessions. I went to court with Jamee and her parents for guardianship proceedings, and watched her zoom down the slope at a ski club. I wanted to experience the existential of corporeality and be in the moment with her. I immersed myself in the life of Jamee.

In her home Jamee has her "spot" at the end of the kitchen table. Her wheel chair fits there perfectly. The table is where she likes to sit. Jamee rules the world from her spot. She asks people to come sit by her. She calls out "Shar nin" (the way she says Sharon), right here" as she points to the seat next to her. She points to a teen magazine and I look at pages with her, I read some of the text and we try to find her favorite Jonas Brother in the teen celebrity magazine. When I find her favorite guy, she yells "yeah!" and her arms go up in the air. I turn the page and ask her if we should look for Kevin, (she thinks he's the cutest) and she laughs so hard. She takes in a breath and her shoulders shake silently in laughter. After a bit, she has enough of magazine time, so she closes it up and says "done." She puts a CD in her player and begins to clap and move to the music. When I start to clap, she finds this hysterical and begins to laugh again.

At eighteen years old, Jamee is the kitchen table queen; from there she rules her home world. She does not have to stay there; she can ambulate through her house and go anywhere she wants. She has a bright pink and green bedroom that is decorated with girly teenage trinkets, and is filled with books, pictures, and games, but she enjoys the kitchen best which is the hub of the family activity. Jamee likes to be in the center of action. The end of the kitchen table is the perfect place for Jamee; she can see the whole main level of her house right from her chosen spot.

After awhile it is getting to be closer to dinner time, she looks up at her mom and asks, "Eat?" Colleen answers, "Not yet Jamee, almost, can you wait a bit?" Jamee nods yes. The phone rings, her mom answers. Jamee hears who is on the phone, and with a big breath she says "Grand-ma." Her mom nods yes, that is who it is. Jamee asks, "Talk?" "In a minute Jamee." After Colleen has finished talking she hands Jamee the phone. Jamee carefully switches it from one hand to the other and watches her own hand as she finds just the correct way to hold the phone. Then this loud "Hi" bellows through the house and phone. She then exclaims: "Graaand-mma, love you" (with another huge grin and a loud chuckle). She listens for a bit, nods her head while her grandma is talking, then after a moment she takes a dramatic breath and says "bby-yye" which is dragged out to be three syllables. After her mom hangs up the phone, she tells her mom, "Grandma, love her." "I know Jamee," her mom replies. One of the few full sentences in Jamee's vocabulary is "I love you."

Phone Calls and Table Fun

Jamee loves talking on the phone. She asks her mom to call people by pointing to the phone and saying the first name of whoever she wants to call. Jamee has a definite list of favorites. On the top of the list is her sister Jenna who is away at college. If Jamee wants to make a call, she thinks it should be "right now," another one of her verbal phrases. Her mom has to tell her at times that it is not a good time to call a particular person.

Her cousin, Amy talked about their phone conversations:

"We talk on the phone and she doesn't have to say anything. I will talk and she'll nod, then I say over the phone: "Quit nodding, I can't see you," and she'll laugh. We are good friends".

Jamee goes through kitchen table activity phases. For a while she will look at magazines, then for weeks she will work on puzzles, or alphabet letters. Currently she likes to color in coloring books. She meticulously colors every page the same way. She picks a crayon from the bin, (the big chunky type so she can grip them) and she colors back and forth using the same stroke on the top of the picture. She puts the crayon back slowly and ponders over the next choice saying, "Ummm" as she is in deep thought. She picks up the new crayon, turns the page and colors the same stroke. This continues over and over again turning, choosing, coloring; turning, choosing, coloring. She would finish the whole book if her mom did not redirect her to engage in another activity. On this particular day Colleen encourages her to put a CD in her player, and Jamee sits in her wheelchair dancing to the music.

Jamee has a small table in her room with all of her favorite items in reach. She chooses what she wants to do, puts the items on her lap and wheels into the kitchen, back to her favorite spot. She does not enjoy TV; it appears she likes to keep her hands occupied. She is definitely a creature of habit.

Schedules and Routines

Jamee has a very structured environment. Through the years her parents and sisters have come to understand that schedules and routines help Jamee negotiate her world. Traditionally, parents and educators have discovered that routine is an important element in alleviating stressful moments for children with disabilities (Springer, 2002). Within predictable schedules, parents can create conditions to assist their child in developing a sense of control and competence. Jamee is able to have control in her environment because of her routine. If Jamee does not have a schedule, or if someone fails to tell her of a schedule change, she becomes very upset. Predictability is an element which Jamee requires in all areas of life. Her sister, Jenna and her mother Colleen talked about Jamee's routine.

J.:   Everything with Jamee is a routine or on a schedule. She has to have it the same way. She will do something for weeks and weeks ... then she will do something different. Her daily routine does not vary either, like her "couch time" with Mom. Before bed every night she has to sit on the couch with my mom. Eating... sleeping... couch time ...it all has to be the same.

C.:   It's weird, she'll do something for months and really like it... and once it is over it is over. She won't want to do it all then...not even for a little while. She does not like to do a couple of activities or mix things up.

In both Colleen's and Jenna's interviews the subject of routine was a critical element.

J.:   Everything with Jamee has to be scheduled partly because it takes so long to do all the physical stuff: dressing, showers, eating, but partly because she needs the routine. If her routine changes or she does not know what to expect, she will get frustrated or cry. She can't explain why she is bothered so she will cry.

Jenna offered an explanation as to why Jamee is typically so calm and happy.

> J.: Jamee does so well and is happy most of the time because my mom is a scheduler. My mom has a way of getting things done. When Jamee gets home from school she has to charge her Dynovox every day... she just knows. Sometimes she freaks if her routine is changed. You have to tell her if there is a change.

Jamee's Dad, Bob, said how she had an emotional moment recently at school. The school staff rarely sees Jamee like that. They did not know what was going on. Her Dad believes she was upset because her teacher stopped in for a visit while she is on maternity leave, and did not stay. He said, "She loves Christine (her teacher) so much, she probably realized how much she missed her." If Jamee does have a meltdown or she "freaks out" as Jenna says, these emotional moments are typically easily remedied. Giving Jamee a hug, or singing a silly song at her, will usually bring an end to her sobbing. Jenna said any time Jamee "freaks out" it surprises people who never see this side of her, because she is usually so happy and easy going.

She's Easy

Jenna and I discussed her role as Jamee's older sister and the relationality between the two siblings. I asked Jenna then, how she would describe being Jamee's sister and her matter of fact reply was: "It's easy."

> J.: It is easy, sounds weird, but she is ... uh... easy on the eyes, she's pretty, she has a nice smile, my mom is...uh... she makes sure she dresses her cute, lets her pick out outfits. Sounds weird, but I think her being pretty makes it easier in some ways for her. She likes people, she likes people to talk to her...and she does not fight back, that's for sure. She's happy to be with you. It is easy to be with her.

People with disabilities have always been subjected to the gaze (Foucault, 1973). If someone looks a certain way or acts in a particular manner they are subjected to labels or categorization. Individuals with disabilities have been marginalized for decades (Shapiro, 1993). Jenna, as she discusses Jamee's physical appearance, is demonstrating an awareness of the how the world looks at people with disabilities. She may be correct in saying Jamee receives positive attention because she is pretty and is typically smiling.

When I told Colleen and Bob (Jamee's parents) that Jenna said Jamee's easy, they laughed, but they said she is, in a way, but then Bob said: "People do not see when she is not easy, when she won't get out of bed and she's swinging her arms at you." Jordan, Jamee's younger sister added: "Yea and when she refuses to take off her coat because she decides only Mom can do it and Mom is at work." Colleen said, "And all the physical stuff and the planning, it may look easy because we had to do a lot to get it that way."

> J.: Jamee's disability is easy in some ways 'cause we don't have to struggle. She really is easy going for the most part-it's her personality. Some parents I met through working with special rec (recreation) made a big thing about it----everything is their child … a real big thing….maybe it is because my parents aren't looking for answers anymore or trying to fix it. Jamee is herself, she's happy. Some parents may have a harder time, but my parents... well uh everyone treats Jamee the same. We don't baby her or belittle her. We just pick her up, put her in her chair and there we go. It's how it is.

Jenna described how she came to know many parents of children with disabilities through her work in special recreation, working in a summer program for children with autism, and in her clinical experiences in her occupational therapy program. She explained that she has met parents who kept trying to change their child or seem frustrated at their child's ability level. She acknowledged that her parents accept Jamee and her disability is part of her identity. Jamee's relationality with her family is reflected when Jenna said: "We just pick Jamee up, put her in her chair and there we go." This philosophy has benefited Jamee in that Jamee is valued for herself.

S.:   So I heard you say she's easy on the eyes or people look at her a certain way, have you experienced negative looks?

J.:   No actually, Jamee is even a buffer or a screener. I would not bring anyone around unless they would like Jamee; I have never had a friend that wasn't nice to her. Everyone at St. Cyril's (Jenna's grade school) growing up knew Jamee. I would never bring anyone home that would not be comfortable. I've never been in a situation where anyone was mean. Too nice, sometimes. She'd say" hug" and strange people at the store would try to hug her......(she laughs) we had to stop her from doing that, and some man tried to give her a hundred dollars, my mom said that it was not necessary and there were poor people with disabilities that could use it more. Little kids in the mall sometimes point or stare or ask their parents what is wrong with her, or why is she in a wheelchair. Some parents just tell the kids "sssh", but others say she needs a wheel chair to get around or she has a disability or whatever. If someone asked I'd explain to them, it's ok...it's just how she gets places.

Jenna, like other individuals with siblings with disabilities, judges others by how they act around her sister (Meyer, 1997; Strohm, 2005). She also discussed how adults are unsure how to respond to Jamee as they encounter her in the community. We talked about Jamee's use of a wheelchair for mobility purposes which led to discussions on Jamee's physical care.

Physical Issues

Jamee is 18 years old and weighs approximately one hundred and twenty pounds. It is physically taxing to get her in and out of her wheelchair, or into bed, or to help her on the toilet, or in the shower. Jamee requires assistance for all physical activities, since she can bear very little weight. Jamee had to undergo an operation for her severe scoliosis, and a rod was inserted to fuse her spine. Since this procedure five years ago, Jamee has lost some of her mobility and body strength. Jamee is the only person in this story who is not able to walk, or ambulate independently. The physicality relating to her disability is difficult for her family to deal with at times, and her care poses grave concerns for her future. I asked Jenna and Colleen about Jamee's physical care.

S.:   What about the physical care?

J.:   There is a lot and it is hard on my parents, she's bigger and she can't do even as much as she use to before her spinal rod. My dad...I worry his legs are already messed up from carrying her...the physicalness I think that is the hardest part...and my mom, I worry how can they always do this?

Colleen shares in the anxiety over the physical aspects of Jamee's disability.

C.:   It's harder now; she can't bear weight as well. I have a hard time, I am used to it. But what about the future? Who will do it for her? Even when we went to Disney World last summer and Jamee loves rides, but it was harder to get her in the seats and to be safe, her feet were hanging or she had posture issues.

Jenna is away at college and worries that something could go wrong with Jamee when she is away. Jenna began to cry and asked aloud:

"What will happen to her?" She told me how Jamee had swelling in her knee recently and was in a lot of pain. The doctors were unsure what the swelling was from. Jenna said "When she had that knee thing and I wasn't home, that freaked me out. I wasn't there (she started to cry again). I told Dave (her boyfriend) that no matter what, we have to be around Chicago, I can't not be in her life."

Jenna is not alone in her desire to share spatiality with her sister with a disability. The literature portrays evidence of siblings making critical life decisions based on their sibling. Examples include choosing a life partner based on the reaction to the disabled sibling, or choosing a permanent place of residence in the proximity of their sibling, or adding rooms to their homes to accommodate their brother or sister (Connors & Stalker, 2003; Meyer, 1997; Strohm, 2005). Jenna further discussed her concerns.

S.:   Being away from her is that difficult....

J.:   I worry... my parents, they do everything, my mom with all the organizing and my Dad he'll search and search to find whatever she needs. They both work to get everything she needs. And Jordan and I will do whatever Jamee needs. Jordan is good with Jamee. I don't know, I always felt old even when I was real young; I'm kinda like an old soul. I am not the typical college student. I do not know if that is because of Jamee or because of me. I just want Jamee happy, and to make choices. My mom gives her choices now, clothes and food and what she wants to do... whatever Jamee does in the future they have to give her choices....Jamee knows.

Jamee is very receptive. She understands language and she knows what she wants. Her family always gives her choices and honors her wishes. Due to Jamee's thin brain stem, she processes information slowly. People who do not know her, or do not understand why it takes her longer to process, do not always wait for her to answer. Waiting for Jamee to answer is critical to her self-actualization. Her family always offers her options. Jamee is included in both important and trivial decisions if they affect her life. Examples of big decisions are, asking her if she wanted to attend camp for a week or if she wanted to switch to a power wheelchair. When Jamee needed a new communication device, the family and school staff had her try a variety of devices before Jamee decided on the one she wanted. Choices are given throughout Jamee's day. She chooses her clothing, what she wants to do for fun and what she wants to eat. The family worries that when others take care of her they do not let her choose, and instead choose for her, or just do whatever is the easiest or quickest, and do not honor Jamee's choices. Choice making is a key part of Jamee's and her family's goals for her future.

S.: So what are your concerns for the future?

J.: Depends on the options, financially, federal funding, maybe she will have to live with me. I don't know, that is why we have to come up with something. So she is ok…happy.

Career Influences

Jenna majors in occupational therapy in college and she is on track to become an occupational therapist within the next year. Jamee has been receiving occupational therapy at school and privately at home since she was two years old. I discussed Jenna's career choice with her.

S.: So do you think Jamee has influenced your choice of becoming an occupational therapist?

J.: Well… maybe, I didn't watch and then say I want to be one of those someday. I did the business thing

took classes, worked at a bank and didn't like it. I
like working with Special Rec. (special recreation). I
volunteered the whole summer of eighth grade and
then I worked there in high school. I had started
working there volunteering with Jamee. So I guess
it started with her. I know I am more understanding because of Jamee. She has a lot to do with how
I understand disability... I do know... I am trying to
figure out how to say this... People in class with me,
the way they describe or talk about disability as if
they are looking in or over it or something or they
are better or normal and disability is over there, removed from them. With me it's just well normal, not
separate. Maybe Jamee and Aunt Jackie made me
think differently; I did not realize it 'til I heard how
they talk.

Jenna is in coursework with students who are aspiring to be occupational and physical therapists. These are the people who will be
working with individuals with disabilities in the very near future. Jenna
has come to the realization that they have been socially constructed to
look at disability in a particular way. In this philosophical view, disability is somewhere over there. It is not me, I can remove myself from it
and stand over here and look at it, but I do not need to immerse myself
in it, because I am not disabled. Jenna's classmates have been trained
as members of the dominant society to look at disability through a
medical model lens (Gliedman & Roth, 1980). Looking at disability in
this manner, they can analyze what is "wrong" with a person with disabilities, and possibly help them, but they do not see the whole person,
just a problem needing to be fixed. Jenna sees disability as life, not a
separate entity. Disability has always been part of Jenna's lived experience. She did not fully realize how the world looked at disability until
she went to college.

Jamee's and Jenna's Cousin Amy, my daughter, changed careers and became a special education teacher. I also asked her if her career choice was made because of Jamee and Jackie.

S.: Did you become a Special Ed. teacher because of them do you think?

A.: Um, yeah… I think. I got involved in Special Rec. when I was in high school because I knew Jamee went to that and I liked hanging out with Jamee. I always was kind of interested in what you did when I was growing up and I just like doing it. I never really thought I wanted to do it as a career, I just felt like doing it for fun. Even all through college, I just worked at Well Spring (Jamee's school) during the summer because I thought people treated Jamee with respect there. I wanted to treat other people's kids and family members with respect. I wanted to help out in any way that I could. I think slowly, but surely, it kind of evolved, like especially when I was away from it for awhile…like how much I just felt like that was what I was supposed to do.

Amy goes on to describe a moment that was like an epiphany when she went to a fine arts fair at Well Spring. She was listening to students singing who she had worked with in the summer and Amy felt like they were singing to her.

A.: And I just remember watching all the kids that I used to work with in Kelly's class. They were singing that little song "I love you more" and I was just thinking about… man what am I doing with my life? And all I heard was… as if there were no other words in the song, but a part in it that said, "Take a look around you, I'm spelling it out one by one" That next week is when I enrolled in my Masters program for special

ed. So, I mean, I just think it's …I just see people for
being people… Jackie and Jamee, they're people.

Amy was very close to my Aunt Jackie and always had a connective
relationship with Jamee. One of Jamee's early words was "Amy" with a
loud emphasis on the "A" sound. Jamee can spell very few worlds, but a
word she can spell is "Amy." As an adult, Amy calls Jamee on the phone
just to talk, and when she was a child she would walk over to Colleen's
house to be with Jenna and Jamee after school. Like Jenna, Amy has
shared Jackie's and Jamee's lived experience; she has been intimately connected to disability all her life. The rhizome symbolizes the linkages;
roots grounded in family and disability. Jackie and Jamee have linked
Jenna and Amy to their lived experiences through proximity, relationality and love.

Jamee's Future

Jenna, at 21 years old is concerned about Jamee's future and has
begun to think deeply about life's consequences. Colleen and I had revealing conversations about her concerns and fears for Jamee's future.
The E.'s had difficulty facing the future and making emotional and financial decisions regarding Chuck. Colleen and Bob coming from a
more open perspective have already begun to prepare for Jamee's future.
The immediate and extended families have all been involved in planning for Jamee's future. Although Colleen is working on preparing for
Jamee's future, this is by no means an easy task. This process has brought
emotions and worries back to the surface, which had been safely tucked
away for a number of years. This is a temporal reaction. The past affects
the future and the present moment. Colleen is forward thinking, yet her
hopes and fears are rooted in her past.

S.:   Jenna shared her worries about Jamee's well-being in
        the future, what are your concerns for the future?

C.:   Going through all his guardianship stuff now is like
        the beginning again… all this uncertainty and the

labels, I never minded what they had to call Jamee as much as the uncertainty or fear. The guardianship brings it all back. The IEP meetings when people didn't know, the three-year evaluations when they say, your child is profoundly retarded. What's that, what does that mean? It's disconcerting not to know something definite and I need to know there's a plan; that she will be okay. I can't be settled 'til I know. Right now with her age, the turning 18 thing, it's like we're back at the beginning. We don't know what's in store, where she will go after high school. For years it's been good. She's been at Well Spring all these years. I know they love her there and are good with her. We are comfortable now, what will happen in the future?

I went with Colleen and Bob to set up a Special Needs Trust for Jamee and the lawyer basically told us that we should move out of Illinois because of the lack of funding for programs for adults with disabilities. We went to the court together for Colleen and Bob to become Jamee's guardians, since Jamee at age 18 is totally dependent on them. I watched Colleen's face as a judge read all the legal speak. Jamee just smiled at the judge and kept saying "hi," but Colleen and Bob both looked solemn and almost fearful. I asked Colleen what she was feeling at that moment.

C.:   It was like those first IEP meetings, it hit you in the face the whole reality of the future, her disability.…. That technically we're not acting as her parents anymore, but as agents of the court. I do not like that they put it like that.

During the court proceedings, the judge told Colleen and Bob that they were now acting as conservators of the court. Rather than being called Jamee's Mom and Dad, Colleen and Bob were referred to as plenary guardians of a disabled adult. As a mother of adult children, I can appreciate Colleen's disconcertion about the words uttered in the courthouse. As parents we do not stop parenting just because our child has reached a particular age. The judge reminded Colleen and Bob twice during the proceedings that as Jamee's court appointed guardians they were responsible to now answer to the court as to how they parent their child and foster her well being. Colleen and Bob must now complete and submit paperwork to the court on a yearly basis updating them regarding Jamee's care. Guardianship for people for disabilities was instituted to protect the rights of the disabled, but the process is very intimidating (Millar, 2008). I witnessed firsthand why parents may want to ignore some of the coming of age requirements and decisions for their disabled children.

Colleen and Bob are two of the most realistic parents of a child with disabilities that I know. As I watched their interactions in the court room and heard the anguish in Colleen's voice as she expressed her worries for Jamee's future, I can further appreciate why parents such as the E.'s are having trouble facing the reality of their mortality and planning for Chuck's future. Laws and government bureaucracy can serve as fences for families with children with disabilities.

Jamee's House

We pulled into the parking lot of the Social Security Office. Colleen, Jamee and I were driving in Jamee's lift van.

"Of course there will not be any handicapped spots open," Colleen let out a sigh and drove through the lot looking for at least a space where we could let the lift down for Jamee.

"There wouldn't be any open spots here anyway half the people in there probably have handicapped licenses. I'll pull up and unload Jamee and then pull across the street."

Colleen drove to the front of the office and dropped Jamee and I off. Sounds simple right? Not really. This whole process took over 10 minutes. Out of the van, push the ramp down, unlock the bands for the wheelchair, push Jamee down the ramp, push the close button and on and on. When I go somewhere with my kids we pull in to a parking space and hop out. With Jamee, it is all about timing. We had a ten o'clock appointment and left early just to have time in case something like not finding a handicapped spot happened.

Colleen is all about schedules and timing. The more time I spent with Colleen and Jamee, the more I came to understand why schedules were and are so important in managing a family which has a member with a disability.

Jamee and I waited on the sidewalk in front of the SSI office which was the last store front in a small strip mall. The place should not have felt scary, but it did. There is something very intimidating about dealing with social services. This wasn't about me or for me, but my stomach felt sick just standing next to Jamee. Colleen came up and we went in-or tried to go in. Five people barged out the door not looking up and ran into the wheel chair. Without an "excuse me or sorry" they went shoving past us.

Colleen went to the desk, and before she could even speak, the attendant said, "Take a number and wait in those seats."

Colleen said, "I have a 10:15 appointment."

"Oh. Name then?", the man did not even look up.

I wondered if they only hire people who make you feel non-human at these places. Or is it a power trip for these workers? Whatever it was or wasn't, it was in the least; rude.

The process didn't get any better with the appointment. As we went through the application process with the counselor, we were reprimanded for not answering a question correctly.

"Where does Jamee reside?" asked the crabby social security worker.

"In her home, with us", Colleen answered.

"I need the exact address, mom," in a very rude tone.

(I thought you could just ask for Jamee's address if that's what you wanted.)

The interview went on and on. Finally, Colleen had answered all the questions and signed the form. Jamee started talking, she figured it was time to be done, too. "Home, bye, eat." Jamee listed her demands verbally. All during the interview Jamee had just sat there with her mouth open, looking puzzled. Typically, Jamee says "hi" to everyone and smiles. Since the worker really never acknowledged Jamee, or ever made eye contact with her, Jamee just sat there. This was all about Jamee and the worker did not even acknowledge the fact that she was there. Jamee was social security number, not a person.

Colleen said "Ok, Jamee we are finished." The woman did look up and said goodbye and said that Colleen would be receiving notification within the month as to Jamee's social security benefits.

Jamee yelled "bye" and started laughing. I wish I could be as spontaneous as Jamee. I wanted to laugh, cry, or something. Colleen just had a determined look on her face and pushed Jamee through the waiting room, out the door.

"I'm so glad to be done with that. Now we have to start looking for adult programs for Jamee. When do you have time?"

Now that we have completed the social security process, Colleen is moving to the next item on Jamee's transition agenda. "I called the PASS agency (Pre admission Screening Service) and they are sending me a list of adult agencies we can visit."

"Ok, let me know." I figured we had some time since Jamee was able to stay in school until her 22nd birthday. It was forward thinking of Colleen to start exploring Jamee's adult options.

When Colleen makes up her mind to start something-you start. We began our visits to adult service providers when Jamee turned 19.

"Wow, this place is beautiful." I was really impressed by a brand new sprawling ranch located on a beautiful block in a swanky suburb of Chicago. The location was highly desirable for anyone to live in.

"Scary that this is our first visit, any others will look like a shack, I'm guessing."

Colleen and I figured we would look at programs and homes while Jamee was in school. Once we had narrowed the options, Jamee and

Colleen's husband, Bob, could come to see them. Jamee does not speak well or much, but she definitely lets you know via her actions when she is comfortable or likes where she is at.

"This may be pretty, but we will still have to see if they have openings and if Jamee would like it here." Colleen rang the bell.

A well-dressed business like woman answered. She actually matched the aura of the neighborhood and home, very well appointed-good clothes, perfect hair, very put together. As the intake director for Northwest Services she was kind and efficient. We got the grand tour of the home. It was new, decorated in the latest styles and a cleaning woman was scrubbing the shiny brown granite counter in the massive kitchen as we walked through the great room.

Everything was beautiful; the 8 people living in the home each had their own bedrooms. We were impressed with the design, cleanliness and the level of accessibility. The hallways were extra wide, the floors were a shiny wood laminate, which would be easy for Jamee to ambulate. The bathroom had a roll- in shower with jets that were like something out of a spa. I was ready to move in myself.

We sat at the dining room table and went through paperwork with Mrs. Efficient. She showed us plans for the next community home the agency was thinking of building. We asked about the day service options the agency would have for Jamee. She started talking about a sheltered workshop site where all the residents "worked" during the day.

Little did she know but her pretty house just lost some of its luster in our eyes. Jamee hated piece work and would not like to spend the day at a workshop.

"Can we visit your worksite?" Colleen asked.

"Of course. We have had the program for over 30 years, it is very successful. Its located in an industrial park about 20 minutes from here."

"Are there any other day options in your agency? I really don't see Jamee as a person who would want to work at a workshop."

"Well, Mrs. F. why don't you look at our program and we can discuss that after your visit."

"How soon could Jamee expect to have a place in a home with you," Colleen asked.

"Well you know with the state funds here in Illinois we have had to be creative in our housing program."

"We are starting to build the next home, we are going to use the same building plans to save money. So we are asking parents to help with the construction by giving monetary support. We are thinking if each family contributed $225,000 dollars we will be able to build and furnish the next home."

"So families are giving money?" Colleen was trying to process what she heard.

"Yes. We have had to be creative to build community homes."

"Ok, could I make an appointment to see the day program?"

A date was set for Colleen to visit the day program and we left the beautiful house.

It was a beautiful house but it didn't feel like a home, there were no family pictures or personal momentous in the living areas. Actually it felt like a motel lobby, very clean, shiny and impersonal.

As we hit the sidewalk, Colleen said "Well I suppose we could figure a way to raise money, if the day program is good, but then maybe we could buy our own house for $225,000 and we know enough people who would help us fix it up."

"Was it me, but it didn't feel right."

"No, I thought it was cold, but then again no one is here, we have to come back when the people are here to really get an idea."

The payment for housing put an idea into our heads. We started brainstorming as to how we could build or buy a home for Jamee and some "yet to be made" friends.

"I want Jamee to be on her own someday or as much as she can be. She will need help, but she deserves her own life."

"I saw what mom went through with Jackie, I don't want that for Jenna and Jordan. They all deserve to be independent. I know Jenna and Jordan will always take care of Jamee, but they shouldn't have to. They shouldn't feel guilty. Plus, Jamee needs to have a chance to have friends and do things with people other than family."

"We will figure it out Colleen, and we will keep looking, there has to be something that feels right for Jamee."

For out next agency appointment, we started at the day program. The room was large and open and there seemed to be divided areas depending on people's interest. The woman guiding us through the building was easy going, dressed casually and had a pleasant tone when speaking. She talked enthusiastically about the different options the agency had for "consumers." (The label adult agencies currently use for the people in their programs). The term "consumers" is suppose to be one of respect or empowerment, since adults with disabilities are "using the services of the program." I, personally, hate labels, but I suppose consumer is kinder than some of the terms historically used to describe or name people with disabilities.

We were taken through what at one time had been a special education school. Construction-wise they had done a nice job of making things open and less school-like. There was a corner with comfy chairs and aquariums filled with colorful fish. The "teacher me" liked all the options that were available for the "consumers". I felt that way until I noticed the consumers. If they were the recipients of the service than how come they weren't partaking in the services? I know adult situations are not the same as school environments. In school, a teacher works to keep all the students engaged and occupied. I know that the adults' choices should be respected and maybe they were happy just sitting there, but no one looked particularly happy to me.

A gentleman was sitting on a rocking chair starring at the wall by the aquarium. A woman sat by herself at the table working on a puzzle. Another woman had her head on the same table. No one was talking to each other.

Our guide continued to talk to us about the program, "Oh see they are having a cooking lesson now in the kitchen."

Colleen and I peered into the kitchen area. Two workers were at the counter stirring batter and the 4 consumers were sitting in chair at least 4 feet away from the cake preparation.

We walked outside into a beautiful greenhouse. Plants were blooming, there were planting stations and abundant materials. A Koi pond sparkled in the sunshine with lilly pads floating on the surface. We crossed the foot bridge over the pond and made our way through rows of plants. There were a couple of consumers sitting in the garden and a worker was digging in the soil.

The guide kept talking... "Our consumers just love the gardening program."

We walked back through the main building following and murmuring yes and no and mmms as we walked.

"So ladies, would you like to get in your car and follow me to our ICF's. We have CILAs too but we do not have any openings in the community homes."

We got into Colleen's car.

"Is it me or-what was wrong in there?" Colleen asked.

"No, it was weird, there was all this stuff, but no one was really busy or even talking to each other." I was trying to figure it out.

"I liked that it wasn't a workshop," Col said.

"Me too, but I think the problem was that the workers seemed to be getting more out of the program than the people. Did you notice the cake baking? The workers were making a nice cake. Let's see what the housing looks like."

We drove onto a road that looked like it led to a forest preserve.We were way off the main road driving through trees. As we drove through the woods, I wondered where we were going.

"I can't believe there's houses back here."

"I know. It would be creepy at night."

"Maybe this is just a short cut and we will get to an open area soon."

The guide turned and we followed. In a small clearing there was covered picnic area with a parking lot. There was a path leading from the lot, at the end of the path were two identical brown buildings, separated by a sidewalk. The buildings were weird. They looked like 1970s style deco doctors offices. There was not a front door, but a side entrance.

Colleen and I just looked at each other.

"Happy guide lady" introduced us to a worker at the door. "Ladies, I'm going to let you look around and you can let Mary know when you are ready to go or have any questions. You can call me and let me know how I can help you. We would love to meet Jamee."

Our guide left and we stepped into a small square room. The room was painted dark brown and the shades were drawn. Two men sat in the room by themselves. Each man sat in an old easy chair, both of them were wearing pajama bottoms and sweatshirts. We tried to say hello, but they weren't social types.

"Don't mind them, they don't like going to the program so they stay back."

We walked into another larger square room which was a weird turquoise color. There were some tables and chairs in the room, with some chairs and couches on the perimeter. One wall was a pass through stainless steel countertop. We could see a kitchen through the open area.

"So this is an all purpose room, they eat here and you know do activities and things here."

We walked to another small square room. This room had an old TV and VCR player with shelves filled with toys and old movies. There was a baby play bed filled with dolls; some of them were broken and naked.

"So this is the TV and rec room."

"These toys and dolls belong to the residents?" Colleen asked from behind Mary and rolled her eyes at me.

"Oh yes, you know these folks all really like their toys. Some of the ladies sit and rock the babies. It's so cute."

"So where are the bedrooms?" I asked. I couldn't figure out this house at all.

"This way."

We followed Mary back to the eating area and turned down a long narrow hallway and there were 15 doors along the hall.

We peered into a small room. It was similar to a college dorm with a large picture window. Compared to the rest of the house at least the bedrooms looked a bit inviting.

"So do you have any questions?" Mary asked.

Colleen asked how many people lived in the home and how many workers were there at a time. There were 10 residents and two or three workers during the times when the residents were home. At night, each house only had one overnight worker.

"What would they do in an emergency with only one worker at night?" Colleen looked concerned.

"Well that is why it is so good to have the house next door."

"Well, thanks Mary."

We couldn't get to the car fast enough.

"Let's get out of here."

"Was that creepy or what?"

"The turquoise walls, yuck!"

"I wonder if those guys just sit and do nothing day after day."

"We'll check that place off the list."

"If these are the options for people with disabilities, I can see why so many families may want to keep their family member at home forever." I was worried if we would ever find a good place for Jamee, but I didn't want to say that out loud to my sister.

"Good thing we have a couple of years to keep looking." Colleen was trying to reassure herself.

"Well we are starting to know what we don't want," I said.

"Somehow Jamee will let us know if she likes a place."

"We will have to think about this Col, maybe that lady had an idea at that fancy house. Maybe we could do something ourselves. Build a house, start an agency, I don't know. We'll think of something."

"I just want to make sure Jamee is happy and safe, that's all."

A life that is safe, secure, with social opportunities; making that happen for a loved one with disabilities shouldn't be so difficult...

Future Concerns

Colleen discussed her inability to "let go" of mothering Jamee. She realized she has to let go for herself, Jamee and her family. Additionally, she believes Jamee should have a life of her own, not one which is so dependent on her mom. Colleen acknowledged that she knows she must do this, but it is not easy for her.

C.: It is hard for me to let go, even with Jamee's part time attendant. It's hard for me to let her help. It's like she's doing my job … I need to. I want her to be in a home of her own and then people will ask me. You'd really let her live in a group home? I think that's OK. Jamee needs her own life. We would like to have a life together, and we had kids young. Just to go away go to Florida let's say, for a weekend, just to be able to go, because our whole life…everything has had to be planned.

S.: So you see her living with an assistant and maybe a couple of other people?

C.: Yea, whatever avenue we take I am going to have to let go a bit. I'm picky, how she looks, her clothes, her physical care. I don't absolutely trust anyone, it's hard. Then I feel guilty about the other girls. I've missed so much… Can't go to Jordan's game…Jamee has therapy. Can't go to see Jenna, Jamee has a wheelchair appointment. I can never work more than I do, even if I wanted to. Bob has kept this job position because he can be home more and if he took the promotions they've offered he'd have to work specific hours. Everything is always a schedule. We've had to schedule and reschedule our whole lives.

Jamee's care is time consuming. She has significant physical needs and the family has always taken the time and energy to address these needs.

Jamee's health status and calm demeanor is due to the energy expended by her parents and sisters to make it all work. The family's schedule and routines have always revolved around Jamee. While routine is important, Jenna and Jordan have never been denied opportunities to be involved in activities. In fact, Colleen and Bob go beyond many parents to foster their interests, but they always have to think of Jamee and her schedule first.

Having a child with a disability is not easy. It is difficult on many levels, from finding accessible buildings and parking, to negotiating IEP meetings, and schedules. I posed the question to Colleen if she ever thought about life if Jamee was not disabled.

S.:   So do you ever think about if Jamee wasn't disabled?

C.:   Sometimes I think what she would be like? Who would she take after? Its kinda like that "Welcome to Holland Story" we hadn't planned for this. It's not bad or good. It's just different. Jamee's fine. She's happy being Jamee. I'm thankful in many ways; nothing really bothers her, even if someone did say something about her, she wouldn't get it. She would understand the tone, but not the full impact of the words. She's happy.

Colleen again, through her words is saying that their life is not bad, but different. While she typically speaks in a noncommittal tone and has a matter of fact approach to raising a child with a disability, she still has fears below the surface. Colleen expressed her worries about Jamee out living her and Bob. With tears in her eyes, as she talked about one of Jamee's friends who just passed away because of complications resulting from having cerebral palsy; Colleen said sometimes she wishes that she and Bob would outlive Jamee. Providing for a child with disabilities after death is worrisome for parents (Gans, 1997; Holland, 2006; Schwartzenberg, 2005). Colleen is not alone in expressing her grave concerns. She worries what Jamee's future will hold; especially medically. She knows the care Jamee requires and wonders if others will care for her the same. Colleen wants Jamee to always have choices and hopes people are patient enough to wait and not just do things for her.

C.:   Jamee needs time to process. She knows what she wants. She does let people know what she needs. People have to let her. This whole year has been hard... the turning 18 thing. She's 18 years old, but she's not. I'm noticing now, how tied down we are. Our friends are getting so they can just go out if they want and we can't make any plans. The house revolves around Jamee... every vacation all the accessible problems. Everything is planning and scheduling.

As much as Colleen may feel tied down with the scheduling, or the hassles of loading up the wheelchair and all the packing, it never hinders her from taking Jamee places. Rather than just run out to the mall by herself, she will ask Jamee if she would like to go. If Jamee says yes, Jamee goes to the mall. Jamee loves to shop. She has definite ideas about her clothes and the material must be soft and warm. She touches the clothes, and if she says "saaaawft" then it has passed the Jamee test of approval. She will shake her head no, when she doesn't want what someone is offering. For a young lady with a working vocabulary of about 50 words, she gets her point across.

Miss Social

Jamee is a people person. As people meet each other they relate to each other. Jamee demonstrates the existential of relationality as she connects to other people on a very personal level. Upon meeting a person once she will remember that person by name. Her "name" vocabulary is probably double that of her functional words. She loves people. If Jamee says someone's name, she expects the person to respond. She keeps yelling the name out until she receives response. At school she has difficulty rolling to class on time. She yells "hi" to everyone she sees in the hallway.

Jamee's "hi" is her connective link to the corporeality of her world.

There are certain people who make Jamee laugh. The crazier some-one's actions, the more she enjoys that person. If a person falls, trips or bumps into the wall, Jamee considers this the ultimate in entertainment. Her laughter will go on forever. If, however, someone gets hurt or has an injury, her face gets very concerned, and she will ask, "Owe?" then, "All better?" If she hears someone is sick or in the hospital she will wheel to the phone and ask her mom to call the person. Jamee will continue to inquire about the person until she hears someone is better. She will ask about that sick person every day.

Jamee enjoys the company of her sisters and cousins. Her cousin Amy shared an interesting Jamee moment:

A.:   I just remember coming back from college, or may-be it was my first year at work, I don't know, but I went over to Col's house and Jamee's got this big grin on her face. She goes rollin' into her bedroom, making me come with her. I asked (Amy giggling), "Jamee, what are you smilin' about ya weirdo?" She lifts up her shirt, flashes me and says "BRA" like any pre-teen, so excited to get her first bra... you know?

Jamee especially enjoys family parties. At the beginning of parties, she is sure to go around greeting all attendees. She has been a bridesmaid for her two cousins' weddings and loved the music and the food. Jamee is definitely a party girl.

A Happy Home Girl

I asked people in the family and at Jamee's school for single words to describe Jamee. The word which was said over and over again was "hap-py." Jamee has a busy life with school, social outings, and family events. She loves roller coasters, snow skiing on a sled, swimming in her pool, country music, and Kevin from the Jonas Brothers music group.

Jamee has traveled on family vacations to Mexico, Disney World, and her Uncle Jim's cabin, but to Jamee, there is "No place like home."

Home Sweet House

"Hi there, I'm Cupcake, who are you?"

A woman with Down Syndrome opened the door for Colleen and I. We did not get a chance to say anything. Cupcake kept talking.

"Well my real name is not Cupcake, it's my nickname you know-so who are you?"

We gave our names, and Cupcake ushered us over to the receptionist's desk - "so here's Colleen and Sharon."

"Oh, ladies who are you here to see?" Cupcake was definitely in charge.

"Kate." Colleen and I said in unison.

"So honey these nice ladies are here to see Kate." She is explaining this to the woman at the desk.

"Hello, sign in please. Kate will be right with you."

We signed in and sat down in the vestibule.

I personally had been at Spring Center before, back about 40 years ago. Spring Center was known as Spring School for Children with Disabilities. The E's had moved to Oak Lawn because of hearing about Spring fifty years ago. Chuck never attended Spring because, Oak Valley opened, but I had volunteered at Spring for a service project as a teenager. The chairs looked the same as they did over 40 years ago, but the atmosphere was definitely different. When Spring was a school, back in the 70's, it felt institutional, this place actually felt fun. People were coming and going; walking, wheeling, shuffling by us. Cupcake plopped herself in a chair next to Colleen and put her arm around Colleen's shoulder.

"So Colleen, you're here to see Kate-Let me tell you I know all her secrets. Kate and I are like this (crosses her fingers)."

Colleen started to laugh. "We are here to talk to her about my daughter, Jamee. We're going to take a tour."

Cupcake was nodding and taking things in. We had a great time bantering back and forth with Cupcake. I hate to be stereotypical, but it was as if Jackie was sitting here with us. Jackie and Cupcake being both woman with Down Syndrome and Cupcake physically resembled Jackie. Plus, she was hysterical, much like our Aunt Jackie.

With "Jackie" welcoming us to Spring Center something already felt very "right" about this place.

Cupcake started whispering in Colleen's ear. Colleen just started laughing.

"Really Cupcake, I don't believe you."

Colleen and I caught eyes and smiled.

Cupcake continued to fill us in on the latest gossip. When people came by, she told us who they were-who loved who-who liked to do what. She definitely had an engaging personality. We were well informed by the time Kate arrived 10 minutes later.

Jamee currently attends a day program at Spring Center. I guess "Jackie" did a great job in convincing us this would be a wonderful place for Jamee. Not only does Jamee attend Spring Center during the day, she currently lives in an ICF (Intermediate Care Facility) which is managed by Spring Center. Jamee has a best friend, Julie at her house. Together, with their families agreement, the ladies decided that they are going to move to a smaller home in the community. So many people worked to make their dream come true. We organized a huge benefit with over 150 volunteers and 500 people in attendance to help finance the purchase of a home and Spring Center will continue to provide service supports for them. Not only did we raise the money to purchase the home, more importantly; we informed.

Hundreds of people now know and understand why it is so critical that individuals with disabilities are regarded as true members of the community. This lesson was learned because people saw Jamee and her girlfriend Julie, as fun, loving individuals not as disabled or *retarded*. They came to know Jamee and Julie as people who have a disability. The disability does not define them, it just part of their identity. Like Laura said, "It is what it is," and like Colleen said, "This is normal to us". The more others see Jamee's lived experience as typical, the more she will be a true member of the community.

Being part of a community means having true relationships with community members. To be part of a community is to be a family member, neighbor, schoolmate, friend, casual acquaintance, church member,shopper, co- worker, significant other. It means being a fellow member of clubs, organizations, and associations and sometimes being a consumer of services as well. Being part of a community means much more than being treated nicely by staff. It means being known as an individual, a unique person, and not a label, a ward of the state, a client of an agency, a consumer of services or a recipient of another's charity. The strongest argument in favor of enabling people to become part of their communities is that they lead better, more fulfilling lives.... (Bogdan&Taylor,1999). Jamee and Julie will be in their new home soon. The house warming party will be a blast! It will not be "Home sweet house, but home sweet home" for Jamee, our home girl.

CHAPTER SEVEN

Life in Metaphors

Rhizomic Possibilities and Safety Fences

Jackie, Chuck, Jonathon and Jamee; four individuals connected by disability, intricately linked, generation to generation, through the connective strands of friendship and families. The family structure of these individuals provided a protective fence to keep each of them safe from many of the social constructions of disability. As I carefully tilled the soil and dug into the experiences, I was compelled to think deeply and examine the life world of my family and friends and their relationship with disability. Through employing hermeneutic phenomenology I sought to give "a rigorous description of human life as it was lived and reflected upon, in all of its concreteness, urgency and ambiguity" (Pollio et al., 1997, p.5). My goal was to write a descriptive metaphorical narrative that told the generational story of the lived experiences of families, friendship and disability. I collaborated in the story telling and connected the root strands. Through interviews I uncovered beautiful compelling narratives that exposed the reality of life for individuals with intellectual disabilities and the people who love them. The four families, connected by rhizomic strands, shared a number of commonalities.

A connective strand which united the families was a fear of the unknown. Typically, when a new baby comes into the world, the family is filled with anticipation and dreams for the future. The birth of a child is a joyful experience. The families in this story had little time to bask in the happiness of a new life. Instead they embarked on emotional quests searching for answers. As loving and concerned parents, they all sought information from medical professionals. As indicated in the literature, this quest for information is a common reaction when a parent realizes their child has a disability (Kinsley&Levitz, 1994/2007; Schartzenberg, 2005). Initially, the parents sought answers so they could understand their role as parents. They wanted to find the means to assist their children. All of the families went through emotional struggles with the professionals. Parents of children with disabilities historically have shared similar anxiety as my grandparents, Mr. and Mrs. E., Laura and Steve, and Colleen and Bob. The parents in this story were all subjected to "category bound activities" (Sacks, 1992).

Parents of children with disabilities are "looked at" in a particular manner. The parents were told by medical professionals they could not handle their child, or that nothing was wrong in Jamee's case. The professionals put the parents in categories. Colleen, Dorothy and Mrs. E. were dismissed as young mothers. Laura was thought of as being too assertive. Social constructs of which the families had no control caused additional anxiety to these families who were already under much pressure. A medical model perspective (Oliver, 1990) does not only define the individuals with disabilities, but places their parents, especially the more involved mothers, in prescribed roles as well. Upon realizing that the professionals did not have all the answers, after time, the parents discovered that they had the answers all along. My grandparents, the E.'s, Laura and Steve, and Colleen and Bob found the strength from within themselves to do whatever was necessary for their children.

Externally the families went about their lives, yet within the spatiality of their homes their experiences were complex. Without any training, my grandmother took on the roles of therapist and teacher. She uncovered that neckties and belts were useful in supporting Jackie as she learned to walk, and match sticks could be used as manipulatives as Jackie learned to count. Mr. and Mrs. E. discovered that elastic bands could be used to stretch Chuck's limbs. Laura and Steve decided their son was not going to die, and found programs to support his growth. Colleen and Bob rubbed Jamee's arm and legs, changed her formula and kept bringing her to doctors to treat her medical difficulties. They all took action, but fear remained under the surface.

Fears

Fear connected the families, but was manifested differently in their lived experiences. As indicated in the literature, parents or siblings of children with disabilities often wondered what they did to deserve this fate, or if they did something wrong for this to occur in their family. My grandmother is representative of this as she was trying to place the blame on someone for Jackie's "condition." Much of this blame had to do with the time in history. People did not understand the medical reasons for Down Syndrome. I cannot fathom the deep anxiety a mother would feel upon realizing their beloved child was viewed by society as sub human, a burden, or a product of sinfulness (Castles, 2004). Parents who gave birth to children with obvious disabilities in this era were often fearful of people trying to come and put their child in an institution. Mere's always insisting that my mom watch her little sister or her walking Jackie back and forth to school up to six times a day, may be outward signs of her deep internal fears. Due to this particular time in history, as a member of the silent generation, (Strauss&Howe, 1992) my grandmother did not discuss her feelings regarding Jackie's disability. She repressed her fears and had emotional breakdowns.

With the progress of medical science over the decades and having a clearer understanding of the etiology of their children's disabilities, the other parents did not have the same type of fears as my grandmother. Yet fear was a connective element experienced by all the families in this research. Mr. and Mrs. E. are not preparing financially or psychologically for Chuck's future. Laura still checks on Jonathon when he sleeps too long. Colleen worries if caregivers in Jamee's future will care for her medical needs and provide her with choices. Chucks' sister Debbie expressed concerns that her role as Chuck's sister may change if she has to become his caregiver. Still feeling anguish over ten years after Jackie's death, my mother pondered if she treated her sister Jackie kindly in her later years. Jenna, Jamee's sister cried as she discussed her worries about Jamee's physical fragility. Jonathon fears being alone and is purposely working on overcoming his shyness. The fear was ever present, but it was accompanied by resilience and resistance.

Resistance

The rhizomic strand of resistance was evident as the stories were told. This was demonstrated by my grandparents refusing to call Jackie anything but Jackie, and demanding that she attend the local Catholic school with her sister. Mr. and Mrs. E. moved to the suburbs to find a school for Chuck, and continued to fight the school district for funding because their son was happy at Oak Valley. Chuck resisted the societal expectations when he is the "man in charge" on his work crew. Laura confronted the doctor when he did not think baby Jonathon should have a prosthesis, because of his fragile state. She continued to resist the expectations of doctors and other professionals throughout his childhood. Jackie was possibly resisting when she wore whatever clothes she wanted after the death of her mother and when she told her sister not to tell her what to do. Demonstrating resistance, Jonathon enrolled in anatomy and physiology classes against the advice of his counselors and received "A's" in the classes. Colleen demonstrates resistance by living in the moment; she does not dwell on the past, but moves forward, providing Jamee with choices in her daily life. Jamee, through making choices and navigating her environment with the support of her communication device and power wheelchair is resisting the social constructs assigned to individuals with significant intellectual and physical disabilities.

Resistance is evident in this story of disability. Without realizing it, the families are demonstrating a particular understanding of the disability experience. A disability studies perspective looks at the entire reality of disability. As an eclectic approach, its ultimate goal is emancipation and self fulfillment in all area of life for people with disabilities. (Finkelstein, 2001; Danforth&Gabel, 2006; Gabel, 2005). The families in this story had unique perspectives and situations, yet self fulfillment for their own child was a personal goal in each circumstance.

Mother to Mother

As I recorded the stories, I noted many commonalities. A common strand, linking story to story, generation to generation is the inner strength of the mothers. The mothers are resilient and strong, taking on doctors, teachers and anyone who denied their children opportunities.

These women played the dominant role while the husbands played the supportive roles (Herbert&Carpenter, 1994). The women were grounded in actualization and hope, negativity was not an option. Each of the women was fenced in by the constraints of the times in which they lived. The historicality served as a fence, for which they had no control. The historicality, the place in actual time, temporality, and lived space represent the contrasts or disconnections in this rhizomic story.

Historicality

Jackie was born in the era of when disability was regarded as sinful, deviant, or a societal burden (Kevles, 1995). In the 1930s, institutionalization was recommended for most people with disabilities. My grandparents did not give in to the societal expectations of the time. As Jackie's parents, they negotiated their lived experience through rebelling. By putting their daughter "out there" in the local catholic school, the community, family gatherings and social situations, they were quietly, but forcefully, rebelling. Particularly revealing was the fact that my grandmother put Jackie out into the world full of pride, but internally she was fighting her own emotional difficulties. The literature (Blancher& Baker, 2007) does indicate that many parents with children with disabilities have internal and emotional struggles. Unfortunately, my grandparents personal and emotional struggles support the studies which indicated that parents could exhibit depression or emotional shock.

While I did not have the exact words of my grandparents in this story, I was told of my grandmother's struggles with depression and break downs by her sister (my great aunt) and her daughter (my mother). As a child, teenager and young adult, I personally saw my grandfather's struggles with alcohol. My mother and Aunt also discussed his drinking in the interviews. I cannot be sure that having a daughter with a disability was the reason for his drinking, but it definitely could have contributed to the situation. Their personal problems may have been because of the narrow minded perspectives about disability which dominated their lived experience. The 1930s and 40s was a difficult era to live openly with a child of disabilities and my grandparents were victims of the societal fences of their times. The fact that Jackie lived in this time, yet portrayed a level of self-confidence and did not see herself as disabled, had much to do with the fences they collectively built to protect their daughter.

Chuck was born in the time of parent involvement (Schwartzenberg, 2005). Down Syndrome now had a biological explanation, so once he was diagnosed; his parents at least had a name and a reason for his particular disability. While the E.'s do not define Chuck by a label they needed to have a diagnosis to understand why Chuck was not developing like his sister Debbie. For Chuck's time in the 1960s, his parents did the best they could with the information they were being given. While medical science had come far since Jackie's time, there were still many misconceptions about Down Syndrome. At the time of Chuck's birth Down Syndrome was still being referred to as "mongoloid" (Trent, 1994). The E.'s were told Chuck would not live long, and were also told to think about placing their son in an institution. The E.'s resisted the advice offered to them and began to make plans for their son. They sought a new life in the suburbs because they had heard there were schools nearby "for children like Chuck". Chuck had a special school to attend, and during his school years laws were written to mandate education for children with disabilities. They, like many parents in the 1960s, joined with other parents to support their child with a disability.

According to Trent (1994), White, middle-class parent advocacy groups were able to help society make the shift from disability being thought of as undesirable, sinful or lower class. The E.'s were representative of their particular time in history, their son was not hidden away and they were creating programs for his support. As a grass root organization, Chuck's school was representative of the time (Kliewer, 1998; Winzer, 1993). My grandparents could be considered "cutting edge" in their accessing an inclusive education for Jackie in the 1940s, the E.'s situation, is representative of the historicality of disability in the mid 1960s.

Jonathon and Jamee went to school in the era of inclusion (Friend, 2008). They were the products of school systems in the infancy stages of such practices. The school districts in both Jonathon's and Jamee's early educational experiences were working through the kinks in their own school settings. Their education was full of fences and rhizomic possibilities, isolation and inclusion involved in an intricate dance with everyone trying to learn the new steps. Initially, both families desired an inclusive school experience for their children. Colleen and Bob while philosophically embracing inclusion for all people with disabilities, had to act in the best interest of their daughter and transfer Jamee to a more secluded school setting. The story of Jamee's public school situation demonstrated the societal conundrum faced by many people with disabilities and those who love and support them. For two years Jamee's parents worked with the school district to bring about changes in the inclusion program. During this time Jamee was actually regressing. The community school was experiencing constant personnel and philosophical changes and lacked the training and understanding to support students with significant disabilities. Colleen and Bob could no longer risk their daughter's personal growth in order to bring about change in the school. There are circumstances when parents have to make difficult decisions to support their child that may not necessarily reflect their philosophical stance.

Another example of a philosophical conundrum was when Jonathon entered high school and Laura and Steve felt it was in his best interest to be in a more secluded freshman program. Laura had fought for the least restrictive learning environment for Jonathon throughout his elementary years and yet supported his placement in the freshman learning center program. Jonathon himself faces a struggle with his own personal philosophy as he accesses support in college. Jonathon told me he does not embrace the label of "disabled", yet he must have a disability label to navigate in the university setting. He also recalled that his high school counselor seemed angry when he insisted on enrolling in a higher level physiology and anatomy class. Mercer (1973) describes this construct and states "people with disabilities are rewarded for behavior that conforms to the social expectations associated with the disability role and are punished for behavior that departs from the expectations" (p.73). Jonathon had his own personal expectations which did not coincide with the counselors desire to keep Jonathon within a particular construction.

Jonathon and Jamee did benefit, however, from a society which had grown in awareness both philosophically and technologically. They both had the benefit of technology to assist them in accessing their education, which was not available for Jackie and Chuck. Computers, graphing calculators, and augmented communication devices have opened the gates of learning for Jonathon and Jamee, and they are able to navigate their educational situations with such support.

Their parents also reaped the benefits derived from a historical era which was beginning to be more open about disability. Laws had been implemented to not only educate, but to include children with disabilities in school. Parents of children with disabilities in contemporary times have the ability to engage in mediation and voice their concerns. Laura and Colleen were not products of the "silent" generation, and as such were able to voice their concerns in a more open forum than my grandmother and Mrs. E.

Exposure

A theme which represents the stories of the families and the corporality and temporality of their situations is: "They were there." All of the families embraced life, and made their presence known. They put themselves and their children out in the community to face whatever life had to offer. Simultaneously, the parents were there to protect their children from whatever society put in their way. They exposed them to opportunity, but put up fences whenever necessary. To these families, life was and is something to partake and opportunities are not only for the strong, but for everyone. The literature noted that throughout history advocates for people with disabilities have predominately been parents (Schwartzenberg, 2005). All of the parents in this story served as advocates for their children. Society in the guise of nuns, doctors, and unkind playmates put up fences of prejudice and ignorance, nevertheless these families found ways to unlock the gates. Metaphorically, the key to the lock may have been finding another doctor, going to see the priest, looking for a school, or confronting the PE teacher, but the barriers kept being knocked down.

Mr. and Mrs. E., Laura and Colleen, stressed over and over, "it is what it is". In fact all of the parents used those words to describe their lives and their lived experience of raising their children. The rhizomic strand which served as a connection in the shared stories is acceptance. The parents sought answers for the purpose of helping their children, and they focused on the possibilities not the disabilities. Laura said she "Wasn't going to have a pity party". Colleen said she never said, "Why me?" Mr. and Mrs. E. told people, "Don't feel sorry for us, Chuck is a gift, not a burden."

Roots

The neighborhood of our youth served as the soil for our rooted experience. Representing the existentials of spatiality and relationality it served as the place where the families became connected. Disability, if one chooses to use the term, was not thought of as something negative, it was life. It was *our* life. The neighborhood was surrounded by busy streets; danger right outside Laura and Debbie's front doors, but it was the grassy alley that protected us, separated us and connected us. We could cross the alley and be together. As children, we had an idealistic view of life. We knew if we yelled loud enough, someone's mother would come and save us, we knew our Dads would come home at the same time for dinner every night, and most importantly we knew we had each other. In our lived space Jackie would entertain us, we would take our siblings uptown or to the park; life was simple. This simplicity and protective fence was difficult to break through. In many ways this fence kept us naïve and unaware of the big world outside. Children were seen and not heard. We did not question why Jackie could not drive, or why Chuck and Debbie always had to play in their yard. We were so blinded by simplicity that we did not even realize that Chuck and Jackie looked alike, until someone pointed that out to us in a cruel way. We held Chuck's hand both figuratively and literally and walked him home.

It's Just Life

Perhaps, because as children we were steeped in this particular lived experience, Laura and Colleen upon giving birth to children with disabilities understood *the experience* as life. They went about the business of mothering their children. It was not different for them, it was *their* normal life. Laura and Colleen share the need to be medically astute in order to provide for their children's well being, because of the physical issues of Jonathon's and Jamee's disabilities. Colleen tagged along with Laura, Debbie and I when she was a toddler. The strands of the rhizome connected Colleen back to Laura as an adult. Laura introduced Colleen to Dr. T. who was both an outstanding doctor for Jamee and an emotional support for the family. Dr. T. was not typical of the doctors and medical professionals in the research and represented in this story. As a world renowned orthopedic surgeon highly regarded in his field, he could have employed an aloof gaze. He instead treated Jonathon and Jamee as individuals and took the time to support their parents. Dr. T. represents what the medical profession could be if they embraced a more social minded concept of disability. Colleen and Laura felt assured and empowered because of the understanding displayed by this one doctor. Jamee continues to receive physical therapy from the therapists recommended by Laura and Dr.T. over fifteen years ago. Jonathon now volunteers at an art gallery that Jamee attends through her agency. Whenever Jamee sees Jon she screams, "Hi" and gives him her biggest smile. She is quite the flirt. She and Jon are now great friends. The rhizomic threads still continue to connect the families generationally, mother to mother, friend to friend.

Colleen revealed in her interview the unique parent to parent connection she feels with other parents of children with disabilities. She discussed sharing conversations with strangers when they reveal they, too, are parents of a child with a disability. Colleen said no one really understands until you have a child with a disability yourself. A connective parent to parent strand prevails. It is this connective parent-to-parent strand which links Laura, Colleen, and Mrs. E. through understanding.

Gardening

I am the gardener, keeping the roots fed, watering the soil, making sure the root strands stay strong. I could never surmise that I truly understand their lived experience, but I know my life is intricately linked to theirs; passing on information, being there to listen, or just being present. We are linked because we were there. We share our beginnings; we know where we came from, surrounded by the fences of strong women, caring men and air filled with the aroma of protection.

More Connections

Jackie, Chuck, Jonathon, and Jamee have taken all of us linked to their lives, places we never thought we would go. They have forced us to look outside ourselves, to be empathetic involved people. Perhaps, I did not become a special educator because of Jackie, but I cannot deny that she helped me realize that different is just different. While others may see difference as wrong, it is normal for me.

My daughter Amy is emotionally connected to her Aunt Jackie and Cousin Jamee. She enjoyed the company of these two family members. Amy felt called to work with children with disabilities. Jenna, Jamee's sister is now an occupational therapist. She currently works at Well Spring where Jamee attended school. Debbie, Chuck's sister has just returned to work after raising her children, and works as a paraprofessional with children with significant disabilities. Megan, Chuck's niece works in the field of special education. She purposely took a difficult teaching position working with teenagers with significant emotional issues. Those of us who have immersed ourselves in careers in the disability field embrace difference as part of life. Normal is a relative term. This is normal for us. Jonathon says he has disabilities, but the disabilities have not disabled him. He personally benefited because people took time in understanding his needs, and desires to make the world a better place for others. Jonathon volunteered for Jamee's benefit and now volunteers at Jamee's adult agency and hopes to improve the well being of others as a medical researcher.

Support

The well being of the individuals with disabilities was, and is critical for the families. Another connective strand exposed in the story telling was the necessity of routine. The families' lives revolved around their routines. Chuck, Jonathon, and Jamee all require different levels of support. The need for routine is particularly imperative for Jamee, because of her physical and medical needs. These three families are schedule driven and Jonathon, Chuck, and Jamee's needs determine the schedule. Jackie however created her own routines: a Pepsi at exactly 10:00pm, Archie Bunker at 10:30pm, and bed at 11:30 pm during the week and 12:30 am on weekends, as examples. She followed her mother and father's life as a young person and my parent's and sibling's schedule as an adult. The "world" did not revolve around Jackie.

Jackie created her own world within her situation. I have been compelled to think deeply if this situation benefited Jackie or if it benefited us. Would Jackie have liked to, "do her own thing" more often? Jackie was very self-sufficient and full of personality. Was she sufficient because the world did not revolve around her, or was further growth stifled because she always answered to someone?

Questioning Jackie's Life

Colleen expressed in the interviews uneasiness with Jackie's circumstance. She ponders if expectations were put on Jackie, without considering Jackie's wants or desires. Yet for Jackie's place in time, my grandmother was very forward thinking by not acknowledging Jackie's disability. Compared to the majority of the individuals born with disabilities in the late 1930s, Jackie led an accomplished life. Now that we have Jamee in our family, we (my siblings and mom) have all wondered out loud if we in some way mistreated Jackie. The following is not an excuse, but we truly never dwelled on the fact she was disabled. Most importantly, Jackie did not think she was disabled, just "short". Disability to Jackie was "poor 'tarded" Chuck across the alley, or the people in wheelchairs at her club, it definitely was not her. Disability was not her identity. Shakespeare and Watson (2002) remind me that "to assume that disability will always be the key to [their] identity is to recapitulate the error made by those from the medical model perspective who define people by their impairment" (p. 22). As far as I am able to ascertain based on conversations with family and sharing much of my life with Jackie, disability did not define Jackie.

Jonathon's Perceptions

Jonathon refuses to call himself disabled. Yet, he is well aware of his blindness and his brain agenesis, along with a myriad of medical issues. He is "supposed" to have an intellectual disability, but he has a different type of intelligence and he has determined how to negotiate school and life using his intelligence. Rapley (2004) suggests that it is not necessary to theorize or re-theorize intellectual disability. "Maybe we should just refuse to do so" (p. 206). Jonathon is an example of just such refusal. He has constructed a fence blocking out disability. The fence has served him well, leading to possibility.

Chuck's World

Chuck is not able to voice his feeling about disability. Based on my observations and immersing myself in the world of Chuck, he appears content with his life. He has activities he enjoys, work which has given him a level of self assurance, his girlfriend Lee, and parents who are very dedicated to his well- being. Chuck does not appear to mind living in a protective environment. His needs are simple and watching his TV programs and swinging his chain brings him a certain level of comfort and joy.

Happy Jamee

Jamee is a happy young woman. Her difficulties with mobility and communication do not appear to affect her spirit. She has never known life as anything different. Jamee has definite interests and is able to express them in her individual manner. Utilizing an augmented communication device she is able to communicate and let her needs be known. Routine is clearly important to Jamee and her family recognizes and honors this need. Within her structured world there are choices, and Jamee is encouraged to make choices in all areas of her life. Her quick smile and pleasant personality denotes a young woman who is content with her life.

Connected Individuals

Jackie, Chuck, Jonathon and Jamee are linked by the off shoots of the rhizome. The rhizome of family and friendship was firmly planted in the soil. Through watering the rhizome with independence and fertilizing with love, these individuals identified themselves as Jackie, Chuck, Jonathon, and Jamee, not as intellectually disabled, retarded, or a person with Down Syndrome. Bogdan and Taylor (1982) proposed "to be called retarded is to have one's moral worth and human value called into question (p .14). Jackie was referred to as Jackie, Chuck is just Chuck, Jonathon is "what he is", and Jamee is a home girl. They are one of *us*.

Final Thoughts

Stories must be written, lives must intersect; able and disabled can meet at the fence and open the gates. Rich stories can serve as a means to reveal multiple perspectives, as a way to allow people who have not been heard to have a voice. Stories can bring about social reform and understanding. Opportunities may emerge because of the stories.

This story was a return to home. I was able to go back to the emotional and physical place where our personalities and our concept of disability were formed. As I wove the stories together, I immersed myself in the connective, fluid experience of our lives. I listened, felt, laughed and cried. As the stories unfolded, I came to understand how intimately I was connected to them, and they were to each other. Their lives became more meaningful to me, their experiences more real. I personally stepped into the fenced-in place of disability. Once inside, however, I found growth, opportunities, love and commitment. I saw how the families faced oppression, and I felt their fears. From those fears, opportunities evolved. Consumed by the stories, I became intimately reacquainted with four individuals with disabilities who are accomplished, secure individuals; their lives steeped in possibilities.

Three childhood friends, four families, four individuals with disabilities connected by proximity, understanding, and love. Together, we wrote a story... *Once upon a time lived three little girls, their lives were connected by friends, family and disability.*

AAIDD. (2008). *Definition of intellectual disability.* Retrieved November 11, 2008, from http://www.aaidd.org/content_100.cfm?navID=21.

Algozzine, B., Browder, D., Karvonen, M., Test, D., & Wood, W. (2001). Effects of interventions to promote self-determination for individuals with disabilities. *Review of Educational Research, 71,* 219-277.

Annells, M. (1996). Hermaneutic phenomology: Philosophical perspectives and use in nursing research. *Journal of Advanced Nursing, 23,* 705-713.

ARC (n.d.). *Introduction to the Arc.* Retrieved October 1, 2008, from: http://www.thearc.org/about.htm

Barton, L. (1998). Sociology, disability studies in education: Some observations. In T. Shakespeare (Ed.), *The disability reader: Social sciences perspective* (pp.53-64). London: Cassell.

Berglund, E., Eriksson, M. & Johansson, I. (2001). Parental reports of spoken language skills in children with Down Syndrome. *Journal of Speech and Hearing Research, 44,* 179-191.

Berube, M. (2004). Family values. In S. Noll, & J. Trent(Eds.), *Mental retardation in America: A historical reader* (pp. 494-500). New York: New York University Press.

Berube, M. (1996). *Life as we know it, a father, a family, and an exceptional child.* New York: Pantheon.

Blacher, J., & Baker, B. (2007). Positive impact on intellectual disability on families. *American Journal of Mental Retardation, 106,* 173-188.

Blatt, B. (1987). The community imperative and human values. In R. Antonak, & J. Mulick(Eds.), *Transition in mental retardation: The community iimperative revisited* (pp. 236-247). Norwood, NJ: Ablex.

Blatt, B., & Kaplan, F. (1966). *Christmas in Purgatory. A photographic essay on mental retardation.* Boston: Allyn and Bacon.

Bogdan, R., & Taylor, S. (1982). *Inside out: The social meaning of mental retardation.* Toronto: University of Toronto Press.

Bogdan, R., & Taylor, S. (1989). Relationships with severely disabled people: the social construction of humaness. *Social Problems, 36*(2), 135-148.

Brown, J. (2007). *Scripture as communication: Introducing biblical hermeneutics.* Grand Rapids, MI: Baker.

Brown, N. (1947). *Hermes the theif: The evolution of a myth.* Madison, WI: University of Wisconsin Press.

Carpenter, B. (2005). *Disabled children: The father's role.* Retrieved March 1, 2009, from Fatherhood Institute: http://fatherhoodinstitute.org/index.php?id15CID=259

Casey, E. (1997). *The fate of place: A philosophical history.* Berkeley: University of California Press.

Castles, K. (2004). Nice average Americans. In S.Noll, & J.Trent(Eds.), *Mental retardation in America* (pp. 351-370). New York: New York University Press.

Conlan, D. (2000). Heuristic research: With thanks and apologies to Clark Moustakas. In P.

Willis, R. Smith, & E. Collins (Eds.), *Being, Seeking, Telling: Expressive Approaches to Qualitative Adult Education Research* (pp. 112-131). Flaxton (Queensland) Post Pressed.

Connors, C., & Stalker, K. (2003). *The views and experiences of disabled children and their siblings.* London: Jessica Kingley Publishers.

Danforth, S., & Gabel, S.(Eds.) (2006). *Vital questions for disability studies in education.* New York: Peter Lang Publishers.

Darling, R. (1979). *Families against society: A study of reactions to children with birth defects.* Beverly Hills, CA: Sage.

Day, M. (1996). *Home in the post modern world: An existential phenomenological study.*Paper presented at The International Human Science Research Conference, Halifax.

Deleuze, G. (1983). *The movement image* (H. Tomlinson & B. Habberjam,Trans.). Minneapolis: University of Minnesota.

Deleuze, G., & Guattari, F. (1987). *A thousand plateaus capitalism and schizophrenia* (B. Massumi,Trans.). Minneapolis: University of Minnesota Press.

Dilthey, W. (1985). *Poetry and experience*. Princeton, NJ: Princeton University Press.

Dowling, J. (2008). Inclusive education, why is it not more prevalent? *Tash Connections, 34,* 2.

Farber, D. & Sherry,S. (1995). Telling stories out of school. An essay on legal narratives. In G. Delgado(Ed.), *Critical race theory: The cutting edge* (pp.283-292).Philadelphia: Temple University Press.

Ferguson, P. (2003). A place in the family: An historical interpretation of research on parental reactions to having a child with a disability. *Journal of Special Education, 36,* 124-130.

Ferguson, P. (1994). *Abandoned to their fate: Social policy and practice toward severely retarded people in America, 1820-1920.* Philadelphia: Temple University Press.

Ferguson, P., Ferguson, D., & Taylor, S. (1992). *Interpreting disability: A qualitative reader.* New York: Teacher's College Press.

Finkelstein, V. (2001). *A personal journey into disability politics.* Retrieved November 8, 2008, from http://www.leads.a-cuk/disability-studies/links.htm

Foucault, M. (1973). *The birth of the clinic an archeology of medical perception (Tavistock, Trans.).* New York: Random House.

Friend, M. (2008). *Special education, contemporary perspectives for school professionals.* Boston: Pearson.

Gabel, S. (2005). *Disability studies in education: Readings in theory and method.* New York: Peter Lang.

Gabel, S., & Peters, S. (2004). Presage of a paradigm shift? Beyond the social model of disability toward resistance theory of disability. *Disability & Society, 19*(6), 571-596.

Gadamer, H. (1989). *Truth and method (2nd ed.).* New York: Continuum Publishing Company.

Gans, L. (1997). *Sisters, brothers, and disability, a family album.* Minneapolis: Fairview Press.

Goffman, E. (1963). *Stigma.* Englewood Cliffs, NJ: Prentice Hall.

Goode, D. (1984). Socially produced identities, intimacy, and the problem of competence among the retarded. In S. Tomlinson & L. Barton

(Eds.), *Special education and social interests*, (pp. 228-248). London: Croom-Helm.

Goode, D. (1992). Who is Bobby? Ideology and method in the discovery of a Down syndrome person's competence. In P. Ferguson, D. Ferguson, & S. Taylor(Eds.), *Interpreting disability: A qualatative reader* (pp. 197-212). New York: Teachers College Press.

Harry, B., & Klinger, J. (2007). Discarding the deficit model. *Model Educational Leadership, 64*(5), 16-21.

Hastings, P., Beck, A., & Hill, C. (2005). Positive contributions made by children with an intellectual disability in the family: Mothers' and fathers' perceptions. *Journal of Intellectual Disabilities, 9*, 155-165.

Heidegger, M. (1977). *Basic writings.* New York: Harper and Row.

Herbert, E. & Carpenter, B. (1994) The secondary partners: Professional perspectives and a father's reflections. *Children and Society, 8*(1), 31-41.

Hornby, G. (1991). Parental involvement. In D. Mitchell & R. I. Brown (Eds.), *Early intervention studies for young children with special needs.* Norwich: Chapman Hall.

Human Science Research Institute (HSRI). (2006, January). *The riot! A national e-newsletter from the self-advocate leadership network. 3*(1). Retrieved August 23,2008, from http://www.hsri.org/leaders/theriot

Husserl, E. (1970). *The crisis of European sciences and transcendental phenomenology.* Evanston, IL: Northwestern University Press.

Kevles, D. (1995). *In the name of Eugenics: Genetics and the uses of human heredity.* Harvard University Press.

Kingsley, J., & Levitz, M. (1994/2007). *Count us in. Growing up with Down Syndrome.* New York: Harcourt, Inc.

Kliewer, C. (1998). *Schooling children with Down Syndrome.* New York: Teacher's College Press.

Kuhn, T. (1970). *The structure of the scientific revolution (2nd ed.).* Chicago: University of Chicago Press.

Kurokowa, K. (2001). Towards a rhizome world or chaosmas. In G. Gensoko,G. Deleuze, & F.Guattari(Eds.), *Critical assessments of leading philosophers* (pp. 1027-1034). London: Routledge.

Linschoten, H. (1968). *On the way toward a phenomenological psychology: The psychology of William James.* Pittsburgh: Duquesne University Press.

Marx, K. (1852) *The eighteenth brumaire of Louis Bonaparte.* Retrieved December 20, 2008, from www.marxists.org/archive/marx/works/1852/18th-brumaire/chol.htm

Meyer, H. (1956). Problems relative to the acceptance and reacceptance of the institutionalized child. *Archives of Pediatrics, 73,* 271-275.

Morse, J., & Richards, L. (2007). *Users guide to qualatative methods (2nd ed.).* Thousand Oaks, CA: Sage Publications Inc.

Moules, N. (2002). *Hermaneutic inquiry: Paying heed to history and Hermes - an ancestoral, substative and methodological tale.* Retrieved November 8, 2008, from International Journal of Qualatative Methods : http://www.ualberta,ca/~ijpm

Moustakas, C. (1994). *Phenomenological research methods.* Thousand Oaks, CA: Sage Publications.

Oliver, M. (1990). *The politics of disablement.* London: Macmillan.

Paul, J., & Warnock, N. (1980). Special education: A changing field. *Exceptional Child, 27,* 3-28.

Peters, S. (1999). Transforming disability through critcal literacy and the cultural politics of language. In M. Corker, & S. French(Eds.), *Disability discourse,* (pp. 103-115). Buckingham, UK: Open University Press.

Phillips, A. (1993). *Democracy and difference.* Cambridge: Polity Press

Pollio, H., Henley, T., & Thompson, C. (1997). *The phenomenology of everyday life.* New York: Cambridge University Press.

Prout, H. & Prout, S. (2000). The family with a child with mental retardation. In M. J. Fine & R.L. Simpson (Eds.), *Collaboration with parents and families of children and youth with exceptionalities.* 2nd ed., (pp. 217-235). Austin, TX: Pro-Ed.

Rapley, M. (2004). *The social construction of intellectual disability.* Cambridge: Cambridge University Press.

Rivera, G. (n.d.). *A personal crossroad.* Retrieved November 8, 2008, from http://geraldo.com.index.php?/archives/18/A personal crossroad.html

Roberts, T. (2001). *Open records for adult adoptees.* Retrieved February 25, 2008 from http://www.finitesite.com/paceswny/articles/open-records.pdf

Rodrigue, J., Morgan, S., & Geffkin, G. (1992). Psychological adaptation of fathers of children with autism, Down's syndrome and normal development. *Journal of Autism and Developmental Disorders, 22*(2), 249-263.

Rothman, D., & Rothman, S. (2004). The litigator as reformer. In S. Noll & J. Trent(Eds.), *Mental Retardation in America* (pp. 445-465). New York: New York University Press.

Sacks, H. (1972).On analyzing the stories of children. In J.Gumper& D.Hynes(Eds.).*Directions in sociolinguistics:The ethnography of commmunication.*(pp.329-345).New York:Holt, Rinehart& Winston.

Schalock, R. (2007). The renaming of mental retardation: Understanding the change to the term intellectual disability. *Intellectual and Developmental Disabilities, 45*(2), 116-124.

Schwartzenberg, S. (2005). *Becoming citizens. Family life and the politics of disability.* Seattle: University of Washington Press.

Scully,J.(2002).Apostmodern disorder:Moral encounters with the molecular model of disability.In M.Corker,&T. Shakespeare(Eds.), *Disability and postmodernity.*(pp.48-61). New York: Continuum.

Seamon, D. (2000). A way of seeing people and place: Phenomenology in environment behavior research. In S. Wapner, J. Kemick, T. Yamamoto, & H. Minami, *Theoretical perspectives in environment-behavior research* (pp. 157-178). New York: Plenum.

Shakespeare, T., & Watson, N. (2002). The social model of disability: An outdated ideology? *Research in Social Science and Disability, 2,* 9-28.

Shapiro, J. (2007, January 22). *Label falls short for those with mental retardation.* Retrieved November 6, 2008, from http://www.npr.org/templates/story/story.php?storyid=6943699

Shapiro, J. (1993). *No pity.* New York: Three Rivers Press.

Siebers, T. (2006). *Disability aesthetics.* Retrieved November 11, 2008, from JCRT: http://www.jcrt.org/archives/07.2/siebers.pdf

Siedman, I. (1998). *Interviewing as qualative research. A guide for researchers in education and the social services.* New York: Teachers College Press.

Skrtic, T. (1995). The functionalist view of special education and disability: Deconstructing the conventional knowledge tradition. In T.Skrtic (Ed.), *Disability and democracy reconstructing [special] education for postmodernity* (pp.65-103).New York: Teachers College Press.

Smith, P. (1999). Drawing new maps: A radical cartography of development disabilities. *Review of Educational Research, 69(2),* 117-144.

Snyder, S., & Mitchell, D. (2001). Re-engaging the body: Disability studies and the resistance to embodiment. *Public Culture, 13,* 367-389.

Spiegel, J., & van den Pol, R. (1993). *Making changes family voices on living with disabilities.* Cambridge: Brookline Books.

Stangvik, G. (1998). Conflicting perspectives on learning disabilities. In C. Clark, A. Dyson, & A. Millward(Eds.), *Theorizing special education* (pp. 137-155). New York: Routledge.

Stoneman, Z., & Gavidia-Payne, S. (2006). Marital adjustment in families of young children with disabilities: Associations with daily hassles and problem-focused coping. *American Journal on Mental Retardation III,* 1-14.

Strauss, W., & Howe, N. (1992). *Generations: The story of America's future 1584-2069.* New York: Morrow & Company.

Strohm, K. (2005). *Being the other one growing up with a brother or sister who has special needs.* Boston: Shambala Publications.

Tolston, A. (1977). *The units of masculinity.* London: Tavistock Publications.

Trent, J. (1994). *Inventing the feeble mind: A history of mental retardation in the United States.* Berkeley: University of California Press.

Turnbull, H., & Turnbull, A. (1985). *Parents speak out: Then and now.* Columbus: Charles E. Merrill Publishing.

Unger, D. (1993). Employer perceptions of the work potential of individuals with disabilities. *Journal of post secondary education and disability, 9,* 278-281.

Van Manen, M. (1997). From meaning to method. *Qualatative Health Research, 9*, 345-369.

Van Manen, M. (1990). *Researching lived experience.* New York: State University Press.

von Eckartsberg, R. (1998). Introducing existential-phenomenological psychology. In R. Valle(Ed.), *Phenomenological inquiry in psychology* (pp. 3-20). New York: Plenum.

Wehmeyer, M., & Meltzler, C. (1995). How self-determined are people with mental retardation? *Mental Retardation, 33*, 111-119.

Wickham-Searl, P. (1992). Careers in caring: Mothers of children with disabilities. *Disability & Society, 7*(1), 5-17.

Wilde, J. (2004). *The disability journey.* New York: iUniverse, Inc.

Winzer, M. (1993). *The history of special education from isolation to integration.* Washington D.C.: Gallaudet University Press.

Wolfensberger, W. (1975). *The origin and nature of our institutional models.* Syracuse and New York : Human Policy Press.

Wright, D. (2004). Mongols in our midst John Langdon Down and the ethnic classification of idiocy, 1958-1924. In S. Noll, & J. Trent(Eds.), *Mental retardation in America, a historical reader* (pp.92-119). New York: New York University Press.

CPSIA information can be obtained at www.ICGtesting.com
Printed in the USA
LVOW07s2304020615

440958LV00001B/65/P